The Body Economic

The Body Economic

LIFE, DEATH, AND SENSATION IN
POLITICAL ECONOMY AND
THE VICTORIAN NOVEL

Catherine Gallagher

PRINCETON UNIVERSITY PRESS

PRINCETON AND OXFORD

Copyright © 2006 by Princeton University Press
Published by Princeton University Press,
41 William Street, Princeton, New Jersey 08540
In the United Kingdom: Princeton University Press,
6 Oxford Street, Woodstock,
Oxfordshire OX20 1TW

Third printing, and first paperback printing, 2008
Paperback ISBN: 978-0-691-13630-1

THE LIBRARY OF CONGRESS HAS CATALOGED THE CLOTH EDITION
OF THIS BOOK AS FOLLOWS

Gallagher, Catherine.
The body economic : life, death, and sensation in political
economy and the Victorian novel / Catherine Gallagher.
p. cm.
Includes bibliographical references.
ISBN-13: 978-0-691-12358-5 (cl : alk. paper)
ISBN-10: 0-691-12358-6 (cl : alk. paper)
1. English fiction—19th century—History and criticism.
2. Economics in literature. 3. Dickens, Charles, 1812–1870—
Knowledge—Economics. 4. Eliot, George, 1819–1880—
Knowledge—Economics. 5. Economics— Great Britain—
History—19th century. 6. Great Britain—Economic
conditions—19th century. 7. Senses and sensation in literature.
8. Body, Human, in literature. 9. Death in literature. I. Title.
PR878.E37G35 2005
823′.8093553—dc22   2005045825

British Library Cataloging-in-Publication Data is available

This book has been composed in Adobe Garamond

Printed on acid-free paper. ∞

press.princeton.edu

Printed in the United States of America

3   5   7   9   10   8   6   4

For Shana and Becca

_____

CONTENTS

ACKNOWLEDGMENTS

This study has benefited greatly from the colleagues and friends who read various chapters—James Chandler, Kim Chernin, Frances Ferguson, Kevis Goodman, Stephen Greenblatt, Thomas Laqueur, David Miller, and Hilary Schor—and from the three readers—Patrick Brantlinger, James Eli Adams, and George Levine—who recommended its publication to Princeton University Press. My editors at Princeton University Press, Hanne Winarsky and Terri O'Prey, have been unfailingly patient and helpful. I am also thankful to the scholars at several universities and to the Dickens Universe at Santa Cruz for giving me the opportunity to develop these ideas in public lectures and for generously correcting my mistakes and suggesting new lines of argument. I would also like to thank the Cambridge University Library and the University of California's Bancroft Library.

Thanks are also due to the young scholars who served as research assistants during the years that this project has gestated: Benjamin Widiss, Emily Andersen, and Amy Campion, and to the staff of the School of Social Science at the Institute for Advanced Study. Ryan McDermott and Leslie Walton read proofs and indexed with minute attention to detail. The research and writing were supported by the University of California's President's Fellowship in the Humanities and by the Institute for Advanced Study at Princeton. Without the constant support of my department at Berkeley, this book would never have been finished.

As always, my husband, Martin Jay, was my best reader, toughest critic, and most loving supporter. My adorable grandchildren, Penelope, Frankie, and Sammy, kept my spirits up throughout the writing, and my daughters, Shana Lindsay and Rebecca Jay, gave me their help and encouragement. I dedicate this book to them.

A part of chapter 3 was first published a very long time ago in *Zone* (5 [1989]: 345–65), and a portion of chapter 2 was first published even longer ago in *Representations* (14 [1986]: 83–106).

The Body Economic

Introduction

There was a time, back in the last century, when most literary critics despised nineteenth-century British political economy. Our disdainful view of it had many sources—the American New Critics, the Leavisites, the Marxists, the early Victorian literati—but it seldom came from any serious encounters with texts by political economists. We preferred to get them secondhand, already packaged as the direct ideological justification of a particularly rapacious capitalism. After all, we had a stake in perpetuating our own image as their humanistic antagonists, the professionals dedicated to the unique, nonfungible properties of things and the autotelic, noninstrumental nature of people. We were the Kantians (or Coleridgeans), they were the Benthamites, and we lacked John Stuart Mill's reasons for attempting a dialectical synthesis.

It is difficult to say just why all of this began to change during the last three decades. The stress that deconstruction placed on displacement in the literary text—the unstable connection between signifiers and signified and the relational nature of all meaning—brought the economic logic of substitution much closer than it had been to the dynamics of textual analysis. Marxist ideology critique also began focusing more intently on the subtle ways in which poets, playwrights, and novelists, despite their overt proclamations, wrote within the dominant ideologies of their times. Reformulations of the concept of ideology also helped: it was seen to be less a set of explicit beliefs than a set of practices, which we repeat even while protesting against them, and which enfold almost inescapable underlying patterns of perception. The Foucauldian replacement of ideology critique with discourse analysis, moreover, allowed us not only to think beyond disciplinary borders to the organizing *epistemes* of a period but also to scrutinize the processes by which various discourses formed and differentiated themselves. The Foucauldian style of analysis had a particularly strong impact on nineteenth-century studies because that century was singled out as the period when the human sciences took their current form, bringing every aspect of human life into discourse. The discovery that literature played a part in the expansion of Man as a disciplinary object was then complemented by Bourdieu's sociological analyses of how different textual practices are constituted in diacritical opposition to others, so that the very nature of literature lies not in its independent substance but in its distinction from—and at times homologous duplication of—intellectual practices like economics. These theoretical innovations were paralleled by new kinds of criticism devoted to the economics of literature, both studies of formal relations between literary and economic writing and studies of the historical development of literature as an economic activity.[1]

Moreover, just as literary critics were exploring these topics, historians, political theorists, and even economists were revising and reinvigorating the history of economic theory. Instead of appearing to spring directly out of the ideological needs of industrial capitalism, the discipline we call "political economy" (that practiced by the "classical" economists, led by Adam Smith, Thomas Robert Malthus, and David Ricardo) has now been reconnected to the complex of late eighteenth-century intellectual endeavors gathered under the term "moral philosophy" (ethics, political philosophy, natural theology, conjectural history, and aesthetics) and has consequently acquired a pedigree that seems respectable to literary critics. We are also beginning to understand its central place among the developing human sciences of the nineteenth century, and its kinship especially with psychology and anthropology brings it closer to the orbit of nineteenth-century literature.

These investigations have produced a lively new subfield of nineteenth-century British studies, combining literary and intellectual history. Works by Boyd Hilton, Stefan Collini, Donald Winch, Mary Poovey, Regenia Gagnier, Christopher Herbert, Philip Connell, Howard Caygill, and Maureen McLane[2] have demonstrated that political economists and their literary antagonists had a great deal in common, which they were frequently unwilling to recognize. The present study is indebted to these earlier works, and it tries to combine their best aspects. For example, I've followed the lead of recent intellectual historians by taking political economy seriously as a discipline and not implying that it was merely a form of early industrial capitalist apologetics. This

[1] Some of the earliest examples of what came to be called the "new economic criticism" include Marc Shell's *The Economy of Literature*, and *Money, Language, and Thought: Literary and Philosophical Economies from the Medieval to the Modern Era*; Kurt Heinzelman, *The Economies of the Imagination*; Jean-Joseph Goux, *Symbolic Economies: After Marx and Freud*; Martha Woodmansee, *The Author, Art, and the Market: Rereading the History of Aesthetics*; Michael T. Gilmore, *American Romanticism and the Marketplace*; Jean-Christophe Agnew, *Worlds Apart: The Market and the Theater in Anglo-American Thought, 1550–1750*; and Walter Michaels, *The Gold Standard and the Logic of Naturalism*. See also my own *Nobody's Story: The Vanishing Acts of Women Writers in the Marketplace, 1670–1820*.

[2] Hilton, *The Age of Atonement: The Influence of Evangelicalism on Social and Economic Thought, 1785–1865* (Oxford University Press, 1991); Collini, *Economy, Polity, and Society: British Intellectual History, 1750–1950*, eds. Stefan Collini, Richard Whatmore, and Brian Young (Cambridge University Press, 2000); Winch, *Riches and Poverty: An Intellectual History of Political Economy in Britain, 1750–1834* (Cambridge University Press, 1996); Poovey, *Making a Social Body: British Cultural Formation, 1830–1864* (Chicago: University of Chicago Press, 1995); Gagnier, *The Insatiability of Human Wants: Economics and Aesthetics in Market Society* (Chicago: University of Chicago Press, 2000); Herbert, *Culture and Anomie: Ethnographic Imagination in the Nineteenth Century* (Chicago: University of Chicago Press, 1991); Connell, *Romanticism, Economics and the Question of "Culture"* (Oxford University Press, 2001); Caygill, *Art of Judgement* (London: Basil Blackwell, 1989); McLane, *Romanticism and the Human Sciences: Poetry, Population, and the Discourse of the Species* (Cambridge University Press, 2000).

has led me to spend more time examining controversies among political economists than literary critics normally do; the book's second chapter, for example, dwells among political economists exclusively. It has also led me to give
them the benefit of the doubt and assume that their theories were motivated
by the same drive that animates most of us as professional intellectuals: a
genuine desire to understand the phenomena they observed. It goes without
saying that they did so within the terms and according to the protocols of
certain historically determined mental operations (otherwise known as "ideologies"), which were by definition outside of their purview.

Like many other literary critics who have lately addressed themselves to
these thinkers, I try to reveal and analyze those operations and to trace their
resemblance to the dynamics we also find in literary works of the period.
Displaying such overarching discursive processes has become a specialty of
literary critics during the last several decades, and it has allowed for a more
synthetic and a less platitudinous picture of relations between nineteenth-
century disciplines and the relatively undisciplined textual practices we call
"literature." This study tries to explain how they were, at first, divided by
common premises and then how their orientations toward each other shifted
as those premises were revised in the course of the century. In the first two
chapters, I trace a development in which political economists and their Romantic and early Victorian critics jointly relocated the idea of ultimate value
from a realm of transcendent spiritual meanings to organic "Life" itself and
made human sensations—especially pleasure and pain—the sources and signs
of that value. I explore the stresses and contradictions attending this fundamental remaking of value within each discourse as well as the interchanges in
which each tended to blame the other for its internal paradoxes.

Political economy, though, was not a static or monolithic entity, even in its
"orthodox" phase, so the first chapters of *The Body Economic* outline the
dynamic through which it developed what I call its "bioeconomics" and its
"somaeconomics." The first term, "bioeconomics," refers to political economy's concentration on the interconnections among populations, the food supply, modes of production and exchange, and their impact on life forms generally. In bioeconomics, "Life" is both the ultimate desideratum and the energy
or force that circulates through organic and inorganic nature. Stressing the
natural limitations on economic activity as well as the tendency of that activity
to rearrange nature, bioeconomics was a set of concerns that derived primarily
from the thought of Thomas Robert Malthus, whose *Essay on Population*
(1797) was both a foundational text of classical political economy and a powerful critique of its theory of value.

I employ the second term, "somaeconomics," to describe the theorization
of economic behavior in terms of the emotional and sensual feelings that are
both causes and consequences of economic exertions. This tradition of
thought is deeply rooted in British empiricism as a theory of action comple-

menting Lockean epistemology: just as we know only what comes through the senses, we are motivated primarily through the sensations (bodily and mental) of pleasure and pain. A long line of British "utilitarian" thinkers argued that we seek those things that produce pleasure and shun those that produce pain, but the "author" of the explicit sensationalism that often informed political economy was Jeremy Bentham. Although Adam Smith did not need Bentham to construct economic man (for Smith drew directly on medical vitalism), later political economists often referred to Bentham's pain/pleasure calculus as the "natural" basis of self-interested behavior. In this tradition, "happiness" or "enjoyment" are the ultimate values, and wealth itself is defined as the "means of enjoyment." As we'll see, Benthamite somaeconomics led political economists into a series of paradoxes and was consequently rejected or minimized by some theorists, but it nevertheless had (and has) remarkable staying power.

The bioeconomics initiated by Malthus, therefore, addressed the issues of life and death; the somaeconomics associated with Bentham dealt with those of pleasure and pain. Together they linked political economy to the life sciences of the early nineteenth century by concentrating on Man in nature, and on natural, corporeal Man. In the first two chapters of this book, I argue that political economy was one of the competing "organicisms" of the opening decades of the nineteenth century, in direct competition with Romanticism, and in subsequent chapters I demonstrate how it interacted with later developments in physiological, ecological, psychological, and anthropological sciences. Chapters 3 and 5 detail later episodes of Benthamite somaeconomics, whereas chapters 4 and 6 carry the story of Malthusian (and anti-Malthusian) bioeconomics into the later decades of the century.

Chapters 3 and 4 also explain how the political economists' somaeconomics and bioeconomics found their way into the plots of Charles Dickens, the most popular novelist of the mid-Victorian period. They did so, I argue, not despite the novelist's overt hostility to political economy, but, more perplexingly, because of it. In readings of *Hard Times* and *Our Mutual Friend*, I try to explain what it was about political economy that ensured the continual return of its literary antagonists to its own logic. And I also analyze what it was about the novel (especially as written by Dickens) that made it such a receptive host for that logic.

The extent of Dickens's hostile takeover of the problematics of somaeconomics and bioeconomics becomes even clearer when we turn to the relatively friendly ways in which George Eliot accommodated them. Political economists were common in George Eliot's milieu, where their connections to evolutionary theory, psychophysiology, and anthropology were understood and appreciated. Chapters 5 and 6 trace the links among these disciplines, revealing the kinship between Eliot's psychological sensationalism and neoclassical somaeconomics as well as the likeness between her plots of cultural development and those of Malthusian anthropological conjecture. George Eliot's acquaintance with political economy was at once direct and refracted through a spectrum of other disciplines, but her novelistic incorporations of it were not uncritical appropriations. Indeed, her knowledge of the varieties and uses of political economy made her a subtle and sophisticated analyst of its limits even as she relied on many of its fundamentals. The book's last chapters, on *Daniel Deronda* and *Scenes of Clerical Life*, attempt to show how political economy penetrated late nineteenth-century thinking about culture in ways that have subsequently become invisible to us.

Somaeconomics and bioeconomics appear in numerous aspects of the four novels analyzed. They have stylistic, structural, and thematic manifestations; they shape the plots and modes of characterization. Above all, though, this book explores their appearance through that elusive creature known variously as the implied author, the authorial persona, or the author effect: the traces of authorial subjectivity left by Charles Dickens and George Eliot. Each of these novels bears the impressions of a creative subject who is emphatically also a productive economic subject as understood by nineteenth-century political economists: one whose life and feelings have been transmitted to the textual product. Moreover, each novel figures the transfer of sensation and vitality differently and presses different questions about the state of the subject. Can productive authors be happy? Can they stay alive through their works? Must their value decline as their careers mature? Does cultural progress depend on their suffering? Unlike the political economists, the novelists wrote themselves into the economic picture, and in so doing they bent the framework of the discourse and pushed its assumptions about life and feelings into the foreground, where they can be thoroughly scrutinized.

This book may strike some readers as deficient in its treatment of the novelists' actual economic situations; admittedly, I have not found time to examine here the quite interesting forms of publishing, ownership, and marketing initiated by both Dickens and Eliot.[3] Their innovative entrepreneurship is, therefore, among the many aspects of their economic lives unexplored in this book. I must also admit that I was unable to spend as much time on the subtle authorial effects of the political economists whose works I analyze as I was on those of the novelists. I plead guilty to having passively followed the lead of the discourses themselves in devoting so much more attention to novelistic than to political-economic authorship. Let me simply note here in passing the irony that authorship is not only a more prominent feature of literary than of political-economic texts but also a feature whose economic dimensions are more likely to be thematized by novelists than by political economists.

---

[3] For a study of Dickens that examines some connections between his publication practices and his literary forms, see N. N. Feltes, *Modes of Production of Victorian Novels* (Chicago: University of Chicago Press, 1986).

The novels therefore gave political economy something it ordinarily lacked: a sustained encounter with the states of vitality and sensation it invented but failed to explore fully. Reading political economy through these novels while also reading the novels through political economy will, I hope, defamiliarize not only those two modes of writing but also the very notions of life and feeling on which they relied.

Chapter One

The Romantics and the Political Economists

How did political economy come to have such a bad odor among the most prominent literary figures of the early nineteenth century? Answering this question has lately proved more difficult than literary historians previously believed, for they used to be content to generalize about the natural antagonism between "organic" and "mechanistic" ways of thinking, or to gesture toward the rift between "enlightenment empiricism" and "Romantic idealism." Now literary and intellectual historians, however, are piecing together a complex picture, which relies less heavily on the self-representations of the "Lake Poets," especially Samuel Taylor Coleridge and Robert Southey.[1] Instead of taking the antagonism for granted, scholars are analyzing it in some detail, and they are uncovering both the multiple contexts of the disagreements and some surprising commonalities between British political economy and Romanticism. In this chapter I will sketch the development of hostilities, from the outraged reaction to the first editions of Thomas Robert Malthus's *Essay on Population*, through disagreements about the national economy during the Napoleonic War years, and into disputes (some might say misunderstandings) about the nature of labor, value, and happiness. But I will also explore the unacknowledged shared premises, the larger discursive agreements that made the terms of the controversies intelligible to both sides.

I hope to show that Romanticism and political economy should be thought of as competing forms of "organicism,"[2] both of which flourished in British

[1] Philip Connell's *Romanticism, Economics and the Question of "Culture"* (Oxford: Oxford University Press, 2001), which is the most authoritative and detailed examination of the topic, notes that early nineteenth-century commentators referred often to hostilities between "'scientific' forms of socio-economic analysis" and "an alternative strain of social criticism, which aligned itself in opposition to the new sciences of society, and which has subsequently come to be identified, above all, with the literary milieu of British Romanticism" (5). And yet we are still trying to understand the "leading causes" of the antipathy (25). For a general analysis of the original proximity between British (primarily Scottish) aesthetic and economic thought in the 1700s and their developing discordance at the end of the century, see Howard Caygill, *Art of Judgement* (London: Basil Blackwell, 1989).

[2] The meaning and history of "organicism" and "organism" in social and economic thought have been much analyzed. For a general discussion of the terms, see Raymond Williams, *Keywords* (New York: Oxford University Press, 1985). Immanuel Kant is said to have been the first to establish criteria for "organic" or natural entities, which, taken together, differentiate them from machines: (1) the whole determines the form and the relation of parts; (2) parts mutually form each other; and (3) the whole reproduces itself (*Critique of Judgment*, Part II, Analytics of Teleological Judgment). For descriptions of the uses of biological sciences and natural metaphors in the history of economic

radical thought at the turn of the century, and both of which fostered skepticism toward what they presented as their immediate predecessors' unrealistic faith in an idealized human rationality. The political economists, like the Romantics, privileged natural processes, operating according to intrinsic and lifelike dynamics, over what they regarded as artificial ones, mechanically constructed and willfully directed from without. Moreover, vital and natural processes served not only as analogies in the social visions of political economists and Romantics but also as the literal forces driving human behavior. Romantics and political economists attributed cohesion, conflict, change, and stability not to political direction from above but to the embodied experiences of the mass of the people: their lives and deaths, desires and frustrations, pains and pleasures.

Finally, I hope to show that Romantic notions of aesthetic value, as well as Romantic social commentary, connected and clashed with classical political economy's theories of value because corporeal and sensational experience were central to both. Each posited necessary conjunctures between the expense of life and the production of value, between suffering and owning, between investing vital energy in an object and making it transferable to others, but they described the connections in irreconcilable ways. This chapter will look at several explanations for the collision between Romantic writers and political economists over these issues—for example, the Romantics tended to take a peculiar form of work (their own) as paradigmatic of labor in general—but the first thing to notice is that the conflict could never have been so sharp if they had not been fighting over common ground.

POPULATION: SEX AND FOOD

The earliest overt controversy between the two groups clearly reveals their joint preoccupation with organic life, for it concerns the basic bodily issues of sexuality, reproduction, and food.[3] When Thomas Robert Malthus's *An Essay on Population* (first published in 1797) provoked their indignation on

---

thought, as well as analyses of economies as physiological organizations, see *Natural Images in Economic Thought: Markets Red in Tooth and Claw,* ed. Philip Mirowski (New York: Cambridge University Press, 1994). For the sources of political economy's organicism in Scottish Enlightenment thought, see Catherine Packham, "The Physiology of Political Economy: Vitalism and Adam Smith's Wealth of Nations," *Journal of the History of Ideas* 63 (2002): 465–81.

[3] Secondary works that discuss the Romantics and Malthus's population principle include the following: Connell, 13–41, 210–12; Maureen N. McLane, *Romanticism and the Human Sciences: Poetry, Population, and the Discourse of the Species* (Cambridge: Cambridge University Press, 2000); Frances Ferguson, "Malthus, Godwin, Wordsworth, and the Spirit of Solitude," in *Literature and the Body: Essays on Population and Persons,* ed. Elaine Scarry (Baltimore: Johns Hopkins University Press, 1988), 106–24; David Kaufman, *The Business of Common Life: Novels and Classical Economics between Revolution and Reform* (Baltimore: Johns Hopkins University Press, 1985).

these topics, Coleridge and Southey were not yet called "Romantics" and Malthus was not yet known as a political economist. Indeed, the resemblances among the three men might have seemed more obvious to contemporaries than their differences, for although the social thought of each was in flux, they were all affiliated with those circles loosely designated "radical." In 1800 Coleridge may have abandoned his faith in the French Revolution, but Southey had not, and both men still hoped for democratic change in Britain, as did Malthus's family and friends. His *Essay* was also the fruit of British radicalism, albeit of a different strain.

In the 1790s, while support for franchise reform was the definitive marker of radicalism, many varieties of the species flourished in relative harmony. Christians like Coleridge and Southey took inspiration from secularists like William Godwin, while Godwin, advocating an eventual voluntary sharing of wealth, seemed to resemble Jeremy Bentham, who put his trust in self-interest, because both supported the widest possible franchise on utilitarian grounds. In the new century, however, divisions among radicals were to become more fixed and obtrusive. In particular, the brand that came to be called "philosophical radicalism," the Benthamite variety championing parliamentary reform while stressing self-interest, was increasingly distinguished from more communitarian radicalisms. And, although the classical canon of political economy was largely unwritten when the century began, its line of development in the next three decades continually intertwined the discipline with Benthamite presuppositions. Malthus (and the political economists who were to follow), therefore, advanced one tendency within British radicalism, Coleridge and Southey advanced another, and the growing antipathy between Romanticism and political economy can partly be traced to their earlier political commonality.

Malthus's *An Essay on Population* and the reaction to it reveal not only that the antagonism between protopolitical economy and incipient Romanticism was internal to British radicalism at the turn of the century but also that several varieties of radical thought were placing a new emphasis on the lived experience, especially the sensational life, of the common people. The *Essay* was conceived inside this radical tradition and drew entirely from its stock of ideas, but it partly framed itself as a quarrel with one of radicalism's greatest heroes, William Godwin. Malthus set out to prove that, contrary to some fatuous remarks made by Godwin in the *Enquiry Concerning Political Justice and Its Influence on Morals and Happiness* (1793),[4] there are known limits to the "future improvement of society"—a thesis that, as many early reviewers noted, was hardly controversial. But Malthus's way of supporting his thesis

---

[4] The immediate irritant was "Essay II" of Godwin's *The Enquirer: Reflections on Education, Manners, and Literature* (1798), but, Malthus tells us in the "Preface," his objections to that essay "started the general question of the future improvement of society" and led him to formulate his own views in opposition to those articulated by Godwin in the *Enquiry.*

and the practical consequence he drew from it were highly controversial, and both challenged optimistic expectations of human progress. His assertion that population increases always outstrip increases in the food supply unless they are brought into equilibrium through misery (starvation, sexual abstinence, late marriage) or vice (prostitution, birth control, infanticide) went directly against Godwin's prediction that people would someday become so reasonable and temperate in their passions that they would be able to control reproduction at will. Godwin forecast a time when men and women, without the prodding of a government, would divide their wealth equitably, form virtuous attachments without the need for patriarchal marriage, and consider their offspring (whose numbers would be limited by the relative passionlessness of the prevailing manners) to be the responsibility of the community as a whole.

Instead of accusing Godwin of sedition and impiety, as conservative critics had, Malthus calmly demonstrated that Godwin's utopian vision was impossible because it rested on the unsubstantiated premise that truly rational social arrangements would diminish the passion between the sexes. Malthus argued that sexual desire is as constant a feature of human nature as the need for food, and he is one of the first modern thinkers to insist that sexual intercourse is both ineradicable and essential to human happiness. Malthus strengthened the side of British radicalism that emphasized the motivating force of bodily pleasure and made the needs of desiring bodies the basis of economic thought. Healthy, procreative sexual passion, he insisted, "seems to be that sort of mixture of sensual and intellectual enjoyment particularly suited to the nature of man, and most powerfully calculated to awaken the sympathies of the soul and produce the most exquisite gratifications."[5] Godwin, he charged, was a desiccated, heartless repressor of this legitimate enjoyment: "Those who from coldness of constitutional temperament have never felt what love is, will surely be allowed to be very incompetent judges with regard to the power of this passion to contribute to the sum of pleasurable sensations of life" (76).

Malthus's intention, historians now claim, was to refute Godwin within the assumptions of latitudinarian English natural theology,[6] but many of his contemporaries were scandalized by what appeared to be his sensual materialism, and he was immediately accused of adopting a base and irreligious view of human nature. That accusation, indeed, is reiterated four times in Robert Southey's angry review of the second edition of the *Essay.* The review appeared in 1803, and it closely follows marginal notes that Coleridge made in his copy of Malthus, so it seems to reflect the views of both poets and exposes another

[5] Thomas Malthus, *An Essay on the Principle of Population: Text, Sources and Background, Criticism,* ed. Philip Appleman (New York: Norton, 1976), 77. Subsequent pages will be given in the text.

[6] A.M.C. Waterman, *Revolution, Economics and Religion, 1798–1833* (Cambridge: Cambridge University Press, 1991); D. L. Mahieu, "Malthus and the Theology of Scarcity," *Journal of the History of Ideas,* 40 (1978): 476–74; and Connell, 13–62.

fissure that had earlier been present within English radicalism between those whose social thought was religiously inflected and those who kept their discourse within secular confines. Even in their most revolutionary youth, Coleridge and Southey had spoken in the idiom of Protestant Dissenting radicalism, modeling their activities on those of the early Christian church, and advocating "The republic of God's own making."[7] They made common cause with secularists in the eighteenth century because both opposed the Anglican Church establishment, but as early as 1796, Godwin's sexual politics had already drawn a reproof from Coleridge, who accused him of pandering to sensuality[8]—just the reverse of Malthus's critique. And the rifts between Christian and freethinking radicals became more apparent in the next century. Coleridge and Godwin became friends again in the 1800s, but by that time, Godwin was moving away from his earlier atheism. So, although Southey's review excoriates Godwin's as well as Malthus's thoughts on reproduction and sexuality, it continues a tendency within British radicalism that sought social change in conformity with a reformed and purified Christianity.

How, then, can I claim that Southey and Coleridge helped locate the happiness of the common body at the center of social discourse? The evidence, at first glance, would tend to point in the opposite direction, toward the promotion of spiritual over physical well-being. "The whole [of Malthus's argument]," Southey claimed, "proceeds upon the assumption, that lust and hunger are alike passions of physical necessity, and the one equally with the other independent of the reason and the will."[9] He hammered away at the *Essay*'s apparent biological determinism, opposing it to a belief in the active power of Christian virtue: "There lives not a wretch corrupt enough of heart, and shameless enough of front to say that this is so: there lives not a man who can look upon his wife and his daughter, who can think upon his sister, and remember her who bore him, without feeling indignation and resentment that he should be insulted by so infamous an assertion" (296). Malthus's sensualism, he insisted, is not only lewd but also blasphemous because it implies that God created human beings who are helplessly in the grip of an overpowering instinct and doomed either to misery or sinfulness. Southey the Christian radical sided with Godwin in blaming corrupt human institutions for the existence of misery and vice, for to blame the human organism is only, by extension, to blame God: "it remains to be seen . . . whether we are to

[7] *Letters of Samuel Taylor Coleridge*, ed. Bart Winer (London: Routledge and Kegan Paul, 1970), 196.

[8] *Watchman, The Collected Works of Samuel Taylor Coleridge*, ed. Bart Winer (London: Routledge and Kegan Paul, 1970), 196.

[9] Rev. of *An Essay on the Principles* [sic] *of Population*, in *The Annual Review and History of Literature for 1803*, 2:296.

complain of the folly of man, or of the will of God, for this is the alternative. Let not the impiety of the question be imputed to us!" (297).

The opposition between Christian free will[10] and materialist determinism that Southey framed in this review may have obscured Malthus's theological intentions, but it remained a continuous underlying current in the stream of attacks on political economy that flowed from the first generation of Romantic writers. It should not, however, lead us to underestimate the Romantics' own commitments to increasing the material welfare, comfort, and pleasure of the general population. Southey accused Malthus of overstating the role of sexual feeling in human happiness, but he did not discount earthly pleasure as a primary goal or recommend that the poor should transcend their desires. Indeed, he censured Malthus's pessimism about making significant improvements in the physical lives of the poor. Ironically, Malthus's seemingly scientific sensualism (however integrated into a meliorist theodicy) guided him to bleak conclusions about the material advantages of political reform, whereas the poets' volunteerism gave them faith in a more general future abundance. So in addition to attacking his sexual determinism in 1803, Southey excoriates Malthus's seeming indifference to the physical plight of the poor. Malthus acknowledged that propertyless laborers (the vast majority of the population) disproportionately suffered the miseries attending the pressure of population. It was they who lacked the resources to raise healthy children and whose offspring went hungry or died in infancy. The vices of the rich (prostitution and birth control, for example, which acted as "preventive checks" to population) were too expensive for them, so their passion often had no outlet other than in reproductive sexuality, which resulted in the "positive checks" of starvation, disease, or infanticide. To decrease the burden of their misery, Malthus argued that they should be discouraged from marrying early and bearing many children; he thought they should be encouraged to suffer the unhappiness of abstinence instead of the greater wretchedness of starvation and death. Consequently, he opposed the practice of giving impoverished couples extra relief for each child they had, noting that, in the long term, such a policy only lowered wages by producing a supply of labor in excess of demand, and he also suggested the eventual abolition of parish relief for able-bodied laborers and their families.

Southey responded to these proposals with all the fervor of a radical who fashioned himself as the defender of the poor, one whose duty was not only to secure more political rights but also to protect certain traditional rights of the propertyless, such as the right to parish relief from destitution. His 1803

---

[10] Not all Christians held this tenet. For a map of the various Christian positions on this topic and their impact on nineteenth-century social controversies, see Catherine Gallagher, *The Industrial Reformation of English Fiction: Social Discourse and Narrative Form, 1832–67* (Chicago: University of Chicago Press, 1985), chapter 1.

review demonstrates how wide the gap was between such communitarian radicals and the incipient philosophical radicals, who were often skeptical about the benefits of state interference in the economy and thought that traditional rights sometimes stood in the way of economic progress. Southey's radicalism had a material aim—the redistribution of wealth—inconsistent with Malthus's (and that of the political economists generally): the augmentation of the sum total of the wealth of the nation. The poor, according to classical political economy, would share in that wealth up to a point, for the total wealth of the country would grow, and the level of subsistence itself would rise. But the law of wages assured that the laboring population would normally earn little more than their subsistence, since it was thought that the labor supply would expand when wages were high, bringing the supply up to demand and lowering wages again. Southey countered that the rich were not compelled by some economic law but instead *chose* to keep laborers' wages down to a minimum. Paying parish rates (taxes on property that would be distributed to the needy poor) was the only way of transferring some additional portion of the wealth they had created back to the laborers' tables. Malthus, according to Southey, did not offer sound advice to the poor but merely sided with the rich, who "have found a place at the table of nature; and why should they be disturbed at their feast?" (300–301). Malthus's treatment of food thus seemed equally abominable to his treatment of sexual passion, for the *Essay* apparently promoted sex as an individual necessity while denying that a share in the community's food is everyone's birthright.

Through all of these substantial disagreements between Malthus and Southey, though, there persisted a similarity of emphasis on the organic lives of the poor, on their miseries and enjoyments, as indices of the commonweal's vitality, as forces propelling its movements, and as sources of its equilibrium. Both parties presented themselves as champions of natural man, whose feelings are as powerful as his thoughts, rejecting the tepid, artificial creature imagined by rationalists like Godwin. Both insisted that only actual experiences of observing ordinary life can serve as a basis for social diagnosis. "Life," "experience," "passion," and "nature": these are their common objects and their common values.

As Southey's political radicalism waned, he nevertheless maintained and nurtured his anti-Malthusianism, which hardened into a generalized opposition to political economy at the core of what has been called "Romantic Conservatism."[11] Southey and Coleridge gave up the newfangled radical idea of equality, but they clung all the more strenuously to their defense of the tradi-

[11] "Romantic Conservatism," writes David Eastwood, "might be defined negatively as the rejection of political economy." See "Robert Southey and the Intellectual Origins of Romantic Conservatism," *English Historical Review* 411 (April 1989): 308–31. See also Geoffrey Carnall, *Robert Southey and His Age: The Development of a Conservative Mind* (Oxford: Clarendon, 1960).

tional rights of the poor, especially their right to an adequate share of the food they produced. The critique of Malthus served as a bridge between radicalism and conservatism, making it fundamental to their social vision in both political phases. Philip Connell has astutely analyzed the context of Southey's review and has linked it to William Wordsworth's use of anti-Malthusian rhetoric in the 1805 *Prelude*, showing that both texts helped the Lake Poets to suppress their earlier affiliations with Godwin. Indeed, Connell demonstrates, Wordsworth even began the "Romantic" habit of disparaging Malthus as a latter-day Godwin, a thinker who considered passion dangerous, or at least dangerous for the poor. Malthus, as we'll see in the next chapter, went to considerable rhetorical lengths to propound both the rightness and necessity of sexual feeling, but, according to Connell, he was nevertheless referred to in the 1805 *Prelude* as among "those who think that strong affections, love / Known by whatever name, is falsely deem'd / A gift . . . / Of vulgar Nature, that its growth requires / Retirement, leisure . . ." (xii. 185–89).[12] Hence, anti-Malthusianism allowed the Lake Poets to salvage what they wanted to preserve from their earlier radicalism while projecting the hyperrationalism of Godwin onto Malthus and, later, political economy.

The success of the strategy seems apparent if we look ahead into the next decade and note that Percy Bysshe Shelley, reviving Romantic radicalism after the first generation had abandoned it, takes up the cry against Malthus in 1816:

> A writer of the present-day (a priest of course, for his doctrines are those of a eunuch and a tyrant) has stated that the evils of the poor arise from an excess of population, and that . . . the soothing, elevating and harmonious gentleness of the sexual intercourse and the humanizing charities of domestic life which are its appendages,—that is to be obliterated.[13]

Absent from Shelley's violent diatribe is any sense of Malthus's sexual radicalism, which had been so prominent a feature of Southey's review; for the later Romantic, Malthus only threatens "to deprive [the poor] of that property which is as strictly their birthright as a gentleman's land is his birthright, without giving them any compensation but the insulting advice to conquer . . . a propensity which persons of the most consummate wisdom have been unable to resist, and which it is difficult to admire a person for having resisted." Shelley here repeats the charge earlier made against Malthus's denial of the "birthright" of parish relief, but he does not at all share the other half

---

[12] Connell, 41–61.

[13] "A Philosophical View of Reform," *The Complete Works of Percy Bysshe Shelley* (New York: Scribner's, 1930), 7:32–33. For a discussion of this text in relation to political economy, see James Chandler, "Ricardo and the Poets: Representing Commonwealth in the Year of Peterloo," *The Wordsworth Circle* 25 (Spring 1994): 82–86. For a discussion of Malthus and Mary Shelley's *Frankenstein*, see Maureen McLane, 84–108.

of Southey's anti-Malthusianism. Instead, he magnifies Wordsworth's claim that Malthus hoped to suppress passion. Malthus, indeed, becomes an antisexual icon for Shelley, a eunuch and a tyrant dispensing a sentence of celibacy on the poor without understanding the misery entailed in sexual abstinence. The last phrase of this passage, in which Shelley expresses his contempt for chastity ("a propensity . . . it is difficult to admire a person for having resisted"), indicates the high value that he, in contradistinction to Southey, placed on sexual activity, and, ironically, it recalls Malthus's criticism of Godwin, Shelley's own father-in-law, for devaluing sexual passion. Without even realizing it, Shelley follows in Malthus's footsteps, propounding, against a putatively unsexed adversary, the necessity as well as the goodness of the passion between the sexes. Romanticism, to be sure, kept defining itself against Malthus, but not against the same Malthus.

As Shelley's unwitting repetition of Malthus indicates, underlying the substantial causes of antipathy, there remained common premises that he, too, shared with the author of *An Essay on Population*. Shelley, too, writes as if the state of laboring bodies is the key factor in the commonweal and depicts the common body as generally miserable. The populousness of a nation had long been thought to indicate its overall prosperity, but the economic instability of the postwar years helped focus attention not only on the *fact* that higher wages bring more babies and lower wages shrink the population but also on the *lived experience* of that generalization. As one historian of economics has recently put it, the actual processes by which life ebbed and flowed were earlier not thought a fit object of study: the laboring family was the "black box" that simply served as "something like a macro-economic production function for the labour market."[14] But the late eighteenth century had seen a flood of representations of common rural existence, in which writers like Wordsworth and Southey had participated. Malthus had only repeated a leading idea to which radicals in both the 1790s and the postwar period subscribed: the poor lived in relative misery even in fairly good times, and that fact was central, not peripheral, to the polity. His most important contribution to the population debate is his claim that the pressure of population operates constantly instead of coming into play in some distant future when the country will be fully inhabited. Population pressure is the daily, oppressive burden felt by 90 percent of the people. Both Southey and Shelley fully conceded that Malthus had not exaggerated either the degree or the significance of the national suffering; their agreement on this fundamental issue made it seem all the more outrageous for Malthus to claim that there was no political remedy.

A second strong connection between Shelley and Malthus was that both were essentially eudemonic or "utilitarian" moralists, maintaining that the best social system, like the best individual action, is that which yields the

[14] Henk W. Plasmeijer, "The Talk of the Town in 1798," *History of Economics Series* (9/24/01): 2.

greatest happiness to the greatest number. The doctrine is most famously associated with Jeremy Bentham, whom Shelley idolized, and the philosophical radicals, but there were also Christian utilitarians, like William Paley, who had a great influence on Malthus. Indeed, eudemonism was standard in both English natural theology and Scottish Enlightenment philosophy. And this broadly conceived "principle of utility" was a mainstay of radical reasoning (both Thomas Paine and William Godwin frequently appealed to the greatest-happiness principle in elucidating their ethical systems), for it seemed to lead to the conclusion that political institutions should be democratized to reflect the interests, and therefore promote the happiness, of the majority. Of course, "happiness" is a notoriously difficult term to define, and, as we'll see in future chapters, there were deep disagreements over its meaning as well as debates over its value. But those very debates disseminated the idea that the felicity of the multitude—the question of how they *feel*—as a collection of sensitive individuals, rather than, for example, the glory of God or the power of the State, was the purpose of civil arrangements.

War: Money, Debt, and Taxes

The next phase of the Romantics' encounter with political economy was shaped by the Napoleonic Wars, which drastically changed the immediate intellectual environment. They shifted the focus of economic thought to fiscal and monetary policy—taxes, the national debt, and paper money—on the face of it not topics that seem likely to generate passion or stimulate fundamental thinking about the nature of collective human life. But they were as hotly contested as the Malthusian controversy, and they served as the platform on which David Ricardo reformulated the discipline's bases and made it a political force. It was in the debates over these topics, moreover, that the competing models of the social organism emerged that would dominate nineteenth-century thought.

After the peace of Amiens in 1802, many proponents of parliamentary reform developed political, social, and economic models that stressed national cohesion and drew as much on Edmund Burke as on Thomas Paine or William Godwin. Already disenchanted by French revolutionary terror, radicals often responded to French imperial aggression in the years between 1804 and 1816 by couching their message in the language of patriotism and warfare. They did not altogether jettison the utilitarian principle of the greatest happiness, which implied that the nation was the sum of its individual members; indeed, they were glad to have an indigenous British concept, free of all references to the "rights of man," on which to base their political program. Jeremy Bentham therefore became an important radical leader, around whom gathered the "philosophical radicals" James Mill, J. R. McCulloch, and David

Ricardo, even as such longtime campaigners for parliamentary reform as Major John Cartwright and Sir Francis Burdett adapted their message to the new circumstances by conceding the legitimacy of the crown in order to produce a "head" for the organism of the nation, softening criticism of the established church, and gaining an ally in the former Tory journalist William Cobbett.[15] Still allied in their support for parliamentary reform, therefore, distinct radical tendencies, which might be as dissimilar as the Benthamites and the Cobbettites, continued to develop in separate directions.

Whether closer in analytic framework to Cobbett or to Bentham, radicals were generally critical of the war economy, but for divergent reasons. Those whose point of view was closer to Cobbett's implicitly began to place themselves in opposition to political economy in the later years of the decade, whereas in the previous decade, when radicals were usually pacifists, they had relied on Adam Smith's argument that warfare was a drain on the productive capacities of the nation. Radicals had not only tacitly accepted Smith's analysis but also claimed that war enriched the Crown and its allies at the expense of the middle and lower classes. However, as free trade became a moot issue, Napoleon's continental system making it impossible, and the war effort gained radical support, many reconciled their patriotism with their attack on the war economy by accusing commercial interests, especially those involved in foreign trade, of encouraging military mismanagement and corrupt administration. William Cobbett, Major John Cartwright, and Sir Francis Burdett attacked the financial system based on high taxes, national debt, and paper money, not as the outcome of financing any war, but as the result of ineffectual generalship, fraud, and profiteering. Developing a form of Little Englandism *avant la lettre*, radical parliamentary reformers of this new stripe maintained that the country needed no foreign trade or empire, no national debt or paper money, and that only a reformed Parliament could deliver the people from administrations principally beholden to commercial interests.

Anticommercial radicalism strongly influenced those Romantics who remained within the radical fold. Witness, for example, Shelley's postwar diatribe against the national debt: an "execrable contrivance of misrule," which multiplies "the number of those who are idle in proportion to those who work, while it increases, through the factitious wants of those indolent, privileged persons, the quantity of work to be done."[16] Shelley apparently swallowed Cobbett's view of the wartime economy whole and, in "A Philosophical View of Reform," waxed as irate about the suspension of payment on banknotes as about the existence of the debt. The Bank of England (then a private corporation) had been instructed by the government to suspend cash (that is

---

[15] See Peter Spence, *The Birth of Romantic Radicalism: War, Popular Politics and English Radical Reformism, 1800–1815* (London: Scholar Press, 1996).

[16] "Philosophical View of Reform," 25.

coin) redemption of its banknotes in 1797 as a temporary expedient to quell panics resulting from rumors of invasion, and the suspension was afterward continued because it helped the government finance the war, a practice Shelley equated with outright deceit and theft: "They declared subsequently that these pieces of paper were the legal coin of the country. Of this nature are all such transactions of companies and banks as consist in the circulation of promissory notes to a greater amount than the actual property possessed by those whose names they bear. They have the effect of augmenting the prices of provision, and of benefitting at the expense of community the speculators in this traffic" (27). His long-term solution was the widest possible franchise, but he also offered a short-term solution to the problem of the national debt, proposing that, since it consists in "a debt contracted by the whole mass of the privileged classes towards one particular portion of those classes," the propertied class should pay only the principal to the investors, who would include some among themselves. "It would be a mere transfer among persons of property" (35), he claimed, and the nation would then be able to rid itself of the parasites that drain its vitality. To be sure, Shelley did not, like some other popular radicals of the time, waste soft words on the monarchy, but he attributed its power to the existence of a "fictitious paper currency" (39), so that the financial revolution, as in Cobbett's analysis, was said to be the source of modern oppression. By identifying public credit as the main enemy, Shelley implicitly places those who live by financial transactions outside the legitimate national community.

Meanwhile, David Ricardo used political economy to mount a very different critique of the war economy. Between the publication of the second edition of Malthus's *Essay* in 1803 and that of Ricardo's *Principles of Political Economy and Taxation* in 1817, no widely read book in the new discipline appeared. Malthus entered into debates over the nature of value and formulated a theory of rent that became a basic tenet of the developing discipline; he also began calling himself a political economist, a fact that may have further alienated the Romantics from the whole enterprise. As the economy underwent dramatic changes, David Ricardo wrote articles and pamphlets criticizing the government's wartime fiscal policies, especially the suspension of specie payments by the Bank of England and the concomitant growth of the national debt. But he did not encourage the conspiracy theorists of paper money or use the national debt as an excuse for attacking commercial interests. Recognizing the necessity of raising taxes in order to support the war, Ricardo thought it would be better to tax subjects directly than to expand the national debt as a form of financing. His concern, unlike that of Shelley and the anticommercial radicals, was not that an idle elite deceived the honest people, exercising undue influence over the government and siphoning off the country's wealth. Indeed, he maintained that paying the interest on the national debt had no effect on the national wealth, but that the debt should nevertheless be speedily liquidated because "the system of borrowing . . . to defray the extraordinary [wartime] expenses of the state" "blind[s] us to our real situation." Called upon to pay only the interest on the debt, the taxpayers forget that they are spending millions and put off the day of reckoning until the end of the war, setting aside no savings to meet their collective obligation. As he later phrased his position in *The Principles*, if people had to pay directly their shares of the cost of the war, "as soon as the war ceased taxation would cease, and we should immediately fall into a natural state of prices."[17]

To Ricardo, therefore, war financing was no fraud perpetrated by a swindling elite against the true nation, but only a form of self-delusion. He had begun to complain of such policies in his debut publications in 1809, which argued that the Bank of England was mistakenly issuing an excessive number of banknotes and thereby causing price inflation and destabilizing the markets in precious metals. Ricardo was interested in finding a money form that would allow the relative values of commodities to appear; establishing the gold standard was intended to remove an obstructing, artificial fiscal system, to neutralize money and make it a transparent medium for exchange values, which originated in the amount of labor required in their production. Whereas Shelley seemed to maintain that paper money and credit were necessarily fraudulent, Ricardo simply wanted them properly regulated so they would not interfere with trade. He achieved his goal in the immediate postwar period; in 1817, consciously appealing to the desire for a scientific understanding of monetary policy but probably also buoyed by popular prejudice against paper money and bankers in general, he led Parliament to reinstate cash redemption of banknotes. Only a tiny group of irresponsible speculators, he prophesied, would lose by the policy. In fact, a deflationary period of deep distress ensued, which Ricardo and other "bullionists" attributed not to their monetary policy but to postwar restructuring of the economy and to the government's protection for agriculture in the form of the Corn Laws, which were passed in 1815 over Ricardo's, but not Malthus's, objections.

Ricardo wanted a fiscal policy that would be ready to shift into free-trade practices as soon as the national emergency allowed, and a transparent currency, one that let commodities trade for their *natural* prices, was therefore necessary. He, too, based his proposals on a holistic, organic understanding of the nation, but unlike Cobbett's or Shelley's, Ricardo's social organism was driven by the commercial urge, although, as we'll see, it contained internal resistance. The economy, he thought, should be encouraged to achieve a homoeostatic balance independently. A faulty currency could misrepresent the

[17] *The Principles of Political Economy and Taxation*, ed. Donald Winch (London: J. M. Dent and Sons, 1973), 163. On the postwar development of political economy, see Cary F. Langer, *The Coming of Age of Political Economy, 1815–1825* (New York: Greenwood, 1987), 230.

organism's well-being and might also attract investment into ultimately un-productive channels, threatening the health of the entire entity.

Inside these general wartime transformations of radical thought—in which, on the one hand, commercial interests were portrayed as cynically profiteering while patriots paid their way, and, on the other, commercial freedom was said to be threatened by wartime expediency—many British writers found themselves with new allies and new grudges. Just as the former Tory anti-Jacobin William Cobbett came around to supporting parliamentary reform, making a convert of Shelley, Coleridge and Southey became more nationalistic and bellicose, and in the second decade of the century, they became unortho-dox Tories themselves. Coleridge, especially, found a distinctive political van-tage point from which to attack both anticommercial and procommercial radicals.

It has often been said that Coleridge counterposed an organic model of the nation against competing mechanistic models, and certainly he strove to give that impression. But in fact one would be hard-pressed to find political and economic commentators who refrained from organic metaphors in those years. The source of nineteenth-century political economy's organicism lay in the vitalist physiology that was developed in the previous century at the Edinburgh Medical School and informed Adam Smith's social and economic theories.[18] It was consequently easy for political economists to line up behind Edmund Burke's attack on the French revolution for trying to substitute an artificial social and political system for a living legacy of national feeling deeply rooted in a distinctive way of life. The ubiquity of holistic and naturalist social thought during the war posed something of a rhetorical challenge for Coleridge, and his reflections on political economy during those years reveal an attempt to wrest organicist rhetoric from both anticommercial radicals and political economists. In an 1809 essay in *The Friend,* Coleridge actually defended the war's financing, and his most surprising display of metaphoric virtuosity is an organicist defense of the national debt:

> What has rendered Great Britain . . . with more than metaphorical propriety a BODY POLITIC, our Roads, Rivers, and Canals being so truly the veins, arteries, and nerves, of the state; that every pulse in the metropolis produces a correspondent pulsation in the remotest village on its extreme shores! . . . I answer without hesitation, that the cause and mother principle of this unexampled confidence, of this *system* of credit, which is as much stronger than mere positive possessions, as the soul of man is than his body . . . has been our NATIONAL DEBT.[19]

---

[18] Packham, "The Physiology of Political Economy."

[19] *The Friend,* I, *The Collected Works of Samuel Taylor Coleridge,* ed. Barbara E. Rooke (London: Routledge and Kegan Paul, 1969), 230.

However, it was not enough merely to develop his own bodily analogies, supplemented by references to credit as the "soul" of the nation; he also needed to denigrate his enemies' organic rhetoric. Therefore, returning to the body-state metaphor in another essay, he associated it with "the sect of Economists"—by which he meant not only the eighteenth-century French *économistes* but also Sir James Steuart and, one might suggest, Adam Smith—and accused them of mistaking their verbal construct of the body politic for an actual living being and of sacrificing real bodies to its merely fictive vigor. As much as the real patriot desires to make a "body politic" out of separate individuals, Coleridge claimed, "he places limits even to this wish," whereas the "sect of economists" allows concrete individuals to become "diseased and vicious, in order that each may become useful to *all*, or the State, or the Society," which is a mere "non-entity under the different words" (299). By the end of the war, Coleridge was urging skepticism toward holistic and organic analogies on the grounds that they often distort organic realities, justifying actual human suffering in the name of a healthy "body politic." Hence his insistence that such metaphors be "more than metaphoric," that they describe economic systems that nourish individual lives. What the political economists called a social body, he complained, was merely "a self-regulating economic machine,"[20] the workings of which severely injured actual people.

Coleridge's desire to gain a monopoly on true organicism is perhaps best demonstrated by the fact that the political economist he reviled most was the very thinker who worried most about the physical well-being of the poor: Malthus.[21] Unfolding a theory of rent and of the rising costs of production in agriculture, Malthus's wartime writings also expressed the concern that capital might abandon agriculture for manufacturing and that the food supply might therefore be threatened. As a consequence of these fears, he supported policies to protect and encourage the landed interests, including the Corn Law of 1815. The economic body politic had to adjust actual bodies to their available nutrients, Malthus insisted: abolish the Poor Laws to keep down the population and protect the landed interests to keep up food production. Although Coleridge opposed those measures, the two writers similarly demanded a constant attention to the health and vitality of laboring bodies. Moreover, as we'll see more clearly in the next chapter, Malthus even outdid Coleridge by inventing a literal form of organicism that concentrated on the biological life of populations as the fundamental social fact.

[20] *Lay Sermons, The Collected Works of Samuel Taylor Coleridge*, ed. R. J. White (London: Routledge and Kegan Paul, 1972), 205.

[21] For more on the similarities between Coleridge and Malthus, see Donald Winch, *Riches and Poverty: An Intellectual History of Political Economy in Britain, 1750–1834* (Cambridge: Cambridge University Press, 1996), 289–306, 396–404, and Connell, 16–17, 30–47.

The Postwar Period: Value, Labor, and Class Conflict

As political economy coalesced in the postwar period around Ricardo's analyses, it increasingly became a kind of life science: the quantity of vital human energy exerted in its production—that is to say, the quantity of labor—was acknowledged to be the only source of a commodity's exchange value, a fact that led to an inevitable conflict between classes over the division of wealth. And the resulting unresolvable tension between the elements of the social organism was further thought to require constant economic expansion. Far from seeming a machine with a fixed input and output, the national capitalist economy was imagined to be a creature facing the distinctly lifelike alternatives of either growing or dying. In the postwar period, political economy was increasingly used to explain the relations among labor, value, and life, as well as the peculiarly conflicted relations among various parts of the social organism. After briefly summarizing the main points of Ricardo's argument, I will discuss, first, some Romantic perspectives on the issue of labor and value, and, second, Coleridge's understanding of the inevitability of class conflict.[22]

Ricardo's *Principles of Political Economy and Taxation* opens with the question of how a society's wealth is distributed among the three parties involved in its production: labor (or the working class), capital (or the owners of the means of production), and rent (or the land-owning class). He did not ask how it should be distributed or how statesmen intend that it be distributed, but how it is distributed, following the internal and natural dynamics of capitalism, without any premeditation. His first step in answering this question was to explain how things acquire their exchangeable value in the first place, distinguishing the origin of value from its measurement. Following but also amending passages in Smith and Malthus, Ricardo clarified and developed the labor theory of exchange value, which his predecessors had confusingly and ambivalently indicated. Adam Smith took labor to be the measure of exchange value and often calculated the value of labor by the value of the commodities (primarily the food) necessary to replenish the body for the hours of labor expended on another commodity. Thus he rooted the exchange value of any commodity in biological need; the worker's body was the primary nexus of exchange through which the value of those commodities that reproduce its labor largely determine the value of all other commodities. Smith, for example, showed that money is merely a representation of labor: "What is bought with money or with goods is purchased by labour as much as what

---

[22] For an account of the differences between Coleridge's social vision and that of the political economists, see David P. Calleo, *Coleridge and the Idea of the Modern State* (New Haven: Yale University Press, 1966); see also William F. Kennedy, *Humanist versus Economist: The Economic Thought of Samuel Taylor Coleridge* (Berkeley: University of California Press, 1958).

we acquire by the toil of our own body."[23] He went on to explain, "The real price of everything, what everything really costs to the man who wants to acquire it, is the *toil and trouble* of acquiring it. What everything is really worth to the man who has acquired it, and who wants to dispose of it or exchange it for something else, is the *toil and trouble* which it can save to himself, and which it can impose upon other people" (47). As Thomas De Quincey often asserted, Ricardo cleared up many inconsistencies in Smith's formulations, distinguishing especially between labor as the origin and labor as the measure of value, and his corrections had the effect of rendering value even more definitively biological. For by insisting that the *quantity* of labor, the measurable sum of the workers' lives, is the sole determinate of a commodity's "natural" exchange value,[24] he further literalized the older metaphors of the economy as an animated being. In the Ricardian theory, human vitality pulses through every exchange.

After establishing this essential rule, Ricardo's *Principles* returns to the question of who gets what share of the produce of labor. The wealth, he explained, is allocated by the vital needs of the economy itself, especially by the imperative that it constantly *grow* in order to stay alive. Integrating Malthus's theory of rent and extending his idea that population growth brings less and less fertile land into arable production, necessitating greater labor for the same crop, Ricardo concluded that there was a general tendency for the rate of profit to drop: *ceteris paribus*, as food becomes more valuable because of the increase of labor required to cultivate it, the share of production going to profits falls, and the incentive to accumulate and invest erodes. This can only be offset by new labor-saving inventions, the creation of new enterprises, and the opening of new markets. Capitalism simply had to grow to survive its own inertial drag, what Ricardo called its "gravitation," and of the three classes contending for the produce of labor, only the capitalists are in a position to make it grow. Obviously, they struggle forcefully against the falling rate of profit, for profit is their share of the produce, and only capital's restless search for the highest return on its investment could augment the overall wealth of the nation by "employing a greater portion of revenue in the maintenance of productive labour . . . or . . . making the same quantity [of labor] more productive" (186). The shares of the produce of labor are therefore apportioned by the constant struggle among the three contending classes in the context of the varying conditions retarding or advancing the rate of profit and contracting or expanding economic activity.

[23] Adam Smith, *An Inquiry into the Nature and Causes of the Wealth of Nations* (Oxford: Clarendon Press, 1976), 1:47.

[24] Several other factors, including the ratio of supply to demand, might influence the market price of a commodity, but these would act as temporary modifications of the "natural" value. On Ricardian economics, see Mark Blaug, *Ricardian Economics: A Historical Study* (New Haven: Yale University Press, 1958); and D. P. O'Brien, *The Classical Economists* (Oxford: Clarendon Press, 1975).

The easiest part of Ricardo's book for contemporaries to accept and assimi-late to various agendas was its apparent restatement of the labor theory of value, with its echoes not only of Adam Smith but also of John Locke, or, for that matter, the Bible. The theory could be taken to buttress commonplace bourgeois pieties: labor is virtuous and should be cheerfully sought; one should work as hard as possible; the industrious are superior to the idle. Work was increasingly valorized, even idealized, as a good in itself, not only a means to an end but also a process through which one realized oneself. Moreover, as the economic distress deepened instead of lifting in the 1820s, a new radical working-class movement used the theory to press its own claims: if labor alone created value then laborers deserve the whole produce of their efforts.

These moral and political uses of the theory, though, operated at a great distance from the political economists' intentions. If we examine their reason-ing about labor and value, we can see that they were by no means touting the independent virtues of work, which for them remained mere toil. In fact, as we'll see in much greater detail in the next chapter, they assumed it was a *painful* necessity, certainly not a joyful activity or a means of self-realization, and it is only as pain that labor factors into the pain/pleasure calculation that economic agents make when deciding how to spend their time. "Aversion," explained Jeremy Bentham, "is the emotion, the only emotion, which labour, taken by itself, is qualified to produce."[25] "Aversion" leads to the division of labor in the first place and then motivates people to keep track of the time spent in various tasks. Although the labor theorists of value seldom dwelt on the quality of exertion expended in production, they nevertheless assumed as axiomatic that everyone strives to counterbalance the affliction of labor by the pleasures of remuneration and consumption. If work were intrinsically pleasurable, economic calculations would be unmotivated, and one would not be able to tell the difference between labor and leisure. The labor theory of value, in short, rested on certain naturalistic assumptions about how our individual sensations, our sensitivity to pain and pleasure, are aggregated into complex economic systems.

The labor theory of value in the hands of political economists, therefore, was not a platform for praising labor. To them, labor was important because it was so *unpleasant* a thing that no one would voluntarily undertake it. For that reason, too, laborers would cease to labor if not compelled by necessity; it was generally believed that abundant remuneration would, even if it did not increase the working-class population and thereby lower wages through competition, decrease the number of hours people were willing to spend work-ing. Instinctive aversion to labor would therefore render impracticable schemes like that of William Thompson to encourage small-scale working-

<hr>

[25] *Deontology, Together with a Table of the Springs of Action, and the Article on Utilitarianism,* ed. Amnon Goldworth (Oxford: Clarendon Press, 1983), 104.

class capital accumulation so that "the industrious become capitalists as well as laborers, each possessed of that portion of capital which is requisite to make his labor productive."[26] To the extent that one had capital, one would use it to stop working, and the same argument could be applied to all schemes for delivering the whole produce of labor to the laborers themselves.

Coleridge noted early on that political economists viewed labor from this peculiar vantage point, although he seems to have missed the reason for their self-imposed limitation. Since the publication of *The Wealth of Nations*, political cal economists had explained that they were primarily concerned with the labor that created *exchange* value; such labor would have to be performed inside a market economy and produce a surplus over the subsistence (or reproduction) of the labor itself. This sort of labor, which yields a profit as well as a wage, Smith called "productive" to distinguish it from other kinds of work, which might nevertheless be both necessary and creative: in his list, "The sovereign, for example, with all the officers both of justice and war who serve under him, the whole army and navy, are unproductive labourers. . . . In the same class must be ranked, some both of the gravest and most important, and some of the most frivolous professions: churchmen, lawyers, physicians, men of letters of all kinds; players, buffoons, musicians, opera-singers, opera-dancers; &c" (295). The division of the population into kinds of laborers was both an extraordinary innovation (since previously many of the people on Smith's list weren't imagined to be laboring at all) and a neutral analytical tool by which those who built up the nation's capital could be distinguished from those who did not. Later political economists disputed the boundaries and usefulness of these categories, but the distinction was never intended to separate valid from invalid, or useful from useless occupations.

But Coleridge, like many other critics of political economy, seemed to think that it was, and he chose to base his critique of the political economists' logic on an early, and superseded, iteration of the distinction, by James Steuart (1767), in which what would later be termed "productive" is called "useful to society" and "unproductive" is identified as "useful only to oneself." Steuart used the example of a vine-dresser who spends half his day growing enough grain to feed himself and his family and the other half growing grapes for the market, to be exchanged for other commodities. Using this example to demonstrate the difference between "Agriculture exercised *as a trade*, and as *a direct means of subsisting*," Steuart concluded, "that as to the last part he is only useful to himself; but as to the first, he is useful to the society and becomes a member of it; consequently were it not for his trade the State would lose nothing, although the vine-dresser and his land were both swallowed up

[26] William Thompson, *Labor Rewarded: The Claims of Labor and Capital Conciliated* (New York: A. Kelly, 1827), 87.

by an earthquake."[27] Influenced, perhaps, more by the closing image than by the logic of the entire passage (in which Steuart is articulating the levels of market, society, and state), Coleridge took Steuart to mean that the man's life is useless, that he is a cipher unworthy to live, and Coleridge goes on to claim that this narrow definition of value in labor can distort and corrupt social existence. Devising a contrasting idyll, Coleridge imagines a countryman who, after spending half the day in subsistence farming, "endeavoured to provide for his moral and intellectual appetites, by physical experiments and philosophical research, by acquiring knowledge for himself, and communicating it to his wife and children." "Would he be useful then?" Coleridge asks, and imagines the negative reply of the political economist: "*He* useful! The state would lose nothing although [he] and his land were both swallowed up by an earthquake!" (300).

It was Coleridge, of course, not Steuart, who moralized the issues; Steuart said only that a man living in complete economic isolation would not be missed by the state if he disappeared, whereas Coleridge seems to think he was being condemned to perdition, cast into some sort of hell. Moreover, Coleridge's competing idyll has all the unreality of the genre: if the man were truly laboring only for subsistence, how could he have the means for "physical experiments and philosophical research?" Steuart's point was that such things come from surplus, exchangeable produce, whereas Coleridge apparently thought that they were just given in the state of nature. He is really picturing an idealized version of himself, a man of middle-class means doing light labor in the morning and spending the afternoon in scholarly pursuits, or in being "neighborly," like the author of *The Friend*.

And that, indeed, was typical of the Romantic train of thought. Coleridge's mind ran so quickly and defensively to a situation like his own—to the value of providing for "his moral and intellectual appetites" and "acquiring knowledge for himself and communicating it"—because political economy seemed to denigrate intellectual and authorial labor. What, after all, does it add to the wealth of the nation? Assuming its paltry contribution to capital and its usual inability even to support the writer's household, what sort of labor is it? It seems neither "useful to society" nor sufficiently "useful to himself." "Men of letters of all kinds" are definitely on Adam Smith's list of "unproductive" workers, to use the terminology later employed by most classical political economists; and even though the mixed nature of the company (ranging from the sovereign to the buffoon) should make it clear that "unproductive" is not a term of moral condemnation, it nevertheless resonated negatively.

It is hard to determine whether political economy created an anxious defensiveness about authorial—especially literary—production or merely provided a focus for a worry engendered by the larger sea change in the general attitude

---

[27] *The Friend*, I, 299.

toward labor, but nineteenth-century writers, starting with the Romantics, certainly felt compelled to describe their labors, while expanding the concept of productivity in ways that countered the economists' apparent reduction. Some, like Coleridge, developed vitalistic accounts of their literary products, which resembled but also exceeded the labor theory of value's accent on the amount of *life* (the quantity of labor) that goes into a product. Literary labor might not appear to be exertion at all, might, as in Coleridge's version of the composition of "Kubla Khan," be accomplished in one's sleep, but for that very reason be the conduit of a powerful visionary force. Just as Coleridge broke down the distinction between acting and recuperating, Wordsworth also confounded the border between leisure and labor, indolence and industry. In contrast to labor's normal, externally coerced condition, its poetic state, as implied in Wordsworth's famous formulation—"spontaneous overflow of powerful feeling"—is unwilled and unconstrained.

The emotion of the poetic worker, like that of the political economists' laborer, is apposite to the product's value as well, but here, too, we see a striking contrast. Unhappiness may subtend labor in political economy and may therefore condition exchange value, but the commodity itself isn't painful; indeed, it is normally pleasurable. In contrast, the poetic product actually *is* the superabundance of powerful, unsubdued feeling, which might indeed be painful and yet mingled with the pleasurable effects of the medium when read or heard. The intermixing of pain and pleasure in both the production and consumption of poetry would, moreover, seem to place it in a realm far from the Benthamite calculus on which exchange value rests, in which the two kinds of sensation must be easily told apart so that we will know what, in Bentham's terms, to "minimize" and what to "maximize." The Romantics, one might *almost* say, might have claimed that their work made a clean contrast with Ricardian labor by being an unalienated expression of the superabundance of affective being (Shelley's "happiest moments" of the happiest of men), in which emotional states are often complex wholes and products are inseparable from producers.

But that is only one side of the Romantics' representation of their labor. On the other side, we should note their emphasis on the suffering of creative work, especially in Coleridge and De Quincey, which seems to share in the labor theory of value's implicit reliance on unhappy work. The very absence of a resistant material medium, which might seem the condition of unconstrained labor, also threatened to mire the poet in fanciful delusions. The precarious state of the poet, his desolation or harrowing experiences in the terrifying depths of the imagination, are sensational versions of the laborer's intimacy with mortality, the constant pressure of necessity in his existence. And the writer's vocational challenges, as Wordsworth's *Prelude* attests, are recurrent themes, as is the complex relation between his own labor and the often economically marginal laboring lives he depicted.[28] Although not highly productive in an economic sense, the lives of Wordsworth's country people receive a different kind of value through their representation, and the poet might be said to "live," through the sympathetic understanding instantiated in the poems, their accumulated struggles. The poet, in other words, came up with a competing answer to the question of how laborers produce value, and he made himself the center of that process; but as in the political economists' account, value still seems to rely on deprivation.

Romanticism, we might say, activated a latent contradiction between eighteenth-century aesthetics, which often privileged the desirable pain of sublimity, and Utilitarianism, which assumed all pain to be undesirable. In his *Philosophical Enquiry into the Origin of Our Ideas of the Sublime and the Beautiful,* Edmund Burke had already linked, while differentiating, toil and the terror of the sublime: "as common labor, which is a mode of pain, is the exercise of the grosser, a mode of terror is the exercise of the finer parts of the system. . . ."[29] And yet the aestheticians were no more paradoxical than the economists in preferring the pain-born product; indeed, it is no mere coincidence that the sublime was elevated above the beautiful in the same decades that labor, old Adam's affliction and the bane of human existence, was discovered to be the source of value. For Edmund Burke's aesthetics rested on the same groundwork of vitalist physiology that supported Adam Smith's economics.[30] By linking the agony of the poet to the unhappiness of the laborer, Romanticism further solidified this kinship between the economists' and the aestheticians' concepts of value.

The Romantics, that is, defended literary labor in two, incommensurate ways: (1) they presented it as an idealized, perhaps utopian, contrast to the economists' miserable but "productive" labor, and (2) they stressed that they felt as alienated in their work, as jeopardized or engulfed in suffering, as any productive worker. Their representation of labor crossed that of the political economists sometimes and at others ran parallel to it. The deeper similarity, though, was that both groups undertook the description of the relations among life, labor, feeling, and value; despite the huge differences between

[28] For discussions of these topics and further elaboration of Romantic poetic labor, see Gary Harrison, *Wordsworth's Vagrant Muse: Poetry, Poverty, and Power* (Detroit: Wayne State University Press, 1994); Clifford Siskin, *The Work of Writing: Literature and Social Change in Britain, 1700–1830* (Baltimore: Johns Hopkins University Press, 1998); Willard Spiegelman, *Majestic Indolence: English Romantic Poetry and the Work of Art* (New York: Oxford University Press, 1995); Thomas Pfau, *Wordsworth's Profession: Form, Class, and the Logic of Early Romantic Cultural Production* (New York: Cambridge University Press, 1993).

[29] *Philosophical Enquiry into the Origin of Our Ideas of the Sublime and the Beautiful,* Part 4, Sec. vi. For more on feeling, labor, and poetry, see Kevis Goodman, *Georgic Modernity and British Romanticism: Poetry and the Mediation of History* (Cambridge: Cambridge University Press, 2004).

[30] Aris Sarafianos, "Pain, Labour, and the Sublime: Medical Gymnastics and Burke's Aesthetics," forthcoming in *Representations.*

them, both felt professionally dedicated to that task. To be sure, most political economists paid short shrift to their own labor or to that of any professional men and/or writers, for they all fell outside of the "productive" fold. Smith, for example, did not seem at all bothered by the fact that he belonged to his own "unproductive" category. The poets, however, looked to their own work as paradigmatic for understanding the right relations among life, labor, and value, and what they found there was no harmonious enterprise, but a seemingly contradictory juxtaposition of states, which eluded the available ideological frameworks. Eventually theirs would come to seem a freestanding discourse, the one we call "Romanticism," which drew on the earlier idea of the sublime and featured the fusion of pain and pleasure in the creator and his product.

We should not leave the topic of value without mentioning the contribution of the one Romantic writer who aspired to be something of a political economist himself and who subscribed to the Ricardian position: Thomas De Quincey. He wrote two important works on the subject; the first, *Dialogues of Three Templars on Political Economy, Chiefly in Relation to the Principles of Mr. Ricardo* (1824), explicates and defends Ricardo, stressing his superiority to Smith and Malthus; the second, *The Logic of Political Economy* (1844), attempts to clarify the theory of value by paying special attention to the concept of "use value." Like Ricardo, De Quincey ignored the emotional state of the producer; the very category of labor assumed that which people generally wish to avoid, and so it did not need to be explicated. The subjective state of the purchaser was normally likewise inapposite to exchange value, but De Quincey claimed that the strength of desire can have an effect on the value of an item whenever supply and demand are not in equilibrium. Then, he argued, exchange value can be shown to consist not only of what he calls the "negative" value of the cost of production (labor) but also the "positive" value of "use," or the value of the commodity to a particular purchaser at a particular time. Use value may normally be submerged in exchange value, but in eccentric markets it reveals itself to be part of the market value.

De Quincey is careful to point out that he is not talking about *intrinsic* usefulness, or some objective utility in the commodity; in order to obviate such misunderstandings, he goes so far as to discuss the market value of a rare poison for one who might want to kill himself. Use value seems altogether personal; it is "the utmost sacrifice to which you would ever submit . . . under the known alternative of losing [the commodity] if you refuse."[31] The extreme subjectivity of the origin of use value, therefore, requires an inordinate amount of narrative; we cannot, for example, conceive the economic logic of a man

[31] *The Logic of Political Economy,* in *The Works of Thomas De Quincey* (New York: Hurd and Houghton, 1878), 10:81. For more on De Quincey and political economy, see Josephine McDonagh, *De Quincey's Disciplines* (Oxford: Clarendon Press, 1994).

who pays one hundred times the "natural" price for a music box unless we know where he is, where he's going, and what his personal tastes are. There is, indeed, so much circumstantial narrative in De Quincey's explication of use value that it overwhelms his abstract point: use value is always there in market value even when the equilibrium of the market keeps it identical with exchange value. And even if one were willing to cede the point—John Stuart Mill thought it had been anticipated from the beginning—it is difficult to know how it could be applied on any but an individual, narrative basis.

The significance of De Quincey's book, therefore, lay less in its direct contribution to the discipline than in its impulse to draw out and examine the issue of subjective desire in political economy. In doing so, he anticipated the political economy of the end of the century, which would try to understand the relation between value and what came to be called the "marginal utility" of a commodity to the consumer. Moreover, unlike most Romantics, De Quincey also broached the question of aesthetic value from the point of view of the receiver of the art work. For example, in describing the relation between what he called "affirmative value" (what someone is willing to pay) and "negative value" (the quantity of labor invested or needed to reproduce the identical item), he seized on an aesthetic instance: "[A] genuine picture of Da Vinci's or Raphael's, sells always on the principle of value in use, or teleologic value" (82). The uniqueness of the works of the dead artist are what take them altogether out of the purview of the labor theory of value; they cannot be reproduced through any amount of labor, and yet they clearly have a market value. That value must be put there entirely by the potential purchasers.

This is one of De Quincey's highly unusual instances of a market value made up entirely of a use value, one that completely escapes the logic of the labor theory of value. In De Quincey's scheme, therefore, the specialness of the value of certain aesthetic works has nothing whatever to do with the agony or the ecstacy of the artist but arises wholly from the desire and the wherewithal of the beholder. It may seem odd that a Romantic who was also a good Ricardian would conclude that the rare aesthetic commodity receives none of its market value in production, but Ricardo himself had excepted "some commodities, the value of which is determined by their scarcity alone" from the general rule that production is the source of value. Like De Quincey, he gave "rare statues and pictures, scarce books and coins, wines of a peculiar quality," as instances because "no labor can increase the quantity of such goods."[32] Ricardo's exclusion of such rarities from the behavior of normal commodities has been identified by John Guillory as a significant indication of the dissociation between economics and aesthetics,[33] but it should also be

---

[32] *The Principles of Political Economy and Taxation*, 6.

[33] John Guillory, *Cultural Capital: The Problem of Literary Canon Formation* (Chicago: University of Chicago Press, 1993), 315. Guillory's persuasive and influential argument uses Caygill's account

noted that Ricardo and De Quincey were giving *economic* explanations for these anomalies, and De Quincey was trying to extend the reach of political economy to include such eccentric markets. It should be noted as well that the exceptions would not include any works capable of mere mechanical reproduction, such as printed literature; "scarce books" are items in the book market, not the literary market. Nevertheless, such commodities do direct our attention to the buyer's desire, and De Quincey's *Logic of Political Economy* therefore allows us to see that even Ricardian political economy was forced to acknowledge the limits of the labor theory of value.

And the labor theory of value was the least controversial part of Ricardo's thought. The social implications of his argument, especially his configurations of class interests and antipathies, were less familiar and more painful to contemplate. He not only divided the nation into two sectors of economic activity, agriculture and industry, but also presented those spheres as opposed. The interests of the owners of land, because their rents increased as the rate of profit declined and stagnation threatened, especially conflicted with the economic interests of all "productive" classes: farmers, agricultural laborers, industrial capitalists, and industrial workers. And the interests of capital and labor in both spheres were also necessarily antagonistic, for any increase in wages led to a drop in profits and vice versa. Since Ricardo believed that capitalists were the only class dedicated to the overall increase of profitable enterprise and were therefore the class that could forestall the tendency of the falling rate of profit, his own allegiance was clear, but free competition was necessary to drive the economy forward. Therefore, no impediment should be placed in the way of the competition between classes; the workers had to be able to combine into unions and bargain for higher wages just as capitalists could combine into trade associations to protect their own interests. Government interference with such combinations or legislative protection of faltering enterprises (e.g., the Corn Laws) would only decrease the incentive for enterprise. In the postwar period, most political economists therefore supported the repeal of both the Combination Acts and the Corn Laws, and their theories seemed, if not to encourage, then at least to tolerate class conflict as an inevitability. Ricardo's body politic was composed of parts that only worked in tension with each other; certainly each part contributed to the whole, but not in a blithely harmonious manner.

Ricardian political economy may not have actively promoted class conflict, but it certainly provided a way of understanding and accepting it. Some working-class radicals in the period (for example, Thomas Hodgskin, John Gray,

---

of the original connection between aesthetics and political economy in the discourse of moral philosophy to explain the incoherence of attempts by aestheticians to construct a concept of "aesthetic value" in the art object that would be wholly independent of economic value.

and William Thompson) may have taken sustenance from Ricardo's ideas[34] or may have built directly on earlier radicals inspired by Adam Smith, but there is no doubt that the popularization of political economy accompanied the growth of trade unionism and the legitimation of contesting class interests. A significant portion of the population began to identify, subjectively, with the social categories that Ricardo had outlined as competing economic classes. Especially in industrial areas of Britain, class consciousness became a primary mode of self-understanding.[35]

Coincidentally, in the same year that Ricardo published *The Principles of Political Economy and Taxation*, Coleridge published a view of the nation's economic forces and their interactions in his *A Lay Sermon, Addressed to the Higher and Middle Classes on the Existing Distresses and Discontents*. In many regards, the two works form an instructive contrast. Coleridge identified "Commerce" and "Agriculture" as separate sectors, but he argued that the "Spirit of Commerce" had slowly infiltrated and overwhelmed the true purposes of Agriculture, "which ultimately are the same as those of the State of which it is the offspring."[36] Commerce, he admitted, propelled the nation's progress and continued to open avenues for industry and talent, but it also encouraged speculative behavior, confused ends and means, and failed to acknowledge a difference between "Things and Persons" (220). Landowners, however, because they held their estates "in trust" for the State, should put the moral, physical, and mental well-being of their dependents ahead of all commercial considerations. Coleridge, therefore, did not believe landowners were primarily a separate economic class; they were, rather, intrinsic units of the State itself, who should resist acting in their own commercial interest. Only because they had surrendered their true purpose and identity to the spirit of commerce, which should properly be confined to its own sphere, had they pursued enclosures, depopulation of the countryside, and impoverishment of their laborers.

Thus Coleridge reversed Ricardo. Instead of regarding the landholders as the most specialized and unproductive of economic classes, Coleridge insisted that, in their deepest essence, they were not an economic class at all, but local instantiations of the Whole which is the State. Instead of basing the good of the nation on the unimpeded activity of the most vigorous elements of commerce, Coleridge concluded that "Our manufacturers must consent to regulations" (229) and asked "Agriculture" to provide a counterweight to commerce

---

[34] See Noel W. Thompson, *The People's Science: The Popular Political Economy of Exploitation and Crisis, 1816–1834* (Cambridge: Cambridge University Press, 1984), 83–110, for the historiographic debate over the amount of influence Ricardo actually had on the thinking of so-called Ricardian socialists.

[35] E. P. Thompson describes this process in detail in his *Making of the English Working Class* (New York: Vintage, 1966).

[36] *Lay Sermons*, 216.

as a cure for the postwar distress, which had been visited mainly on the laboring populations of both the towns and agricultural districts.

And yet the very neatness of the contrast between the two works attests to their deep structural congruity. In both, the nation is divided into two sectors (or spheres). For Ricardo, these were agriculture and industrial production, while for Coleridge they were Agriculture (with a capital "A") and what he calls "Commerce." Ricardo's "industry" looked forward to nineteenth-century discourse, whereas Coleridge's "commerce" maintained continuity with eighteenth-century social thought, especially that of Edmund Burke. But despite their differences in orientation, Ricardo and Coleridge name roughly similar divisions. Moreover, each imagined three classes: landowners, capitalists, and laborers, even though Coleridge insisted that the first of these was more than a class. Finally, and most surprisingly, both envisioned the relations among these groups as antipathetic; neither thinks that landlord and capitalist can act harmoniously in concert, and both point to the strife between capital and labor. To be sure, the antipathy arose for different reasons in the two writers' accounts, but both thought it natural for the possessors of the land and the owners of capital to counteract each other, and both believed that the "commercial spirit" automatically instrumentalizes the laboring population. Ricardo may have fretted less than Coleridge about the necessity of a society in conflict, and Coleridge may have hoped to reform "our Agricultural system" into an island of amicable paternalism in a sea of expanding commercial strife, but in confronting the postwar realities of industrializing Britain, they both depicted a nation whose vitality depended on the contention of opposing forces. Indeed, Coleridge's hopes for Agriculture were belied by his later call for the artificial creation of a special order, a "clerisy,"[37] that could transcend all interests and represent the State in its entirety.

In the immediate postwar period, though, the organicism of both thinkers resembled less the early modern hierarchical model of a smoothly coordinated body politic, with an undisputed head and numerous subordinate parts, than the model that Darwin (with Malthus's help) would come to articulate in the 1850s. With the substantial prodding of political economy, British organicism, even in its Romantic form, underwent a transition from imagining the nation on the model of a unified single organism to imagining it as a vital autotelic system, not only tolerating but also requiring dynamic conflict.

By the 1830s, the controversies I've described here had themselves come to seem "natural." It appeared that a "humanist" literary sensibility instinctively opposed the scientific objectification of human activity; or, conversely, it appeared that an empirical understanding of the optimal modes of accumulating

---

[37] Coleridge develops the idea of a clerisy in *On the Constitution of the Church and State: According to the Idea of Each*, vol. 10, *The Collected Works of Samuel Taylor Coleridge* (London: Routledge and Kegan Paul, 1969).

and distributing social wealth came under fire from moralists who wanted to interfere with those processes. And yet both sides promoted the nineteenth-century apotheosis of "Life" as an ultimate good, and both looked to the feelings of the mass of people to measure the success of a way of "Life." As Michel Foucault argued in *The Order of Things*, the nineteenth-century "*episteme*" (the ordering principles of its knowledge) initially organized the world according to biological models: "[M]an, his psyche, his group, his society, the language he speaks—all these exist in the Romantic period as living beings."[38] And the prevailing models of knowledge throughout the century remained biological; as late as the twentieth century, Alfred Marshall remarked that "the Mecca of the economist is economic biology."[39] Even the seemingly intractable controversies we've been examining over the competing *varieties* of "organicism" helped establish its ubiquity and laid the basis for many of the distinctive traits of Victorian literary realism and social science.

We have so far merely looked at the most obvious "organic" features of political economy; a fuller exposition will, I hope, bring some of the paradoxes and complexities of the discipline into view. Consequently, before turning to the interchanges between political economists and the two most influential novelists of the early and later Victorian periods—Charles Dickens and George Eliot—I'll examine in the next chapter several paradigmatic political-economic perspectives on "Life" and "sensation" more carefully, explaining why their critics had so much trouble escaping the gravitational pull of their discourse.

[38] Michel Foucault, *The Order of Things: An Archeology of the Human Sciences* (New York: Random House, 1970), 359.

[39] Foucault argued that the biological model in the human sciences was followed by economic and anthropological models, but he also recognized that both of these built on certain premises about life. Moreover, Foucault names Ricardo not just as an author of the discourse of economics but also as the thinker who located the source of value in physiological labor, thereby rooting it in the productive body. See *The Order of Things*, 253–63. Alfred Marshall's remark is in *The Memorials of Alfred Marshall*, ed. Alfred Pigou (London: Macmillan, 1925), 318.

Chapter Two

Bioeconomics and Somaeconomics

Life and Sensation in
Classical Political Economy

If political economy had its own peculiar organicism, its own way of imagining society as a vast, living system, and of basing its calculations on the certitudes of vital need, were its critics simply mistaken when they accused it of being "mechanical in heart and mind"? Not quite. The Romantic and early Victorian writers who feared that a moribund system was replacing a vigorous body politic were not entirely deluded, for they were following through on certain insights of political economy itself, which implied that the creation of wealth routinely rendered life and sensation dormant. Political economy's organicism looked peculiar to them not only because it predicted unceasing strife but also because it privileged abeyant forms of vitality and feeling. This chapter will give you a picture of this odd organicism, outlining what political economists said—primarily to each other—about economic *life* (as a biological entity) and about its sensations.

Before novelists like Charles Dickens and George Eliot incorporated them into extended narrative forms, which I'll analyze in subsequent chapters, political economy's organic premises were already structured as plots, as highly consequentialist, if extremely schematic, stories about the processes of life and death, pain and pleasure. I'll divide these plots into two broad categories. First I'll examine what I call the "bioeconomic" plots of political economy, the stories of how the economy circulates Life, with a capital *L*. Then I'll explore their "somaeconomic" plots, their accounts of how pleasure and pain, happiness and unhappiness, desire and exhaustion, stimulate economic activity and are in turn modified by it. Bioeconomic plots trace the interconnections among human life, its sustenance, and modes of production and exchange; they track the reciprocal effects of economic activity and life forms generally. Somaeconomic plots describe more intensively the feelings that are the sensual and affective causes and consequences of economic exertion. Obviously the two sorts of explanation overlap, for telling biological stories about the economy required attention to the sensations of economic actors, whose accumulated feelings, in turn, were used to explain both the quality and the quantity of economic life.

Nevertheless, the two kinds of narrative diverged in the major works of the political economists, and the divergence is symptomatic of the discipline's inability to integrate the levels of analysis: the life of the organic whole, to take an obvious example, develops independently of, and frequently at odds with the welfare and happiness of the individual organisms peopling it. Or, to take another simple example, enjoyment as an individual economic motivator is in tension with the necessity for delaying gratification while accumulating wealth. But political economy's organic plots are often quite a bit more surprising, paradoxical, and controversial than these easy examples would predict. By analyzing the stories political economists argued about, I hope to demonstrate how ready they were for the attack launched against them by early Victorian writers. Almost everything Thomas Carlyle, John Ruskin, or Charles Dickens accused them of had been anticipated in their internal controversies, and that fact will help explain why the literary critiques kept reproducing the contradictions that the political economists had (more rigorously and self-consciously) encountered.

BIOECONOMICS OF POPULATION

I'll begin with Malthus because his *Essay on the Principle of Population* radically reconceptualized the social organism. By telling a strange new story about how healthy bodies eventually generate a feeble overall population, Malthus departed from nearly all his predecessors and contemporaries.[1] Adam Smith and David Hume, who also wrote of the "power of population" and its "checks," had certainly been cognizant of population size as an important factor in social well-being. However, they maintained a two-millennia-old tradition of seeing the individual body as sign—both as metaphor and as source—of the health or infirmity of the larger social body. Hence they viewed rapid reproduction as simply an index of a healthy state. Hume, for example, writes, "For as there is in all men, both male and female, a desire and power of generation more active than is ever universally exerted, the restraints must proceed from some difficulties in men's situation, which it belongs to a wise legislature carefully to observe and remove."[2] Thus, he continues, "Every wise, just and mild government, by rendering the condition of its subjects easy and secure will always abound most in people, as well as in commodities and

---

[1] In the second edition of the *Essay,* Malthus names the following eighteenth-century writers who had also noted "the poverty and misery arising from a too rapid increase of population": Montesquieu, Benjamin Franklin, James Stewart, Arthur Young, and Joseph Townsend. These writers, however, do not emphasize the connection Malthus makes between physical vigor and eventual social decline. Robert Wallace's *A Dissertation on the Numbers of Mankind in Antient and Modern Times* (1753) was often said to have anticipated Malthus's argument, but it too presented a large population as a sign of stability and morality.

[2] David Hume, "Of the Populousness of Ancient Nations," in *Essays Moral, Political, and Literary* (Edinburgh, 1825), 1:376.

riches." Hume is typical of eighteenth-century writers in seeing no apparent contradiction, either actual or latent, between individual physical potency and social vitality. In this one particular, his social vision is uncharacteristically static ("Every wise, just and mild government will always abound most in people") and based on the assumption that human biological nature itself is not at fault ("the restraints must proceed from some difficulties in men's situations").

For Enlightenment utopians, the link between healthy individual and social bodies was even more direct; in the works of Condorcet and William Godwin, whom Malthus explicitly takes as antagonists, hopes of the perfect society were often founded on the possibility of biological perfectability. Malthus's *Essay,* as I pointed out in the last chapter, countered this utopianism, not with reminders of the fallen state of the human race, its imperfections and frailties, but with a far more devastating evocation of its most redoubtable power, the power it shares with all other animal species and that exercises itself almost automatically as a biological function: "the power of population." The fact that populations have a tendency to increase to the limits of their means of subsistence and are only held in check by misery or vice is the single principle on which Malthus tries to erect a "juster philosophy" of social questions. His aim is to avoid the "mere conjectures" of both the "advocate for the present order of things" and the "advocate for the perfectability of man,"[3] and his method is a revaluation of the social meaning of the healthy body, a revaluation fundamental to nineteenth-century social discourses and practices.

Malthus's theory destroyed the homological relationship between individual and social organisms by tracing social problems to human vitality itself. For him, the human body is a profoundly ambivalent phenomenon. He admits that Hume and even such utopians as Godwin are right to see the rate of increase in the number of human bodies as a sign of *present* physical prosperity and even healthy, "innocent" social institutions. But Malthus simultaneously sees the unleashed power of population, the reproducing body, as that which will eventually destroy the very prosperity that made it fecund, replacing health and innocence with misery and vice.

Thus, for example, he asks what would be the effect on population of the actualization of Godwin's utopian society and, in turn, what would be the effect on his utopia of the power of population. Malthus hypothesizes almost all the elements of Godwin's perfectly rational society, even granting the supposition that marriage could be abolished without immediately causing social

---

[3] Thomas Malthus, *An Essay on the Principle of Population: Text, Sources and Background, Criticism,* ed. Philip Appleman (New York: Norton, 1976), 17. I concentrate on the first edition of Malthus's argument because it is the most coherent version. I have tried in the footnotes to indicate where, in the later works, Malthus revised or contradicted the first *Essay.* All quotations from the *Essay* are from the Norton Critical Edition, and subsequent page numbers are given in the text.

chaos: "Each man would probably select himself a partner to whom he would adhere as long as that adherence continued to be the choice of both parties" (68). Everything else in the society likewise both attests to and promotes equality, rationality, and health. Malthus makes no claims for any a priori weakness or depravity in human nature when he supposes

> all the causes of misery and vice in this island removed. War and contention cease. Unwholesome trades and manufactories do not exist. The greater part of the happy inhabitants of this terrestrial paradise live in hamlets and farmhouses scattered over the face of the country. Every house is clean, airy, sufficiently roomy, and in a healthy situation. The necessary labours of agriculture are shared amicably among all. The number of persons, and the produce of the island, we suppose to be the same as at present. The spirit of benevolence, guided by impartial justice, will divide this produce among all the members of the society according to their wants. Though it would be impossible that they should all have animal food every day, yet vegetable food, with meat occasionally, would satisfy the desire of a frugal people and would be sufficient to preserve them in health, strength, and spirits. (68)

Malthus begins his demonstration, therefore, by granting the time-honored homology: healthy individual bodies represent a healthy social organism. Unlike Hume's scheme, however, Malthus's is temporally dynamic; the strong body entails a present and a future social condition: first a society of innocence and health and then one of vice and misery. The degeneration from one society to the next, moreover, is effected neither by inner corruption nor by external adversity. It is solely a product of the procreative vigor of the body itself.

The spirited health and strength of the utopian body leads within two generations to social chaos, want, warfare, and, finally, starvation. For after fifty years, the very felicities of Godwin's utopia would overpopulate it: "The irremediableness of marriage, as it is at present constituted, undoubtedly deters many from entering into that state. An unshackled intercourse on the contrary would be a most powerful incitement to early attachments, and as we are supposing no anxiety about the future support of children to exist, I do not conceive that there will be one woman in a hundred, of twenty-three, without a family" (68). Thus in half a century the population would quadruple (according to Malthus's famous dictum that animal populations increase geometrically) while the stock of food to support them could only—under near miraculous conditions—triple (following his maxim that increase in the vegetable kingdom takes place according to an "arithmetic" ratio). The healthy, and consequently *reproducing*, body is thus the harbinger of the disordered society full of starving bodies: "Provisions no longer flow in for the support of the mother with a large family. The children are sick from insufficient food. The rosy flush of health gives place to the pallid cheek and hollow eye of misery" (70).

By rhetorically melting one generation into another in this way, Malthus occludes the possibility of using the healthy particular body to signify the healthy group. The healthy body here has lost, in the very power of its fecundity, the integrity of its boundaries and hence comes to be a sign of its opposite. The blooming body is only a body about to divide into two feebler bodies that are always on the verge of becoming four starving bodies. Hence, no state of health can be socially reassuring. Malthus's argument ruptures the healthy body/healthy population homology. Simultaneously, by making the body absolutely problematic, he helps place it in the very center of social discourse.

At the end of his argument, Malthus actually uses the same body/nation analogy he has been rendering so untenable, and his use of it exposes its accumulated difficulties. Predictably, he centers the metaphor on the instability of vigorous physical states. Also predictably, he imagines the social body as female, since only the number of women of childbearing age in a society gives an indication of its rate of increase. The relationship of the social theorist to the society, then, is that of an anxious lover to the body of the beloved:

> A person who contemplated the happy state of the lower classes of the people in America twenty years ago, would naturally wish to retain them for ever in that state, and might think, perhaps, that by preventing the introduction of manufactures and luxury he might effect his purpose; but he might as reasonably expect to prevent a wife or mistress from growing old by never exposing her to the sun or air. The situation of new colonies, well governed, is a bloom of youth that no efforts can arrest. There are, indeed, many modes of treatment in the political, as well as animal body, that contribute to accelerate or retard the approaches of age, but there can be no chance of success, in any mode that could be devised, for keeping either of them in perpetual youth. (114–15)

At first glance, the analogy seems to work; social bodies, like individual bodies, are subject to decay. But the sentence "The situation of new colonies, well governed, is a bloom of youth that no efforts can arrest" betrays the paradoxical nature of even this negative body/society homology. The sentence's ambiguity reveals Malthus's double vision, for the woman's bloom of youth is both the prized thing that one wants to "arrest," in the sense of fixing forever, and the culprit whose "arrest" would be necessary to stop the enfeebling process of reproduction. The ambiguity points to the underlying paradox that would immediately strike any careful reader of the preceding argument: the social body is growing "old" precisely insofar as the actual demographic proportions of the society are increasingly weighted toward youth, since, under optimal conditions, each generation would be twice as large as the generation preceding it. To be comprehensible in the terms of Malthus's argument, this body/society homology can only be read as a body/society opposition. The social body is an "old woman" insofar as it is populated by young women.

Malthus, thus, turns the body into an absolute social problem. All individual bodily states, without exception, mean trouble for the state of society. This
problematization of the body does not in itself, however, completely account
for its centrality in the social discourse of the nineteenth century. The body,
after all, had been problematized before in both classical and Christian ascetic
traditions that had made the flesh a treacherous enemy of man's "ultimate"
good. If Malthus had stopped at merely making all states of the body problematic, we might be able to see him as just a secularizer of those older traditions,
one who substituted "social good" for "spiritual good." But Malthus breaks
definitively with those traditions by accomplishing the problematization of
the body in the context of its complete valorization. Indeed, the body can
only become absolutely problematic when it is completely valued.

Far from making war on the body and its appetites, as earlier enumerators
of its dangers had done, Malthus casts himself in the role of the body's champion. As we saw in the last chapter, instead of following the lead of conservative contemporaries by accusing Enlightenment utopians of crass materialism,
of the denial of the spiritual dimension of human nature, Malthus launches
an attack from the opposite quarter, accusing the "advocates for the perfectability of man" of being indifferent, indeed hostile, to the just claims of
the body, which he sets out to vindicate. His two opening postulates set the
direction for the entire argument: "First, That food is necessary to the existence of man. Secondly, That the passion between the sexes is necessary and
will remain nearly in its present state"(19). Despite the seeming obviousness
of these propositions, even despite the fact that he calls them "postulates,"
Malthus actually spends some time justifying them. For it is the most basic
facts of biological existence that he finds denied in the works of Condorcet
and Godwin, his two examples of utopian thought.

In the *Essay,* these two writers represent different aspects of a single utopian
desire to radically alter human biological nature. Condorcet is presented as a
biological engineer, planning organic perfectability through selective breeding.
Malthus's task is to belittle this scheme without belittling the body itself by
concentrating on its imperfections and without appearing to be an "advocate
for the present order of things" who dismisses all novelty and scientific experi-
mentation. He must expose, under the desire for a scientifically perfected
body, a blatantly unscientific disregard for the body as it is. He accomplishes
this by harnessing a Swiftean satiric rhetoric to a rigorous methodological
argument.

Malthus ostensibly centers his attack on Condorcet's faulty induction.
From the evidence of biological improvement noted in plant and animal
breeding, Condorcet concludes (according to Malthus) that species might be
perfected even to the point of producing the feature of physical immortality.
Malthus leaves aside the disastrous effects on population of such an "improvement" as too obvious to need mentioning, and explicitly concentrates on the
fallacy in Condorcet's reasoning: the latter has failed to distinguish between

"an unlimited progress and a progress where the limit is merely undefined" (63). That is, the fact that no limit has been reached in the development of a certain feature does not imply that no limit exists. Indeed, it does not even imply that (taking into account the known rules of the physical universe) one cannot predict "a point at which [improvement] will not arrive" (63).

Although this argument seems to question only Condorcet's logical failures and to leave untouched his devaluation of the empirical body, Malthus uses this logical structure as a framework for a satirical rhetoric that implicitly accuses Condorcet of contempt for the whole of biological nature. In illustrating "points at which improvement will not arrive," Malthus creates a series of grotesque forms of life, biological absurdities, that, although entirely of his own fabrication, seem somehow the perverse results not just of his opponent's faulty reasoning but of the underlying desire to direct biological progress:

> In the famous Leicestershire breed of sheep, the object is to procure them with small heads and small legs. Proceeding upon [the maxim that you might breed to any degree of nicety you please], it is evident that we might go on till the heads and legs were evanescent qualities, but this is so palpable an absurdity that we may be quite sure that the premises are not just and that there really is a limit, though we cannot see it or say exactly where it is, I should not scruple to assert that were the breeding to continue for ever, the head and legs of these sheep would never be so small as the head and legs of a rat. (63)

Monsters proliferate in this section of the argument; counterfactual beings are created as the possibilities of their existence are denied. We see a carnation "increased to the size of a large cabbage" (63), human bodies with four eyes and four legs, and trees that grow horizontally (83). The very comic grotesqueness of these bodies implies that Condorcet is attempting a ridiculous and impertinent interference with nature. Malthus thus manages to incorporate the satirical rhetoric of a Swiftean antiscientific tradition into a defense of proper empirical reasoning. Without ever directly attacking the validity of Condorcet's aims or the morality of his means, Malthus is able to cast his opponent as an overreaching distorter of the equilibrium of the natural world and to fashion himself the protector of the "delicate materials of a carnation stalk" and a friend of heads and legs that are more than "evanescent qualities."

Malthus is even more obviously the vindicator of the rights of biological nature in his critique of Godwin. When, for example, he duplicates Godwin's utopia, he refuses to grant one of his opponent's central hypotheses: that "the passion between the sexes will become extinct" (76). As I pointed out in the first chapter, he denies this not on the traditional grounds that man's fallen nature makes him incapable of rising above base, animal instincts, but rather on the grounds that the instincts are not base. Just as Condorcet had been indirectly characterized as an impertinent disrupter of nature's course, Godwin becomes the desiccated, heartless repressor of the body's just demands, one of "[t]hose who from coldness of constitutional temperament have never felt what love is" and who "will surely be allowed to be very incompetent judges with regard to the power of this passion to contribute to the sum of pleasurable sensations of life" (76). Malthus even indulges in passages of lyrical rhapsody in defense of these pleasures: "Perhaps there is scarcely a man who has once experienced the genuine delight of virtuous love . . . that does not look back to the period as the sunny spot in his whole life, where his imagination loves to bask, which he recollects and contemplates with the fondest regrets, and which he would most wish to live over again" (76).

To be sure, the justification of sexual passion as rational, pleasurable, and essential was a rhetorical necessity, for it made sexual abstinence seem like "misery," and therefore supported his larger argument that all checks to population growth can be classified as misery or vice. And we must also keep in mind Malthus's proviso that any practice severing sexual pleasure from reproduction would be vicious and degrading to the passion itself. These points, however, only remind us that Malthus's argument must continually valorize the body's needs and natural reproductive processes. Our physical strengths rather than our weaknesses, our virtuous passions rather than our vices, underlie the endemic imperfections of our social state. Hence, even after he was attacked as a sensualist and loosened the tight logic of his original argument by admitting, in later editions, a third category of "moral restraint" (delayed marriage) to those of misery and vice, he never revised his valuation of sexual passion. Indeed, even after recommending late marriage and conceding that one might remain chaste without being completely miserable, he was unable to withhold the qualification that moral restraint would at least cause "temporary unhappiness."

Malthus's attack on Godwin, furthermore, carried his vindication of organic nature beyond the confines of sexual pleasure. He presents all of Godwin's schemes for self-discipline, for the exercise of the "power of mind over the body," as so many recipes for self-enfeeblement. Just as Condorcet seemed the creator of many monsters, Godwin seems the deviser of many tortures. Malthus takes Godwin to be arguing that the body is only "real" insofar as the mind experiences it. Thus, a man who had just walked twenty miles but who did not feel tired because he was enlivened by some urgent purpose would not, in Godwin's argument, be admitted to have any "real" muscular fatigue. Godwin, according to Malthus, holds that the mind's ability to render the body "unreal" and thus overcome its exigencies is practically limitless. Malthus, in contrast, argues that bodily states persist regardless of the mind's cognizance. As in his argument against Condorcet, he attempts not to define the positive limits of bodily endurance but to infer them from the existence of impossible feats: "A motive of uncommon power acting upon a frame of moderate strength, would, perhaps make the man kill himself by his exertions,

but it would not make him walk an hundred miles in twenty-four hours"
(79–80). Similarly,

> When a horse of spirit is nearly half tired, by the stimulus of the spur, added
> to the proper management of the bit, he may be put so much upon his
> mettle, that he would appear to a stander-by as fresh and as high spirited as
> if he had not gone a mile. Nay [note how Malthus mimics the sound of the
> horse as he enters its consciousness] probably the horse himself, while in the
> heat and passion occasioned by this stimulus, would not feel any fatigue;
> but it would be strangely contrary to all reason and experience to argue from
> such an appearance that if the stimulus were continued, the horse would
> never be tired. (80)

Thus Godwin's line of reasoning seems to implicate him in the crimes of
walking men to death and spurring on exhausted horses. As Malthus's argument advances, Godwin seems guilty of depriving people of food and sleep,
and even of inhumanely denying the reality of Malthus's very own toothache,
which he happens to have at the exact moment of composing this argument
even though "in the eagerness of composition, I every now and then, for a
moment or two, forget it" (80). In short, Malthus exults in the body's power
to triumph, through both its strengths and weaknesses, over every insolent
utopian scheme to improve, rearrange, suppress, or discount it.

BIOECONOMIC VALUE

In the first edition of Malthus's *Essay*, utopians were not the only perverters
of organic nature; commercial and industrial society seem just as culpable.
The essay starts another durable plot line of classical political economy, in
which the gross organic entity is less a metaphorical individual, such as "the
nation" or "the population," than what we now call an "ecosystem" ("the
biome [i.e., the biotic community of plants and animals] considered together
with all the effective inorganic factors of its environment" [*OED*, 1.1]. In two
sections of the *Essay*'s first edition that were later heavily revised or altogether
scrapped, he shifted his focus from inevitable biological constraints to alterable
market forces, and this shift is accompanied by a movement away from the
topic of sexual reproduction to that of food production. To be sure, reproduction remains inevitable; indeed, it is so automatic that it altogether disappears
as a discrete event. However, its disproportion to the increase in food follows
not so much from physiological necessity as from economic contradictions.
The oppositions earlier seen to be inherent in biological drives (the sexual
instinct versus misery and vice) are recast in economic categories (productive
labor versus unproductive labor or agricultural production versus industrial
production). And once reconceived in this way, the problem of population

pressure, although always an impediment to perfect happiness, appears at least partially responsive to human will. These sections of the *Essay's* earliest edition might be said, on the one hand, to lighten the vision of the preceding chapters by proposing that the mass of people could be both larger and better fed than they were in 1797. Indeed, Malthus even goes so far as to suggest some remedies, such as greater investment in agriculture, an end to primogeniture, and smaller land holdings. But this analysis might also be said to deepen the gloom of the population plot by showing that modern society compounds nature's hardships with its own artificial methods of increasing numbers of people while discouraging food cultivation.

In these sections, moreover, Malthus takes a surprisingly critical view of the fundamental principles of political economy, its concepts of wealth, productive labor, and value. Despite the later importance of his contributions to the discipline, the first two editions of his *Essay* reveal a profound distrust of several of its most basic precepts. Indeed, in his analysis of contemporary problems, Malthus might almost be said to put Adam Smith in the place filled by Condorcet and Godwin earlier in the *Essay,* the place of the enemies of natural organic processes. For, according to Malthus, Smith's theories condoned a distribution of wealth that tended to separate value, the fruit of labor, from the valuable, laboring bodies that produced it. He questioned Adam Smith's assurance that all increases in the wealth of nations would ultimately augment the fund for the maintenance of the poor, and this skepticism led on to the rejection of Smith's definition of productive labor, and, by implication, to a denial of the nascent labor theory of value. Even though Malthus later gradually adopted Smith's views on these topics, his early resistance points to a fundamental paradox in political economy's treatment of labor's physicality, and it will, therefore, help us to understand why a discourse that seems centered on working bodies and mindful of biological life in the aggregate was so often accused of disregarding them.

When considering the contemporary state of the laboring population, Malthus, indeed, sounded less like a budding political economist than like the critics of modernity. Indeed, the story he told resembled those later developed by Cobbett, Coleridge, and Southey: working people were probably better off in the past, not because they were increasing too rapidly in the present, but because the fund out of which they were supported—the national granary— was either stationary or dwindling. Moreover, he claimed that the plight of the poor was the result of commercial and industrial wealth. To be sure, Malthus argued more dispassionately than Cobbett or Coleridge, and he had a more precise explanation for the suffering of the poor in commercial society— that economic processes obscured the inadequacy of the actual size of the fund for the support of labor—but he shared with them a general account of decline due to urban and industrial development. The false promises of an economy dominated by commerce and industry were, in his view, tricking the feeble

poor into reproducing themselves, not necessarily beyond the country's potential ability to feed them, but certainly beyond its realized agricultural capacity.
This relatively new ability of a society to misrepresent the resources available
to laborers—that is, to promise prosperity through high money wages and
then betray the promise by a scarcity of provisions—was a novel plot element
in the narratives of national prosperity and ruin, and to it Malthus attributed
a new steady state of working-class misery: "The increasing wealth of the
nation has had little or no tendency to better the condition of the labouring
poor. They have not, I believe, a greater command of the necessaries and
conveniences of life, and a much greater proportion of them than at the period
of the revolution is employed in manufactures and crowded together in close
and unwholesome rooms" (105–6).

In Malthus's version of this story, classical political economy played a vil-
lainous role, for it encouraged people to believe that the nation's wealth equals
its *exchangeable* value. The more a society thinks in the abstract equivalencies
expressed, for example, in monetary terms, the more enfeebled the body of
labor will become, for the differences between kinds of products will no longer
seem important: "It is evident . . . that two nations might increase exactly
with the same rapidity in the exchangeable value of the annual produce of
their land and labour, yet if one had applied itself chiefly to agriculture, and
the other chiefly to commerce, the funds for the maintenance of labour, and
consequently the effect of the increase of wealth in each nation, would be
extremely different" (109). If the exchangeable value were primarily the produce of land *and* labor, that is, if it were agricultural produce, primarily grain,
destined to be eaten by workers, "the poor would live in great plenty"; but if
the exchangeable value were mainly commercial, the poor may not benefit at
all, and indeed, might even suffer increasingly. Exchangeable value in the
abstract, therefore, is not the true gauge of a nation's real wealth because it
does not accurately indicate the prosperity of the great majority of people.
"The gross produce of the land" he reasons, is "a more accurate definition" of
the nation's wealth. In keeping with his tendency to root all value in the very
body he found problematic, Malthus insisted that Adam Smith had commit-
ted a fundamental error in "representing every increase of the revenue or stock
of a society as an increase in the funds for the maintenance of labour" (103).
A stock or revenue "will not be a real and effectual fund for the maintenance
of an additional number of labourers," he states, "unless the whole, or at least
a great part of this increase be convertible into a proportional quantity of
provisions; and it will not be so convertible where the increase has arisen
merely from the produce of labour, and not from the produce of land" (104).
In other words, the only stock whose increase is truly destined for the maintenance of labor is the stock of working-class food, that which can be converted
most directly and immediately into working-class bodies. Denying Smith's emphasis on the efforts of labor alone to produce the nation's wealth, Malthus

agreed with the French "physiocrats," the *economists,* as their English contemporaries called them, that a nation's true wealth was the produce of labor in conjunction with the natural environment, or labor on the land.

We might say that Malthus was trying to make the fundamental bioeconomic plot of political economy consistent by giving it a central protagonist whose fate would be of primary importance from the beginning to the end of the story. In his view the protagonist would be the aggregate of productive workers. It may sound paradoxical, but this attempt to create a consistent collective hero led Malthus to challenge one of Smith's most important, albeit problematic, claims: that everything costs what the labor of producing it costs. Labor was the "measure" of value, according to Smith and his followers, and later Ricardo would strengthen and define the role of labor, insisting that it was the origin of value. Malthus's objections to these labor-centered theories of value uncover an ambivalence toward human physiology at the heart of political economy. On the one hand, the discipline takes labor to be the measure or source of all value and calculates the value of labor by the value of the commodities (food, clothing, lodging) necessary to replenish the body for the hours of labor expended on another commodity. Thus the exchange value of any commodity seems rooted in biological need; the worker's body is the primary nexus of exchange through which the value of those commodities that replenish its ability to labor largely determines the value of all other commodities. Moreover, since labor is itself a commodity, its value will be partly determined by its abundance or scarcity in relationship to demand, that is, by the size of its working population. Hence, like Malthus, the labor theorists of value placed biological sustenance and reproduction at the center of their system. But on the other hand, the very ability to calculate, through the common measure of labor, the relative values of all commodities led away from a hierarchy of commodities based on ultimate biological usefulness. The labor theory of value could "equate" a bushel of corn, for example, with a bit of lace, even though, from another physiological point of view, the corn would seem more intrinsically valuable. Thus Malthus can argue that it is precisely the *bodies* of laborers, their collective material needs, that the preoccupation with exchangeable value allows one to discount or overlook. This paradoxical treatment of laboring bodies by political economists—making them simultaneously central and irrelevant to discussions of value—helps account for the fact that, in the nineteenth century, issues of bodily well-being and of economic circulation are frequently articulated both through and against each other.

Malthus blamed the habit of regarding all commodities as abstractly fungible items, the conflation of value in general with exchangeable value, for encouraging unhealthy towns, inflating the money economy, proliferating non-agricultural enterprises, and, ultimately, lowering the overall standard of living among the working population. Against these pernicious tendencies, he opposes a theory that allows him to maintain his emphasis on the body as the only sure locus of value by distinguishing between commodities on the basis of their "usefulness," by which he means their direct capacity to sustain human life. He took from the French *economists* not only their definition of wealth but also their distinction between productive and nonproductive labor, a distinction that Adam Smith's habit of always thinking in terms of exchangeable values had obscured: "It appears to me that it is with some view to the real utility of the produce that we ought to estimate the productiveness and unproductiveness of different sorts of labour" (110). While rejecting the *economists'* reason for labeling most forms of manufacturing labor "unproductive"—they thought industry yielded no clear rent—Malthus reiterates his own justification: "The consumable commodities of silks, laces, trinkets, and expensive furniture are undoubtedly a part of the revenue of the society; but they are the revenue only of the rich and not of the society in general. An increase in this part of the revenue of the state cannot therefore be considered of the same importance as an increase of food, which forms the principal revenue of the great mass of the people" (112). Cleaving to his equation of the nation's real wealth with its granary, Malthus implies that the manufacturer is not only an unproductive laborer but also a kind of parasite:

> He will have added nothing to the gross produce, and has left a bit of lace in return; and though he may sell this bit of lace for three times the quantity of provisions that he consumed whilst he was making it, and thus be a very productive labourer with regard to himself; yet he cannot be considered as having added by his labour to any essential part of the riches of the state. (111)

The lace-maker seems a metaphorical pack rat, who has broken into the food supply, eaten more than his share, and left behind a mere shred of fabric from milady's bedroom. Such luxuries—almost all manufactured goods in the *Essay's* first edition are luxuries—bear too attenuated or frivolous a relationship to the bodies of producers to be easily reincorporated into them. Hence only the fiction of the abstract equivalence of exchange allows them to be imagined as part of the general society's wealth, as things that are convertible into working-class sustenance.

In making this argument, Malthus manifested a general distrust of far-ranging attenuated economic circuits. The process by which more land might be put under cultivation in England in response to a rise in the cost of provisions is depicted as slow and subject to various kinds of interference (105).[4] The possibility of importing a larger food supply is seen as too costly a process owing to the mere size of the country. In both cases, the longer the circuit of

---

[4] In both this section of the *Essay* and the earlier sections that concern the difficulties of increasing agricultural production, Malthus's arguments tend to be vague, for he had not yet formulated the theory of rent on which Ricardo would base the "tendency of the rate of profit to fall."

exchange leading from the laborer's body (where the organic plot should stay centered) in the form of a commodity and back to it in the form of food, whether that circuit be a certain number of exchanges or a certain amount of literal space traversed, the more inflated is the cost of food and the less productive is the labor.

Once again we note that it is the centrality of the actual physical bodies to Malthus's theory of value that causes his distrust of such elongated circuits. The most productive labor is that which can be converted back immediately into the laboring body; the plot should not become distended with extraneous characters and incidents. But the habits of thought encouraged by the use of money and codified by Adam Smith caused the actual protagonist of the piece to disappear in a cloud of abstraction denominated "labor." The abstracting mentality asks how much labor was required to produce the commodity and how much labor the commodity can command in the marketplace in order to define its value. But Malthus, resisting this tendency, asks instead into how many laborers, or more precisely, how many pounds of laboring flesh the commodity can be easily converted? In the first edition of the *Essay*, healthy laborers, and not abstract units of labor, are the measures of value.

This bioeconomic plot predicted the leakage of organic life out of social systems distorted by industrial and commercial enterprise, as we saw in the conversion of grain into lace. Another variation on the plot envisioned the reshaping of the biosphere itself. Pounds of healthy flesh, rightly destined for productive bodies, become stuck in the wrong places, such as manufacturing towns, which prevent the flow of capital back to the countryside, and consequently soil is left uncultivated (113). Moreover, "Life" is misplaced even in agriculture, a scenario most graphically illustrated by Malthus's description of how a surplus of commercial wealth turns into cattle by increasing demand for butcher's meat, encouraging farmers to use arable land for grazing (107). This new distribution of land results in a "diminution of human subsistence, which might have counterbalanced the advantages derived from the inclosure of waste lands and the general improvements in husbandry" (107). Thus money reshapes the relative proportions of vegetable, animal, and human matter:

> The present price will not only pay for fattening cattle on the very best land, but will even allow of the rearing many on land that would bear good crops of corn. The same number of cattle [as were formerly raised in waste lands] or even the same weight of cattle at the different periods when killed, will have consumed (if I may be allowed the expression) very different quantities of human subsistence. A fattened beast may in some respects be considered in the language of the French economists, as an unproductive labourer: he has added nothing to the value of the raw produce that he has consumed. The present system of grazing undoubtedly tends more than the former

system to diminish the quantity of human subsistence in the country, in proportion to the general fertility of the land. (107)

The biological economy envisioned here is one in which cattle, rather than the proverbial sheep, "eat" men. So many potential pounds of human flesh are converted (through the conversion of land from tillage to pasture) into so many pounds of animal flesh, which, by an undeniable caloric arithmetic, can never be converted back into an equal number of pounds of human flesh. That beast thus stands as an impediment to value as Malthus imagined it; or, more precisely, it stands for the displacement of value. Created by a surplus of money flowing from nonagricultural sources, it is the explicit embodiment of unproductive labor. We might call it the fatted beast of modern commercial society, a striking contrast to the emaciated body of productive labor. The protagonist, productive labor, seems to have been forced into a Minoan labyrinth to be eaten by a new kind of Minotaur.

Malthus subsequently modified his definitions of value and productive labor, gradually bringing them into line with Smith's in subsequent revisions of the *Essay*.[5] But the dire narratives he developed nonetheless haunted the

---

[5] In the 1803 edition, for example, he asserts the difficulty of choosing between the definitions of wealth given by Smith and the *economists*, but continues to call manufacturing unproductive labor compared with agriculture, for the latter issues in "a new production, a completely new creation" whereas the former "are merely the modification of an old one." Agriculture, that is, brings new matter into existence whereas manufacturing only reworks stuff already generated. Even though Malthus's hierarchy remains unchanged in the 1803 edition, this reformulation of its terms points the way toward his ultimate capitulation to Smith's views. Once the issue is *new matter* fit for the consumption of the working class, Malthus gradually accepts the possibility that manufacturers might produce not only luxuries for the rich but also "conveniences and comforts" for the poor, which (although wrought from preexisting materials) would nevertheless bring matter back to one place of its origin: the husbandman's cottage. By 1826, he had reversed his earlier negative evaluation of the effects of commercial wealth on the laboring body:

On an attentive review, then, of the effects of increasing wealth on the condition of the poor, it appears that, although such an increase does not imply a proportionate increase of the funds for the maintenance of labour, yet it brings with it advantages to the lower classes of society which may fully counterbalance the disadvantages with which it is attended. . . . A rapid increase of wealth indeed, whether it consists principally in additions to the means of subsistence or to the stock of conveniences and comforts, will always, *ceteris paribus*, have a favourable effect on the poor. (447)

His *Principles of Political Economy* reiterates Smith's definitions of productive and unproductive labor, as well, with a special insistence on the creation of a durable material product. In a lengthy response to Say and other theorists who accommodated producers of such immaterial goods as knowledge in their definition of productive workers, Malthus urged the necessity of some tangible result. Having given up on the criterion of food, he clings to the more normal materialism of political economy as conceived by Smith, in which bodies are productive insofar as their labor replenishes their own expenditure and creates a surplus of value embodied in some exchangeable item. Malthus had begun to trust the extended circuits of exchange that he once deemed threatening to the food supply on which the mass of people depended, and the only hint of his former apostasy in the *Principles* is

discipline of political economy. In later iterations of his vision of diminishing returns, he prophesied that, as town populations grew, agriculture would become less productive since tracts of land with little natural fertility would need to be laboriously cultivated to feed the town populations. More expensive food would drive up wages, and the ratio of the country's produce that could be reaped as profit by capitalists would decline. The classical political economists never resolved this tension between the vital needs of human groups and the dynamics of capitalism; instead the problem was formalized by Ricardo in the idea of the falling rate of profit, which used Malthus's insight (that food would become increasingly expensive to produce) to explain why capital constantly seeks greater profitability in order to stave off the ever threatening decline of its share of the national product.[6] As a life science, then, political economy elaborated the behavior of capital as an element in an ecosystem, albeit one that constantly remade its biome and sought to elude the very biological limitations on which it was based.

Somaeconomics: Productive Desire versus Unproductive Enjoyment

Capital looked like a life form in another sense as well: it seemed to be the aggregate of numerous individual persons responding—as all living organisms do—to the stimuli of pain and pleasure. It was a megabeing whose telos was expanding wealth and whose motive was believed to be the promise of individual happiness. There was little doubt in the minds of political economists that "wealth" could be defined as the means of enjoyment or pleasure, a definition that rested on Utilitarian hedonistic premises. It is to this second level of analytic narratives—which concern the feelings of individual economic agents—that I will now turn.

I am calling the political economists' underlying plots about the role of pain and pleasure in economic life "somaeconomics" not because pain and pleasure were always thought to be physical in a narrow sense of the word but because even the most cerebral economic operation was assumed to be *sensational,* tinged with actual or anticipated suffering or enjoyment. An idea completely detached from sensation would not be relevant to economic be-

his continuing defense of protective legislation (the Corn Laws) for agriculture. Indeed, he goes so far as to claim that Smith's version of the distinction between productive and unproductive labor is the most fundamental postulate of political economy.

[6] Ricardo used Malthus's theory of rent to support free international trade in grain, whereas Malthus himself used it to support protectionism. For the development of economic theory on this issue and its impact on policy, see Boyd Hilton, *Corn, Cash, Commerce: Economic Policies of the Tory Governments, 1815–1830* (Oxford: Oxford University Press, 1977). For more on this dispute, see Keith Tribe, *Land, Labour and Economic Discourse* (London: Routledge and Kegan Paul, 1978). For a general overview of Ricardo's theories, see Mark Blaug, *Ricardian Economics: A Historical Study* (New Haven: Yale University Press, 1958).

havior. Most political economists were metaphysical materialists who denied any mind/body dichotomy, but even supposing they had not been, supposing they had believed in the possibility of mere ideas or pure rationality, they still would not have regarded such phenomena as *economic* motivations, for they thought economic actors, no matter how enlightened, strive ultimately for the maximization of their pleasurable sensations. With such a belief in place, it might seem that the basic plot linking the individual to the group would be relatively straightforward: people would compete and thereby grow the total amount of wealth so that increasing numbers of people would probably find enjoyment; wealth would be converted into enjoyment and enjoyment into wealth.

But it was never that simple because—leaving aside for the moment the obvious difficulty of how to translate units of wealth into units of enjoyment—political economists faced the paradox that the rapid conversion of most wealth into pleasure would, in fact, impoverish the country. In order to sustain the idea that wealth and pleasure are related, the *potential* for enjoyment had to be given priority over *actual* enjoyment and located outside of people in entities such as "the nation's wealth," "the annual produce," or, simply, "capital." "The economy" would not be a fully developed concept until the 1930s, but an organic totality far larger than the sum of its human participants was under construction to explain where the pleasures and pains went while they were not being felt.

As a way into this paradoxical state of suspended feeling, I'm going to return to the debate over the productive/unproductive distinction, for it clearly demonstrates the need for an entity that could hold sensation in abeyance.[7] Political economists used the hedonistic calculus, the familiar pain/ pleasure ratio, to determine whether labor was productive or unproductive: labor was productive if it resulted in more potential pleasure than actual pleasure. As John Stuart Mill put it in an 1844 essay, "Sources of enjoyment may be accumulated and stored up; enjoyment itself cannot. The wealth of a country consists of the sum total of the permanent sources of enjoyment, whether material or immaterial, contained in it: and labour or expenditure which tends to augment or to keep up these permanent sources, should, we conceive, be termed productive."[8] The desire for enjoyment is thus the engine that drives the entire economic narrative, moving it forward, however, only if the right relation between desire (represented by the accumulated means of future enjoyments) and actual sensations of enjoyment is maintained. The debate over what should be deemed productive labor turned on how one perceived that

[7] For other overviews of this distinction in political economy, see Karl Marx, *Theories of Surplus Value* (Moscow: Progressive Press, 1969), 1:152–304; Blaug, *Ricardian Economics*; Phyllis Dean, *The Evolution of Economic Ideas* (Cambridge: Harvard University Press, 1978); Samuel Hollander, *The Economics of David Ricardo* (Toronto: Heinemann, 1979).

[8] "On the Words Productive and Unproductive," *Essays on Economics and Society, Collected Works of John Stuart Mill* (Toronto: University of Toronto Press, 1963–91), 4:284.

relation; it tried to determine the most effective proportions of the sensations of desire and satisfaction in *homo economicus*.

The emphasis on accumulating a secure supply of future enjoyments led many disputants to privilege the production of material objects over other sorts of labor, such as services or the production of knowledge. The story sanctioned by James and John Stuart Mill, for example, insisted that a nation investing its surplus in stockpiling palpable things would become richer whereas one bent on consuming its surplus (immediately experiencing "mere pleasure," in the phrase of J. S. Mill),[9] would become poorer. A favorite illustration of the principle contrasted the owner who spent his profits on wages for workers with one who spent them on wages for servants: "The wages which a man affords to a ploughman, are given for the sake of production; the wages which he gives to his footman and his groom, are not given for the sake of production."[10] The plowman increases the store of things; the footman depletes it. The plowman helps accumulate for the future; the footman merely serves and consumes what was previously stored. In both cases, the master's ultimate end is identical:

> It is true that mankind are, for the most part, excited to productive industry solely by the desire of subsequently consuming the result of their labour and accumulation. The consumption called unproductive, viz., that of which the direct result is enjoyment, is in reality the end, to which production is only the means; and a desire for the end, is what alone impels any one to have recourse to the means.[11]

But despite the underlying oneness of aims, the two kinds of labor set in motion bring opposite sensations as well as opposite material effects: in the first instance accumulating wheat requires the master's abstinence from enjoyment; the wheat is a physical embodiment of pleasures not taken. And in the second instance, the disappearance of food consumed by the groom and footman is the physical absence denoting enjoyment obtained. The production and endurance of things, of objects, figures the persistence of the sensation of desire; the disappearance of things figures the ephemerality of the sensation of enjoyment.

Since maximizing the former and minimizing the latter was thought to be the essence of growing prosperity, it should have followed logically that, in a prosperous society, feelings of desire would predominate above those of enjoyment. In the long run, to be sure, the absolute amount of immediate pleasure might increase, but at any particular time, this story would predict, the aggregate amount of desire for enjoyment should be considerably greater than the

---

[9] From this point on, I will refer to J. S. Mill simply as Mill.

[10] James Mill, *Elements of Political Economy*, 2nd ed. (London: Baldwin, Cradock, and Joy, 1824), 221.

[11] Mill, "Words," 287.

aggregate amount of satisfied desire. To put the point slightly differently, wealth accumulates not only if enjoyments are deferred but also if they never equal or surpass the desire for them. The nonpleasure/pleasure ratio would have to remain top heavy in the wealthy society.[12]

This narrative in which wealth accumulates by denying enjoyment seems discrepant with the eudemonic Utilitarian presuppositions of many, although not all, political economists, in which optimal national well-being was equated with the greatest happiness of the greatest number and happiness was thought to consist in the predominance of pleasure over pain. Did political economy's privileging of "productive" labor imply that wealth and happiness were at odds?[13] Some of their controversies indicate such a rift. Jean-Baptiste Say, for example, tried to break down the mutually exclusive stories of production and consumption by denying the emphasis on material wealth in the definition of productive labor. If external materialization were not a key feature of productivity, he reasoned, one might conceive of kinds of wealth that do not disappear when used or consumed, such as knowledge or skill, so that the accumulation/consumption antagonism would not operate. Starting from the widely held premise that we are powerless to bring matter into being but can only cause it to assume forms that make it useful to us, he reasoned that, since "utilities" are all that labor ever produces, labor resulting in any kind of utility should be accounted productive. He named surgeons, teachers, judges, and legislators among productive laborers whose efforts are not embodied in an external physical item. He did, however, imply that such "immaterial" wealth—call it mental capital—must have relative permanence, and hence Mill partly incorporated Say's argument into his own redefinition of wealth in the *Principles*:

> [Wealth is] any product which is both useful and susceptible of accumulation. The skill, and the energy and perseverance, of the artisans of a country are reckoned part of its wealth, no less than their tools and machinery. According to this definition, we should regard all labour as productive which is employed in creating permanent utilities, whether embodied in human beings, or in any other animate or inanimate objects.[14]

---

[12] Following Howard Caygill, John Guillory argues that, prior to the nineteenth century, the difficulty presented to a Utilitarian theory of wealth by this realization was dealt with by David Hume's distinction between immediate and deferred enjoyment and later by Adam Smith's idea of a "harmony between the realm of production and the realm of need or desire" (Guillory, 310–13). It is clear from the nineteenth-century writings, though, that the "proportion between production and consumption"—and thus between wealth and happiness—remained highly problematic.

[13] For another discussion of this paradox, see Donald Winch, "Higher Maxims: Happiness versus Wealth in Malthus and Ricardo," in *That Noble Science of Politics*, ed. Stephan Collini, Donald Winch, and John Burrow (Cambridge: Cambridge University Press, 1983), 63–89.

[14] *Principles of Political Economy* in *Collected Works of John Stuart Mill* (Toronto: University of Toronto Press, 1963–91), 2:48.

What Mill seems to offer here as an escape from the criterion of material embodiment, though, he quickly qualifies:

> But in applying the term wealth to the industrial capacities of human beings, there seems always, in popular apprehension, to be a tacit reference to material products. The skill of the artisan is accounted wealth, only as being the means of acquiring wealth in a material sense; and any qualities not tending visibly to that object are scarcely so regarded at all. (49)

For Mill, the sign of all accumulation worthy of the name of "wealth"—even the accumulation of mental and moral attributes—was still the aggregation of material objects fabricated for human enjoyment.

Other political economists besides Say also contradicted John Stuart Mill's story about the opposition between accumulation and consumption. They anticipated some modern theorists of consumer society,[15] who point to the pleasurable qualities of anticipation, putting desire in the pleasure rather than the pain column, and they suspended the whole question of whether or not pleasures in general really make people "happy." Indeed, Nassau Senior boldly cut the discipline off from its Benthamite attachments and announced "that wealth and not happiness" was its subject.[16] That declaration of independence was designed to obviate the sorts of discussions about the ultimate causes of human happiness foisted on political economists by moralists who used the greatest-happiness principle against them. Even critics like Coleridge appealed to eudemonism, the ethics of happiness, when attacking their preference for accumulating a surplus of exchangeable value:

> Let the sum total of each man's happiness be supposed—1000; and suppose ten thousand men produced, who neither made swords or poison, or found corn or clothes for those who did—but who procured by their labour food and raiment of themselves, and for their children—would not that Society be richer by 10,000,000 parts of happiness?[17]

The battle against such moralists was an old one for political economy, dating back to its founding arguments with those who condemned luxury. Indeed, Smith's idea of productive labor was designed to counter the prejudice of which Malthus's first edition was an instance: that labor invested in luxury

---

[15] See, for example, Zygmunt Bauman, "Consuming Life," *Journal of Consumer Culture* 1 (June 2001): 9–29.

[16] Nassau William Senior, *An Outline of the Science of Political Economy* (New York: Farrar and Rinehart, 1939), 2.

[17] Coleridge, *The Friend*, I, ed. Barbara E. Rooke, vol. 4, *The Collected Works of Samuel Taylor Coleridge* (Princeton: Princeton University Press, 1969), 300. It must also be noted, however, that Coleridge attacked Utilitarian ethics for failing to distinguish between the good and the pleasurable: "Is *Good* a superfluous work . . . for the pleasurable and its causes—at most a mere modification to express degree and comparative duration of pleasure?"

goods was somehow misspent. By calling all labor that "fixes and realizes itself in some particular subject or vendible commodity" productive, Smith set aside hierarchies of products and discussions of their relative merits or ultimate usefulness. And yet, the productive/unproductive distinction itself carried a trace of the old antiluxury bias. Consider, for example, Smith's contrast between the manufacturing laborer and the servant:

> A man grows rich by employing a multitude of manufacturers; he grows poor by maintaining a multitude of menial servants. . . . The labour of the menial servant . . . does not fix or realize itself in any particular subject or vendible commodity. His services generally perish in the very instant of their performance, and seldom leave any trace or value behind them.[18]

Smith may be translating the distinction into a technical one, but this and most subsequent uses of the contrast nevertheless retained the flavor of attacks on opulent establishments, bursting with a surplus of servants who cater to the mere sensual enjoyment of their masters.

J. R. McCulloch, detecting the residue of antiluxury moralism in Smith's productive/unproductive differentiation, assailed it in his hugely popular *Principles of Political Economy*, which went through numerous editions between 1825 and 1844. Like Nassau Senior, he insisted that political economy could not be a science of happiness, could not determine what the ultimate causes of human felicity might be. Perhaps moralists were right to argue that people could only be happy by reducing their desires and remaining content with the simplest possible life; the felicific calculus might in truth be most securely weighted toward happiness if the level of wants were kept below the number of sure enjoyments. But such a state of contentment, McCulloch assures us, would never lead to the accumulation of wealth, for

> To make men industrious . . . they must be inspired with a taste for comforts, luxuries, and enjoyments. When this is done, their artificial wants become equally clamorous with those that are strictly necessary, and increase exactly as the means of gratifying them increase. Wherever a taste for comforts and conveniences is generally diffused, the desires of man become altogether illimitable. The gratification of one leads directly to the formation of another. (528)

In McCulloch's view, the somatic state of man, consisting of appetites, pains, and pleasures, is not fixed by nature but is plastic and revisable. Wealth, as in J. S. Mill's definition (the means of enjoyment), both presupposes and stimulates a constant sense of unsatisfied desire, and it does not at all bother McCulloch that such a state may entail unhappiness:

---

[18] Quoted in McCulloch, *The Principles of Political Economy* (London: A. Murray and Son, 1970) 536–37.

But whether the attainment of wealth . . . be favourable or unfavourable to happiness, there can be no doubt of its pursuit being eminently congenial to human nature. . . . "The natural flights of the human mind are not from pleasure to pleasure, but from hope to hope"; and at every step of this progress man discovers new motives of action, new excitements of fear and allurements of desire. (532–33)

Indeed, as he waxes enthusiastic about perpetual dissatisfaction, he decides that it is, in itself, the goal:

When, indeed, the end is compassed, when the object of our exertions has been attained, it may, perhaps, be found not worth the trouble of acquiring; or, though prized at first, the enjoyment may pall upon the sense. But this, instead of discouraging, invariably tempts to new efforts; so that the pursuit of even imaginary conveniences of riches, distinctions, and enjoyments that can never be realized, is productive of an intensity of gratification, unknown in the apathy of a fixed or permanent situation. (533)

McCulloch thus fashioned a political economic plot that seemed to reverse the usual causality. The products that represent the desire for enjoyment become merely the means of stimulating the desire, which is the primary desideratum; and the products may be merely imaginary, for the appetite can be easily roused "by enjoyments that can never be realized." The never-to-be-realized enjoyment, paradoxically, keenly gratifies us, it seems, by fulfilling our natural human desire to desire.

By inverting the usual relation of desire to its object, by making consumption just another stimulus to desire, McCulloch collapsed the neat binary—"means of enjoyment" versus "enjoyment"—on which the productive/unproductive distinction relied. Hence, having established that the pursuit of enjoyment is what we seek and that enjoyment is merely one means to that end, he explicitly proceeded to dismantle Smith's contrast. All labor is productive, he next claims, which either immediately or indirectly creates the conditions for further desire and accumulation. The footman who serves you one meal whets your appetite for another and consequently stimulates you to increase your wealth; the whole apparatus of the state ensures the security of property and thereby encourages your industry; even the last of those mentioned in Adam Smith's list of unproductive workers, "players, singers, opera-dancers, buffoons, &c.," are productive, according to McCulloch, because "the amusements in question—how trifling soever they may seem in the estimation of cynics and *soi-disant* moralists—create new wants, and by doing so, stimulate our industry to procure the means of gratifying them" (541). Wants, not enjoyments, are the telos of this system, and their predominance over satisfaction creates the heady tumult and discontent that replace happiness (read contentment) as the normative emotional state.

An affective aim of this sort does indeed reconcile means and ends by making them indistinguishable, and so the contradiction between a wealthy society and a happy one recedes as a problem within the purview of political economy. Despite Mill's contempt for this disposal of the problem ("Mr. McCulloch has asserted, *totidem verbis*, the labour of Madame Pasta was as well entitled to be called productive labour as that of a cotton spinner"),[19] McCulloch's reasoning may be said to be more consistent than Mill's as well as more prescient: he gives an accurate description of the sensations generated in a mature consumer economy, where economic subjects are openly encouraged to savor constant stimulation and the manipulation of desires, where anticipation is a pleasure. McCulloch's celebration of the pleasure of wanting "enjoyments that can never be realized," though, also turns pleasure into a more imaginary, a less palpably physical, sensation than the enjoyments Mill had in mind. Although McCulloch's somaeconomic plot seems, in many ways, more pleasurable than Mill's, its account of motivation is also less sensuous and more imaginary. By abandoning the endurance and materiality of the product as criteria of productive labor, McCulloch also decreased the body's weight in the pain/pleasure ratio. The narrative becomes more psychologically dynamic and ironic, featuring economic actors who may be seeking "happiness" but are likely only to find disenchantment; and it becomes more open-ended, for political economists need no longer reconcile the pursuit of wealth with happy endings.

SOMAECONOMICS: THE PAIN THEORY OF VALUE

What we might call the psychologization of one somaeconomic plot, therefore, did seem to yield a society with a surplus of pleasure, although it would no longer follow that such a society would necessarily be "happy." But could labor itself, like the mere desire for consumption, also become pleasurable? The implicit answer given by the political economists seems to have been no. Labor, by definition, entailed suffering, and unpleasant sensations were the only kind that properly belonged to any activity qua labor. For example, one may have plenty of disagreeable feelings while gardening, but if one gardens as recreation, those sensations are incidental to the activity; if, on the other hand, one's labor is to garden, the feelings are essential. The first page of Mill's *Principles* states the axiom in an unusually explicit form:

> Labour is either bodily or mental; or, to express the distinction more comprehensively, either muscular or nervous [note Mill's materialist monism]; and it is necessary to include in the idea, not solely the exertion itself, but all

[19] "Words," 280–81.

feelings of a disagreeable kind, all bodily inconvenience or mental annoyance, connected with the employment of one's thoughts, or muscles, or both,
in a particular occupation. (25)

Agreeable feelings, bodily convenience, and mental elation may also accom-
pany the activity, but they do not make part of the *labor*.

In the last chapter, I gave some of the reasons for this definition of labor,
noting that it supports a number of the discipline's important distinctions:
between labor and leisure, production and consumption, labor and the reproduction of labor. It also allowed political economy to erect its theory of value
on what seemed to be self-evident somatic premises. The simplest version of
the story states that because we naturally avoid pain and seek pleasure, we
would shirk toil if we did not expect to enjoy its fruits. And since we dislike
labor, we have a natural tendency to measure the time we spend at it and to
calculate how much of it will purchase the things we want. Wanting to minimize it, we invent labor-saving devices and learn to master a limited set of
tasks and then exchange our surplus produce for the surplus of others who
have likewise specialized out of an instinctive aversion to labor. This simple
individual story then becomes the narrative of economic development in
which the possibility of exchange, human inventiveness, and the division of
labor all proceed naturally from our instinctive antipathy to labor. Labor is
that exertion for which we seek, in McCulloch's phrase, "some sort of equivalent advantage" (72). If we delighted in labor itself—as, for example, a mode
of self-expression, an experience of mastery, or a means of self-realization—
we would not be counting the hours and trying to make them pay. As Karl
Marx pointed out, the political economists tended to define "labor" restric-
tively, limiting it to its "alienated" variety; intrinsically pleasurable labor was
simply an oxymoron.

Very little of this needed to be said; indeed, Mill was unusual in defining
labor at all. The central idea of a disagreeable activity was carried in the term
itself. "Labour" then, as now, meant "exertion of the faculties of the body or
mind, especially when painful or compulsory" (*OED*'s first definition); and it
can be contrasted with the synonym "work," which is more neutral regarding
pleasure and pain and has a wider variety of meanings: "industry," "employment," "task," "operation," "creation," and "finished product." Perhaps the
breadth of meanings in "work" discouraged political economists from using it
to name the exertion expended in producing something. Smith, for example,
sometimes uses "toil," which has even stronger connotations than "labor" of
"hard and continuous . . . exertion which taxes the bodily or mental powers"
(*OED*), and he frequently uses "trouble" to indicate the inconvenience of
effort, but "work," which appears often in *Wealth of Nations*, is seldom used
as a synonym for "labor." In this passage, which uses both words, their difference is apparent:

This great increase of the quantity of work which, in consequence of the division of labour, the same number of people are capable of performing, is owing to three different circumstances; first, to the increase of dexterity in every particular workman; secondly, to the saving of the time which is commonly lost in passing from one species of work to another; and lastly, to the invention of a great number of machines which facilitate and abridge labour, and enable one man to do the work of many.[20]

"Work" here means tasks, or industrial operations; its quantity can thus be said to increase while labor itself (the exertion that goes into each task) is abridged. The claim is not that one man is laboring as hard as many but that his labor produces the results (the work) of many. Unpleasantness was conveyed in the very use of the word "labor" and hence did not need to be further elucidated.

Nor was it necessary to explain that, just as labor was a pain, the enjoyment of its products was a pleasure. We've just seen that the accumulation of wealth implied the ratio of delayed or anticipated enjoyment over realized enjoyment, and unless one could find a way of making anticipation just as pleasurable as consumption, one had to admit that a wealthy society was not, in the main, a pleasurable one. McCulloch's way of finessing this problem could not be applied to the equally obvious difficulty that a wealthy society was also generally one in which laboring was a more frequent activity than consuming, and hence the social body as a whole was experiencing more pain than pleasure. Even McCulloch assumed the unpleasantness of labor; in his story about what makes people work, pleasurable anticipation was a necessary goad to labor, which in itself implied that one would not be industrious merely for the sake of industriousness. In theory, of course, wealth accumulates if production outweighs consumption, and production might increase without any increase in the amount of labor expended. That, after all, was the point of the industrial revolution: more output with fewer hands equaled higher productivity. But machinery, like capital in general, was thought of as labor stored, and the labor that was saved in one machine-driven enterprise went into making machines or into whatever new enterprise the accumulated capital found most profitable. Since, as we've also seen, capital had to grow to stay alive, there could be no cessation of industry, no overall reduction of the painful expenditure and storage of labor.

If labor were painful and its very painfulness made it the measure (Adam Smith) or source (Ricardo) of exchange value, and if the amount of wealth gained in any given amount of time would equal the exchangeable value produced minus the amount consumed, the usual economic scenario would pre-

[20] Adam Smith, *An Inquiry into the Nature and Causes of the Wealth of Nations* (Oxford: Clarendon Press, 1976), 17.

dict the predominance of sensations of pain over those of pleasure in the wealthy society. Mill might retort that the amassed produce, the wealth, is painful labor converted into the means of enjoyment, for pain, like pleasure, is a fleeting thing that cannot be stored. And yet, in the first place, the amount of potential enjoyment in the unused commodity can only be estimated by the amount of labor, of "toil and trouble," it cost its producers. And in the second place, the wealth (in its myriad liquid and solid forms) might just as easily be thought of as the "means of labor" instead of the "means of enjoyment." To quote once again Adam Smith's formulation, "What everything is really worth to the man who has acquired it, and who wants to dispose of it or exchange it for something else, is the *toil and trouble* which it can save to himself, and *which it can impose upon other people*" (emphasis mine) (47). Ricardo objected to this formulation because it implied that the amount of labor expended on a commodity equaled the amount that could be obtained in exchange, but he did not dispute the idea that wealth is a means of employing others to undertake "toil and trouble," and he certainly advocated that as much of the nation's wealth as possible should be invested as capital, to set more labor in motion, rather than expended in personal consumption. Ricardo was extremely sparing with the language of sensation—"happiness" appears twice, and "enjoyments" refers to things that laborers might obtain over and above subsistence—but his labor theory of value is implicitly a pain theory of value, and his imperative to increase capital can be restated as the necessity to multiply "toil and trouble."

· · ·

How do the bioeconomic and somaeconomic plots I've been examining fit together? From Adam Smith to John Stuart Mill, political economists imagined vitality and sensation collecting into a great reserve of wealth and then sluicing out through further production or consumption. They dealt with the creation, distribution, exchange, and expense not only of objects and values, goods and services, credits and debits, but also of life itself and its feelings of pleasure and pain. Adequate vitality, they thought, could only be stored for further use if present enjoyment was withheld and more pain than pleasure released into the system. Even Malthus, who at first seemed to favor a bioeconomics of rapid embodiment, gradually admitted that *potential* vigor and sensation must, at each moment, vastly overbalance actual life and sensuous experience, for it is in the surplus that capital is constituted and finds its resilience, mobility, and continuity. Capital, therefore, could easily be imagined by the political economists as a repository of vigor and sensation, a guarantee of the corporate entity's future life, but it could just as easily be attacked by its critics as a force withdrawing life and feeling from the people and withholding them for its own aggrandizement.

In either the negative or the positive version of its operations, capital appeared to place sensate life in abeyance, to abstract it from biotic form while preserving its potential force, and a fascination with this apparent power to extract, suspend, and transfer emotion and vitality seized the literary as well as the economic imagination of nineteenth-century Britain. The next chapters explore the forms this fascination took in the novels of Charles Dickens and George Eliot as well as in the works of Thomas Carlyle, John Ruskin, and numerous other commentators. At times, these writers engaged political economy explicitly; at other times, they unconsciously shared the imaginative universe of that discipline simply by cohabiting with it in a larger realm of conjecture about the circulation of life, value, death, pain, and pleasure. The bioeconomic and somaeconomic plots available to Dickens were essentially those outlined in this chapter, whereas George Eliot drew as well on the later developments of neoclassical economic theory. The underlying and often conflicting narratives about the workings of organic and psychic life were not the exclusive property of any discipline; they belonged as much to imaginative literature, aesthetics, philosophy, biology, medicine, organic chemistry, and psychology as to political economy. Consequently, the following chapters will describe the parallel play and mutual pressures among various plots instead of arguing for the precedence of any one mode of thought. Of all the relevant discourses, though, political economy and the novel claimed to have special obligations to model a lifelike totality, as well as unique credentials and resources for doing the job, and so we might reasonably say that the plots they both fought over and shared were fundamental to the Victorian social imagination.

Chapter Three

Hard Times and the Somaeconomics
of the Early Victorians

There is no joy in the Coketown of Dickens's *Hard Times*. Its people are unhappy, like the city dwellers in other industrial novels, but the source of their misery is atypical. Their suffering does not seem to derive from uncommonly wretched living and working conditions. Our first walk through Coketown's deadening regularity contrasts tellingly with, for example, the constantly obstructed passage through Manchester's chaotic squalor in one of the early chapters of Elizabeth Gaskell's *Mary Barton* (chapter 6). Whereas Gaskell's narrator gives us a complete sanitarian's nightmare—a street soaked with urine, cluttered with rubbish heaps and ashes, and lined with fetid, oozing cellar dwellings—Dickens's narrator gives us a dry and schematic *premise* in the place of a human environment. Coketown is made of figures almost as abstract as those of the despised statisticians, and they are laid out for us in the keynote paragraph with a repetitiousness of sentence structure as monotonous as a ledger book's:

> [I]t was a town of red and black like the painted face of a savage. It was a town of machinery and tall chimneys, out of which interminable serpents of smoke trailed themselves for ever and ever, and never got uncoiled. It had a black canal in it, and a river that ran purple with ill-smelling dye, and vast piles of buildings . . . where the pistons of the steam-engine worked monotonously up and down like the head of an elephant in a state of melancholy madness. It contained several large streets all very like one another, and many small streets still more like one another, inhabited by people equally like one another, who all went in and out at the same hours, with the same sound upon the same pavements, to do the same work, and to whom every day was the same as yesterday and tomorrow, and every year the counterpart of the last and the next. . . .
> You saw nothing in Coketown but what was severely workful.[1]

In this novel the most pervasive problem attending industrialism is not factory hours, low wages, child labor, dangerous machinery, unsanitary housing and

---

[1] *Hard Times*, eds. George Ford and Sylvere Monod (New York: W. W. Norton, 1966), 17. All subsequent quotations from the novel are from this edition and page numbers are given in the text of the essay.

neighborhoods, pollution, unemployment, class conflict, unsympathetic masters, or even the cash nexus. Many of these are mentioned, but the most pervasive problem is, quite simply, labor itself in its repetitious invariability. In *Hard Times*, monotonous work by itself makes people unhappy. Unlike the political economists, Dickens makes no distinction between work and labor; all endeavors touched by toil are equally unpleasant.

Like much of the prose of *Hard Times*, this keynote paragraph carries the point stylistically. It's a melancholy piece of writing, and its melancholy is created by the labored tedium of the paragraph's rhythms. The uniformity of sentence pattern, moreover, is not just an instance of imitative form, although Dickens was surely making use of that device in the repetitive grammatical constructions ("It was," "It was," "It had," "It contained") and in the gradual settling down of the word "like" from a marker of "fanciful" similitudes ("like the painted face of a savage," "like the head of an elephant") into an indicator of the merely iterative: "like one another," "like one another," "like one another" (three times in one sentence). The prose doesn't just mime the monotony of the environment but also announces that the novel is both product and producer of the severe workfulness it seems to criticize. *Hard Times* relentlessly belabors its effortful prose and its unhappy (in both senses of the word) allegories. Workfulness is not just an attribute of people in this novel; it is a mode of representation and an angle of vision on the world in general.

The narrator takes the connection between toil and melancholy so thoroughly for granted that he never feels the need to explain it. The instances of people who are unhappy because they work very hard just mount up. Why are the hands of Coketown unhappy? Because, we are repeatedly told, they are incessantly working. Why are the children of Thomas Gradgrind unhappy? Because they are constantly forced to be "somethingological." "Folkth can't be alwayth working, thquire. They mutht be amutht," we are told by Mr. Sleary the circus proprietor, but the amusers themselves are severely workful and often appropriately gloomy. The horse-riders, as they are called, are not idle (and therefore potentially happy) drifters, as the factory owner, Bounderby, imagines, but people in a regular trade, to which children are apprenticed at very young ages, with comically melancholy results: Josephine, according to the narrator, was "a pretty fair-haired girl of eighteen, who had been tied on a horse at two years old, and had made a will at twelve, which she always carried about with her, expressive of her dying desire to be drawn to the grave by the two piebald ponies" (28). Signor Jupe, Sissy Jupe's father, is a more serious instance of the misery encountered in the amusement business. After years of working to entertain others, he can no longer effortlessly perform his tricks; the harder he has to work, the unhappier he becomes, until he is almost insane with misery. Even James Harthouse, the rakish MP who works at indolence and attempts one of English literature's most grimly determined seductions, finds that the labor of seeming never to exert himself causes considerable ennui.

The early Victorian writers we normally associate with Charles Dickens seldom portrayed labor—labor in the abstract—as a misery-inducing activity that should not be allowed to dominate life. If the Romantics, as we saw in chapter 1, claimed to seek self-expression and self-realization through work, the literati of the early Victorian period pursued that end with a quasi-religious fervor. They extolled work as the source of well-being and spiritual grandeur, as the numerous paeans to work, especially in writings about industrialism, attest. "Qui laborat, orat," says the eponymous heroine of Disraeli's *Sybil.* And she goes on to quiz a character she suspects of not working (as in so many Victorian novels, said character is a lawyer): "Is yours that life of uncomplaining toil wherein there is so much of beauty and of goodness, that . . . it is held to include the force and efficacy of prayer?"[2] Disraeli's heroine is echoing a famous passage from Thomas Carlyle's *Past and Present:* "[A]ll true Work is Religion. . . . Admirable was that [saying] of the old Monks, '*Laborare est Orare,* Work is Worship.' "[3] And not even the shortest list of hymns to work would be complete without Carlyle's exhortation in *Sartor Resartus,* which is often cited as a definitive expression of Victorian productivism: "Produce! Produce! Were it but the pitifullest infinitesimal fraction of a Product, produce it, in God's name! 'Tis the utmost thou hast in thee: out with it, then. Up, up! Whatsoever thy hand findeth to do, do it with thy whole might. Work while it is called Today; for the Night cometh, wherein no man can work."[4]

To be sure, Carlyle, the most influential and enthusiastic early Victorian chorister in praise of workfulness, never claimed that enjoyment was among its effects. Whereas most of the choir, which consisted of voices from all classes, denominations, professions, and political persuasions, sang of its happy consequences—the prosperity, well-being, and autonomy it would bring—Carlyle scorned such craven eudemonism: "Does not the whole wretchedness, the whole *Atheism* as I call it, of man's ways, in these generations, shadow itself for us in that unspeakable Life-philosophy of his: The pretension to be what he calls 'happy'?"[5] Recommending a "Greatest-Nobleness Principle" in place of Utilitarianism's "Greatest-Happiness Principle," he exhorts his readers to seek the *suffering* of work:

All work, even cotton-spinning, is noble; work is alone noble: be that here said and asserted once more. And in like manner, too, all dignity is painful;

---

[2] *Sybil: or The Two Nations* (London: Oxford University Press, 1970), 252.
[3] *Past and Present,* intro. G. K. Chesterton (London: Oxford University Press, 1960), 206.
[4] *Sartor Resartus: the Life and Opinions of Herr Teufelsdrockh. In Three Books* (London: Chapman and Hall, 1871), 136.
[5] *Past and Present,* 159.

a life of ease is not for any man, nor for any god. The life of all gods figures itself to us as a Sublime Sadness—earnestness of Infinite Battle against Infinite Labour. Our highest religion is named the "Worship of Sorrow." (158)

Coketown's severe workfulness and concomitant disregard for happiness, Dickens's apparent objects of satire, would seem to accord fully with Carlyle's ideal of human life.[6]

It is, therefore, odd that *Hard Times*, which presents itself as an explicitly Carlylean satire on Benthamism and political economy, blames the Victorian cult of work on the very people who were most innocent of such bombastic mystifications. Charging the Utilitarians with ardent workism, as this novel does, is especially inappropriate because Jeremy Bentham, as I've noted in previous chapters, forthrightly denied that work possessed any intrinsic glories. In Bentham, indeed, one finds clear anticipations of *Hard Times's* maverick skepticism about the spiritual wonders of labor. In 1817, Bentham published *A Table of the Springs of Action*, in which he unequivocally states that people do not derive happiness from labor itself (but only from the wealth it creates) and hence cannot truly be said to love, desire, or gain satisfaction directly from work: "[D]esire of labour *for the sake of labour*—of labour considered in the character of an *end*, without any view to any thing else, is a sort of desire that seems scarcely to have place in the human breast."[7] Those who would eulogize the love of wealth, Bentham explains, claim to love " 'Industry' . . . and thus it is that, under *another* name, the *desire of wealth* has been furnished with a sort of *letter of recommendation*, which under its own name, could not have been given to it" (104). To the founder of Utilitarianism, praise of labor was mere cant and hypocrisy. Labor in his view, moreover, was not simply a neutral thing improperly promoted through eulogy. In the great ledger book of his mind, where he balanced pains against pleasures to calculate the net happiness of any phenomenon, labor was automatically entered in the pain column: "*Aversion*—not *desire*—is the emotion, the only emotion, which *labour*, taken by itself, is qualified to produce. Of any such emotion as *love* or *desire*, *ease*, which is the *negative* or *absence* of labour, *ease*, not *labour*, is the object" (104).

Since, according to Bentham, we are naturally averse to labor, prolonged doses of it inevitably result, not in the sanctified "Sorrow" of Carlyle's imagination, but in a much less meaningful *un*happiness. Bentham, therefore,

---

[6] For a useful short history of "happiness" as the professed goal of ethics and social arrangements, see Darrin M. McMahon, "From the Happiness of Virtue to the Virtue of Happiness: 400 B.C.–A.D. 1780," *Daedalus* 133, no. 2 (Spring 2004): 5–17. For philosophical discussions of the utilitarian and eudemonic positions, see J. L. Cowan, *Pain and Pleasure: A Study in Philosophical Psychology* (New York: St. Martin's Press, 1968), and Elizabeth Telfer, *Happiness* (London: MacMillan, 1980).

[7] *Deontology, Together with a Table of the Springs of Action, and the Article on Utilitarianism*, ed. Amnon Goldworth (Oxford: Clarendon Press, 1983), 104.

seems a better guide than Carlyle to the logic behind the allegory of the melancholy mad elephant in *Hard Times*, an image for the incessant motion of the steam engines. To be working is to be unhappy. To be industrious is to be working continuously and thus to be in a sustained condition of unhappiness: that is, melancholy. To be willingly industrious is to choose to be melancholy and is hence to be mad. When Dickens blames Coketown's unhappiness on its severe workfulness, when he figures the spirit of the town as animal vitality bent into ceaseless rhythmic motion, he unwittingly adheres to Bentham's view.

When Carlyle contravened the Utilitarian emphasis on felicity by avowing that it would be nobler to embrace labor, transforming the unhappiness into an *imitatio Christi*, than to avoid work in the pursuit of ease, he at least got Bentham and Adam Smith right; he knew that Utilitarianism and political economy, whatever else they might be, were no gospels of work. Indeed, Carlyle's definitive break with eudemonism made him one of the most consistent and effective anti-Benthamites of the early Victorian period. He went far beyond Coleridge's and Southey's comparatively mild complaints about Utilitarians confusing the commonwealth with the commonweal, complaints that, as we saw in earlier chapters, sometimes invoked a greatest-happiness-as-greatest-contentment principle. Born in 1795, Carlyle belonged temperamentally as well as chronologically to the younger generation of Romantics and shared their often contemptuous attitude toward the Lake Poets. Coleridge, the first English writer to anglicize the German Romantic tradition, was clearly his most important forebear, and probably for that reason came in for Carlyle's unsparing criticism: "Coleridge's talk and speculation was the emblem of himself: in it as in him, a ray of heavenly inspiration struggled, in a tragically ineffectual degree."[8] Coleridge was incapable of bringing light to England, according to Carlyle, because he could not defeat the unmanly desire for ease: "Harsh pain, danger, necessity, slavish harnessed toil, were of all things abhorrent to him" (322). Despite his apparent anti-Utilitarianism, in other words, Coleridge remained a hedonist, sunk in "indolences and esuriences" (322). Coleridge was not up to the task of driving the Greatest-Happiness Principle from its hold on the British mind because he acceded to it in the very conduct of his life. Ironically, the avoidance of pain produced its own ultimate misery, proving itself to be not only ignoble but also self-defeating,

> For pain, danger, difficulty, steady slaving toil, and other highly disagreeable behests of destiny, shall in no wise be shirked by any brightest mortal that will approve himself loyal to his mission in this world; nay precisely the higher he is, the deeper will be the disagreeableness, and the detestability to

[8] *The Life of John Sterling*, in *Thomas Carlyle's Works* (London: Chapman and Hall, 1885), 4:50–51.

flesh and blood, of the tasks laid on him; and the heavier too, and more tragic his penalties if he neglect them. (322)

Clearly, Carlyle was not about to neglect them. He had reconceived happiness as a mere ephemeral chimera ("The night come, our happiness, our unhappiness—it is all abolished; vanished, clean gone"), and he had elevated work to an eternal principle ("But our work . . . for endless Times and Eternities, remains").[9]

Was all of this simply lost on Dickens when he so completely bent the logics of Benthamism and Carlylism that he attributed the latter's gospel of work and disregard for happiness to the former? Was Dickens just mistaken, not paying attention to the details of the controversy, as several commentators have claimed? In 1877, E. P. Whipple, for example, wrote that Dickens was innocent of any knowledge of either political economy or Utilitarianism, an opinion that has been seconded by many.[10] But, rather than settle for a mere plea of ignorance, we should also recall that between Bentham's death in 1834 and the composition of *Hard Times* in 1854, Utilitarianism underwent changes. Uppermost in Dickens's mind might have been the fact that the most important piece of Utilitarian legislation, the New Poor Law that went into effect on Bentham's demise, produced misery on purpose (as a disincentive to improvidence), so philosophical radicalism's purported emphasis on maximal enjoyment might easily have seemed merely a cruel irony. To Dickens the satirist, ever on the lookout for hypocrisy, Benthamite talk of happiness would only have made its punitive policies seem all the more egregiously heartless.

Bentham's version of the greatest-happiness principle, moreover, had found critics other than Carlyle, even some within the ranks of the utilitarians and political economists themselves. Mill famously censured the limitations of Bentham's felicific calculus in an 1838 article:

Man is never recognised by [Bentham] as a being capable of pursuing spiritual perfection as an end. . . .

The sense of *honour*, and personal dignity—that feeling of personal exaltation and degradation which acts independently of other people's opinion, or even in defiance of it; the love of *beauty*, the passion of the artists . . . the love of action, the thirst for movement and activity, a principle scarcely of less influence in human life than its opposite, the love of ease: —None of these powerful constituents of human nature are thought worthy of a place among the "Springs of Action."[11]

[9] *Past and Present*, 161–62.

[10] E. P. Whipple, "On the Economic Fallacies of *Hard Times*," *The Atlantic Monthly* 233, no. 29 (1877): 353–59.

[11] "Bentham," *Dissertations and Discussions: Political, Philosophical, and Historical* (New York: Henry Holt and Company, 1874), 1:385.

Mill's point is not that Bentham's greatest-happiness principle is itself altogether mistaken,[12] but that his understanding of human pains and pleasures, the components of happiness and unhappiness, was deficient, and we should note especially that Mill makes room here for an active desire to exert oneself—perhaps to work—instead of always seeking "ease."

By the 1850s, then, even if Dickens knew that Bentham had proclaimed general felicity the goal of his system, he could ignore that fact on the grounds that Benthamites had no adequate understanding of what actually made people happy. Or, more precisely, he could satirize "the greatest happiness for the greatest number" (a formulation Bentham took from Priestley)[13] as a meaningless abstraction, associated with the statistical chimera that Sissy Jupe has such trouble comprehending:

> "And [Mr. M'Choakumchild] said, Now, this schoolroom is a Nation. And in this nation, there are fifty millions of money. Isn't this a prosperous nation? Girl number twenty, isn't this a prosperous nation, and an't you in a thriving state?"...
>
> "I said I didn't know. I thought I couldn't know whether it was a prosperous nation or not, and whether I was in a thriving state or not, unless I knew who had got the money, and whether any of it was mine. But that had nothing to do with it. It was not in the figures at all," said Sissy, wiping her eyes. (44)

In 1854 it was already a cliché to note that general prosperity depended on the distribution of wealth, and not its mere accumulation.[14] Indeed, Bentham himself worried the issue and decided to drop the ending phrase "for the greatest number" from his formulation of the greatest-happiness principle when he realized that "distributing a minority of 2000 men as slaves among the majority of 2001 promotes the happiness of the greatest number, but not the greatest happiness in aggregate."[15] But when Sissy asks if any of the wealth were hers, she points to a slightly different question raised by the greatest-happiness principle; why should individuals identify their well-being with that of some corporate entity, or, to use Bentham's terms, why should their

[12] In his 1863 essay "Utilitarianism," Mill goes to great lengths to defend it as the only coherent moral principle.

[13] In his introduction to *Bentham's Political Thought* (New York: Barnes and Noble, 1973), Bhikhu Parekh explains that Bentham used Priestly's phrase in 1776, but then dropped it for forty years. It reappears frequently in his writings between 1816 and 1829, when he cut off the "greatest number" phrase.

[14] One way to look at Malthus's objections to Smith's theory of value and later to Ricardo's insouciance about the price of provisions is that he thought wealth might increase without making the majority of people happier. See Donald Winch, "Higher Maxims: Happiness versus Wealth in Malthus and Ricardo," in *That Noble Science of Politics: A Study in Nineteenth-Century Intellectual History,* eds. Stefan Collini, Donald Winch, John Burrow (Cambridge: Cambridge University Press, 1983), 63–89.

[15] Bentham, *Bentham's Political Thought,* 16–17.

self-interest be "enlightened"? Sissy here comes dangerously close to sounding like her putative contrast, the young Bitzer, who confronts Mr. Gradgrind with his Benthamite creed at the novel's end:

> I am sure you know that the whole social system is a question of self-interest. What you must always appeal to, is a person's self-interest. It's your only hold. We are so constituted. I was brought up in that catechism when I was very young, Sir, as you are well aware. (218)

Bentham never successfully negotiated the psychological gap between particular felicific calculations and general ones, which is why he came to rely on the government to close it. Lawmakers, he argued, should see to it that particular self-interests tend toward the general good, for they do not naturally converge. Dickens need not, and as numerous critics of the novel have demonstrated, does not, come up with his own solution to this dilemma, but instead he rests content with exposing the untranslatability both of aggregate prosperity into individual happiness (Sissy) and of individual well-being into the general good (Bitzer).

Furthermore, by the 1850s, as I mentioned in the last chapter, many political economists had disencumbered themselves of the greatest-happiness principle in their attempt to achieve disciplinary focus. Nassau Senior fixed the "Limits of the Science" in 1836 and republished them in three subsequent 1850s editions of *An Outline of the Science of Political Economy*. The passage merits extensive quotation here because it seems to resonate throughout Dickens's satire:

> [T]he subject treated by the Political Economist . . . is not Happiness, but Wealth. . . . The business of a Political Economist is neither to recommend nor to dissuade, but to state general principles, which it is fatal to neglect, but neither advisable, nor perhaps practicable, to use as the sole, or even the principal, guides in the actual conduct of affairs. In the meantime the duty of each individual writer is clear. Employed as he is upon a Science in which error or even ignorance, may be productive of such intense and such extensive mischief, he is bound, like a juryman, to give deliverance true according to the evidence, and allow neither sympathy with indigence, nor disgust at profusion or at avarice—neither reverence for existing institutions, nor detestation of existing abuses . . . to deter him from stating what he believes to be the facts, or from drawing from those facts what appear to him to be the legitimate conclusions.[16]

Senior's attempt at disciplinary modesty was supposed to shield him from the "unfavourable prejudices" that had arisen against the science for seeming to

---

[16] *An Outline of Political Economy, with Appendices*, in *The Library of Economics* (New York: Farrar and Rinehart, 1938), 2–3.

prefer wealth to happiness or virtue: "It must be admitted that an author who, having stated that a given conduct is productive of Wealth, should, on that account alone, recommend it . . . would be guilty of the absurdity of implying that Happiness and . . . Wealth are identical. But his error would consist not in confining his attention to Wealth, but in confounding Wealth with Happiness" (4).

And yet, if *Hard Times* is any indication, disclaimers like this seem to have backfired, supplying instead the image of an endeavor for which complete moral indifference and the suppression of sentiment were requirements: neither sympathy nor disgust, neither reverence nor detestation will deter the political economist from stating "the facts."[17] "Now, what I want is, Facts. Teach these boys and girls nothing but Facts," demands Thomas Gradgrind in the opening words of *Hard Times*, and although the next sentence—"Facts alone are wanted in life"—makes the very opposite of Senior's point (i.e., much else is wanted, which political economy cannot supply) Dickens's satire finds a warrant in the political economist's readiness to dissociate facts and values in the first place. In *Hard Times* the diminished ambitions of the science, which, according to Senior, must "disregard all consideration of Happiness or Virtue" (3), ineluctably reduce its practitioners' capacity for human understanding, restricting their sagaciousness within its narrow limits.

All of this discursive history is by way of moving us to the 1850s and excusing Dickens for not seeming to notice that Benthamites, rather than Carlyleans, were supposed to care about happiness. In the thirties and forties, eudemonism seems to have been fugitive in both camps. Carlyle railed against it, distinguishing himself from Coleridge, and Nassau Senior as well as McCulloch declared its irrelevance to political economy, distinguishing themselves from Bentham. These early Victorians, that is, were not taking part in exactly the same controversy that had occupied their immediate predecessors. The greatest-happiness principle was too puny for Carlyle's purposes and too ambitious for the political economists'; it was beneath Carlyle and beyond Senior. And so, for opposite reasons, both rendered the question of felicity moot.

This peculiar convergence may, in part, account for the melancholic aimlessness of *Hard Times*, its almost complete lack of narrative hope. Not a single plot is set in motion that has the chance of a pleasant outcome or promises any gratification of the reader's desire for pleasure. For all of its strict consequentialism (its three books, for example, are titled "Sowing," "Reaping," and

---

[17] For a general history of the divorce between facts and values in British social discourse, see Mary Poovey, *A History of the Modern Fact: Problems of Knowledge in the Sciences of Wealth and Society* (Chicago: University of Chicago Press, 1998). For a history of the concept of fact that stresses, as Senior does in this quotation, the need to weigh and interpret them as a legal process would, see Barbara Shapiro, *A Culture of Fact: England, 1550–1720* (Ithaca, N.Y.: Cornell University Press, 2000).

"Garnering"), it gives us nothing to look forward to. Our expectations are not frustrated; they are grimly fulfilled. To paraphrase Dickens's own satire of the didactic literature of his day, All the little Utilitarians grow up to be selfish, criminal, dead, or barren. Wherever marriage plots might have begun (in the story of Sissy Jupe, for example, or that of Stephen Blackpool and Rachel), they are suppressed. In Dickens's notes for chapter 16, he queries, "Lover for Sissy?" then answers, with double underscoring, "No. Decide on no love at all" (236, Norton). In the place of the emphatically rejected love plot, we have only its negatives: Louisa's incestuous fixation on her brother, the dissolution of the Louisa-Bounderby marriage, and the simultaneous threat of an adultery plot. "Time the Manufacturer," to use the novel's own metaphor for its plot machinery, "not minding what anybody said" (69), cranks out life stories with deadening regularity and utter indifference. The novel's satire of heedless, anaesthetized work notwithstanding, it seems powerless to produce or even anticipate enjoyment at the end of its own process. My point is not just that *Hard Times* lacks a happy ending but rather that it makes no attempt to engage the gears of hope and fear, avoidance of pain and anticipation of pleasure. Instead, it relies on an inertial movement, unstoppable and unmotivated, for which the appropriate metaphors are the mere passage of time and the grinding of the mill. The economy of reading, paralleling the depicted economy of working, is propelled by no expectation of enjoyment, and hence it practices an affective economics in which the drive to put in time has become utterly independent of any other goal.

And yet, the ambient denigration of satisfaction as an ultimate aim, even if it did invade Dickens's underlying vision, need not have resulted in such a disengaged narrative. After all, J. R. McCulloch lit on the perfect affective predisposition for the Victorian novel reader after abandoning the idea that our efforts in economic life are rewarded by happy conclusions. His description, examined in the last chapter, of our motivation for working to accumulate more than we reasonably expect to enjoy can be easily applied to novel reading: "The natural flights of the human mind are not from pleasure to pleasure, but from hope to hope." By redescribing desire as both a good in itself and the "natural" state of the civilized mind, and by insisting that we are usually more gratified by anticipation than achievement, McCulloch asserted that we do not work just to reach the goal of consumption. Nor, by extension, is the gratification of reading experienced only at the end of the narrative. Instead of an economy driven by the simple dialectic of pain and pleasure, labor and consumption, McCulloch imagined one in which the sensation of desire dominates and finds merely temporary objects for its continuation, discarding them once they are gained, very much as a novel reader moves from episode to episode, no sooner at the resolution of one than impelled toward the next.

Reflections of this sort, paralleling unsatisfiable desire in life and in reading, were certainly available to Dickens; since the publication of Thackeray's *Vanity Fair* (1847), they had been the substratum of the Victorian novel's complex irony, and Dickens was to explore them thoroughly only four years later in *Great Expectations*. And yet, in *Hard Times* he comes close to what one Victorian called the fallacy of "Sisyphism," the view that modern industrial conditions impose "unceasing and fruitless labor," which admits of no pleasurable anticipations.[18] This representation of work is by no means typical of Dickens's novels, but in *Hard Times* he seems to have taken the insight that wealth depends on a top-heavy ratio of nonenjoyment to enjoyment, or productive pain to unproductive pleasure, and extended it into a plot about futility. Why such despair in this book alone; why such a studied refusal to credit or exploit the operations of modern desire? Given Dickens's need to distance himself, and his novelistic endeavor, from the dynamics of industrial capitalism, why would he stress its futility and then mimic it in his narrative mode?

We can begin to answer this question by first acknowledging what readers have long recognized: *Hard Times* is a transparent advertisement for the amusement business, the business to which it supposedly belongs.[19] This project of self-legitimation—justifying "fancy," "imagination," and "amusement"—tends, indeed, to override the novel's other ideological commitments. What has gone unrecognized, however, is that the novel, in a particularly daring move, mounts its defense of imaginative activity in its enemy's own territory, developing its raison d'être in political-economic terms.[20] Seemingly unable to validate amusement for its own sake, *Hard Times* represents the somaeconomics of providing pleasure, and in doing so it takes up and works out two of the concepts whose history I've been tracing: (1) the theoretical expansion of the category of labor, and (2) the affective implications of the labor theory of value. Dickens's novel imagines the melancholy confluence of these two ideas. Whereas political economists like McCulloch dealt with the topics separately, without seeming to notice the implications they had for each

[18] Under "Sisyphism," the *OED* quotes G. R. Porter, tr. *Bastiat's Popular Fallacies* (1846): "We beg the reader to excuse us if we designate this system hereafter under the name of Sisyphism"; and it quotes Reade, *Never Too Late* (1846), I, 231: "The ancients imagined tortures particularly trying to nature, that of Sisyphus to wit. . . . We have made Sisyphism vulgar."

[19] The most informative and well-developed work on this topic is Paul Schlicke, *Dickens and Popular Entertainment* (London: Allen and Unwin, 1985), 137–89. Schlicke places Dickens's portrayal of the circus in *Hard Times* in the contexts of both changes in popular entertainment in nineteenth-century Britain and the trajectory of Dickens's novelistic and journalistic career. He subscribes to the received opinion that "Dickens presents the circus in polar opposition to the perversities of the schoolroom and the factory" (143), even though he notices the commercial flavor of the enterprise.

[20] It has been noticed that Dickens's recommendation of amusement is an inadequate response to the problems of industrial society. See, for example, John Holloway, "*Hard Times*: A History and a Criticism," in *Dickens and the Twentieth Century*, ed. John Gross and Gabriel Pearson (London: Routledge and Kegan Paul, 1962), 159-74.

other, Dickens put them together narratively, and his novel is accordingly a deep envisioning of the discipline's paradoxical pronouncements about economic sensations.

Every character in *Hard Times* works; there are no exceptions. The novel thus adheres to one of political economy's innovations, introduced, as we've seen, by Adam Smith in the very act of distinguishing between productive and unproductive labor: everyone is some kind of laborer, from "[t]he sovereign . . . with all the officers both of justice and war who serve under him," down through the professions, and including even "players, buffoons, musicians, opera-singers, opera-dancers; &c."[21] Before the rise of political economy, it was not normal to view every occupation as labor. Certainly, everyone was supposed to have a station and a duty, perhaps even a vocation, but many were considered exempt from labor per se. Those who governed, planned, directed, invested, as well as those who played for a living were generally contrasted to those who labored; they were not thought of as different kinds— that is, unproductive kinds—of laborers.

Even long after the rise of political economy, Smith's nomination of almost everybody as some sort of worker was unusual. For many Victorians, his delightfully eclectic list would have seemed a roll call of shirkers, parasites, and vagabonds. Indeed, the critics of political economy, who were most enthusiastic about the spiritual advantages of work, were especially apt to define it more exclusively. Carlyle, for example, divides the world into workers and *un*workers,[22] a categorization that surely owes something to Adam Smith's distinction between productive and unproductive labor and yet denies that almost everyone toils. John Ruskin, to name another of orthodox political economy's critics, ranged all activities on a continuum from death enhancing to life enhancing, or from negative to positive work. Negative work, he writes in *Unto This Last*, produces death, positive work produces life, and idleness is neutral regarding life and death. Murderers and mothers are thus his typical examples of negative and positive workers (certainly not a normal way of thinking about the issue). Although he gives us no instances of idlers, he insists that there are such things theoretically, for any negative-positive continuum must have a zero point. In short, Victorian critics of political economy seem to have been both inspired and challenged by the inclusiveness of the category of labor, inspired to come up with their own idiosyncratic redefinitions and challenged to impose some moral order on this economic classification.

In *Hard Times*, however, Dickens does not crisscross the category of labor with ethical distinctions or tailor it to exclude particular occupations, classes, or genders. The novel echoes the almost comical inclusiveness initiated by *The*

---

[21] Adam Smith, *An Inquiry into the Nature and Causes of the Wealth of Nations* (Oxford: Clarendon Press, 1976), 1:331.

[22] See *Past and Present*, especially book 3, chapter 8.

Wealth of Nations, representing Mrs. Sparsit, the Gradgrind children, Stephen Blackpool, and the horse-riders all as some sort of laborers, and this consistency helps account for the novel's famous unity of vision. In Adam Smith's view, neither kings nor beggars escape the destiny of work, and the same might be said of the inhabitants of Coketown. Mrs. Sparsit, for instance, drolly exemplifies Smith's point by *working* at her aristocracy, enacting her pedigree for a yearly salary (by mutual consent unacknowledged as such) paid by Mr. Bounderby. Thus, Carlyle's "unworking aristocracy" is pressed into the service of his "working aristocracy." Moreover, instead of making moral distinctions between kinds of toil, Dickens seems intent on drawing parallels: Bounderby and Sleary, and Stephen Blackpool and Mrs. Sparsit are only two of the unlikely pairs that the novel unites, imagistically and thematically, on the basis of similarities in their labor and economic relations. Certainly there are moral distinctions separating the two characters in each of these pairs, but the characters are, in one case, equally industrious in employing their own and others' labor, and, in the other case, equally laborious in their employer's service. In short, Dickens's sense of the capaciousness and moral neutrality of the classification "worker" resembles Adam Smith's more closely than it resembles Carlyle's.

Furthermore, his apparent reluctance to draw even the distinction Smith elaborated in his famous passage—the productive/unproductive differentiation that was crucial, as we saw in the last chapter, to considerations of economic sensation—represents no break with political economy but rather an alignment with the very thinker he once referred to as "that Great Mogul of imposters, Master McCulloch."[23] Indeed, if it were not so implausible that Dickens might have read McCulloch's *Principles of Political Economy,* one might speculate that its critique of Smith's categories inspired *Hard Times.* Arguing in favor of "the productiveness of the labour of players, singers, opera dancers, buffoons, &c.," the political economist explains:

> A taste for the amusements they afford has exactly the same effect on national wealth as a taste for tobacco, champagne, or any other luxury. We wish to be present at their exhibitions; and, in order to get admittance, we pay the price or equivalent demanded by them for their services. But this price is ... the result of industry. And hence it is, that the amusements afforded by these persons—however trifling they may seem in the estimation of cynics and *soi-disant* moralists—create new wants, and by so doing necessarily stimulate our industry to procure the means of gratifying them. They are unquestionably, therefore, a *cause* of production; and it is very like a truism to say that what is a cause of production must be productive.[24]

---

[23] To John Forster, 12–14/8/1855, *The Letters of Charles Dickens,* eds. Madeline House, Graham Storey, Kathleen Tillotson (New York: Oxford University Press, 1965), 7:687.

[24] J. R. McCulloch, *Principles of Political Economy* (London: Ward, Lock, 1886), 215.

Truism or not, *Hard Times* goes to great lengths to demonstrate a similar point, although the emphasis in the novel is slightly different:

> That exactly in the ratio as they worked long and monotonously, [the narrator tells us] the craving grew within them for some physical relief— some relaxation, encouraging good humour and good spirits, and giving them a vent—some recognised holiday . . . —some occasional light pie . . . which craving must and would be satisfied aright or would inevitably go wrong. (19)

The horse-riding is less an explicit stimulus to the operatives' desire in this passage than it is a release for the pent-up frustration of overwork, but the "light pie" of Sleary's amusement nonetheless complements and rewards labor, and, the implicit argument runs, should therefore form part of its reproduction. The contrast this passage foreshadows ("which craving must and would be satisfied or it would inevitably go wrong") between the "encouraging" amusement and the discouraging trade-union meeting that follows its departure from Coketown, moreover, reinforces the stimulating role that the circus plays in the productive process. When Sleary comes to town, the people work; when the trade-union organizer comes, they strike.

Hard Times aligns with other remappings of the productive/unproductive border as well. Mill's tortured discussion in his *Principles of Political Economy* instances the accumulation of skills as a kind of productive labor because, "we should regard all labour as productive which is employed in creating permanent utilities, whether embodied in human beings, or in any other animate or inanimate objects."[25] And Mill, too, turns to performers to illustrate his point. The player learning his trade, he writes, labors productively. As we saw in the last chapter, Mill ultimately backs away from this position partly because it seems absurd to claim that as long as the performer is only practicing to acquire skill he is engaged in productive labor whereas his display of that skill in public performance (because it "leaves nothing behind") is unproductive. But Mill gives no cogent reason for his retreat, and one might just as easily conclude from his discussion that both the acquisition and the pleasure-giving, remunerative display of skill in a performance are productive labor.

At least one contemporary reader of political economy concluded that the distinction must rely on whether or not the labor produces a profit as well as a wage, that is, whether or not it augments capital. Karl Marx's copious notes on what other political economists said about productive and unproductive labor, the fruit of which would be *Das Kapital*, catch the political economists in numerous inconsistencies as they try to ground the difference in some intrinsic quality of the labor or its product. But the only way to make their

---

[25] John Stuart Mill, *Principles of Political Economy* in *Collected Works of John Stuart Mill* (Toronto: University of Toronto Press, 1963–91), 2:48.

theory consistent, he urges, is to admit that the distinction relies on the situation in which the activity is accomplished: "An actor, for example, or even a
clown . . . is a productive labourer if he works in the service of a capitalist (an
entrepreneur) to whom he returns more labour than he receives from him in
the form of wages."[26]

Hard Times is equally intent on transforming its players into workers even
though it ostensibly recommends that its workers play. Turning the players
into workers at first looks like one of Gradgrind's category mistakes:

> "Cecilia Jupe. Let me see. What is your father?"
>
> "He belongs to the horse-riding, if you please, sir."
>
> Mr. Gradgrind frowned, and waved off the objectionable calling with
>   his hand.
>
> "We don't want to know anything about that, here. You mustn't tell us
>   about that, here. Your father breaks horses, don't he?"
>
> "If you please, sir, when they can get any to break, they do break horses
>   in the ring, sir."
>
> "You mustn't tell us about the ring here. Very well, then. Describe your
>   father as a horsebreaker. He doctors sick horses, I dare say?"
>
> "Oh, yes, sir."
>
> "Very well, then. He is a veterinary surgeon, a farrier, and horsebreaker."
>   (2–3)

The irony of this exchange is that, in the name of fact-finding, of describing
Sissy Jupe's father in terms appropriate to the venue of the school (the "here"
so frequently stressed), Mr. Gradgrind comes up with an utterly fantastic Signor Jupe. He does this by stripping away everything that might have been
thought of as "playful" about the horse-riding and translating what's left into
a cluster of vocations related to horses. The redescription works thematically
to set up an obvious contrast: the circus is really playful, but Coketowners try
to remake it in their own workful image.

This contrast, however, soon collapses when the Utilitarian steps into the
lair of the horse-riders, and the novel becomes just as intent on making the
players into productive workers as Gradgrind had earlier been. The dialogue
in the parallel later scene stresses that all the performers had been apprenticed
early, and that their very bodies are shaped by their labor. Mr. Childers seems
to be the top half of a centaur, with short, muscular legs and stiff knees,
expressive of the fact that he was always on horseback. Sleary's voice is, he
explains, "a little huthky, Thquire, and not eathy heard by them ath don't
know me; but if you'd been chilled and heated, heated and chilled, chilled
and heated in the ring when you wath young, ath often ath I have been, *your*
voithe wouldn't have lathted out, Thquire, no more than mine" (28). Sleary's

---

[26] *Theories of Surplus Value*, vol. 1 (Moscow: Progress Publishers, 1968), 157.

speech impediment, which the novelist seems to exploit whenever he realizes
that this is not a very entertaining book, is presented to us here as a vocational
malformation. All members of his troop work, husbands and wives, parents
and children. Even the infants do "the fairy business when required" (27).
And they do it for the profit of Mr. Sleary, whom we first glimpse as "a stout
modern statue with a money-box at its elbow, in an ecclesiastical niche of
early Gothic architecture."

Hard Times reinforces the idea that what counts as productive work changes
with the situation in which an activity is performed by paralleling the scene
of Sissy's schooling with that of Gradgrind's. Just as Sissy had to learn a new
vocabulary in the school to describe her father's work, Gradgrind has to learn
a new one to understand what skills make up the clown's apparent play—
that is to say, his labor—among the horse-riders.

> "Jupe [one of them explains] has missed his tip very often, lately."
> "Has—what has he missed?" asked Mr. Gradgrind. . . .
> "Offered at the Garters four times last night, and never done 'em once,"
>   said Master Kidderminster. "Missed his tip at the banners, too, and
>   was loose in his ponging."
> "Didn't do what he ought to do. Was short in his leaps and bad in his
>   tumbling," Mr. Childers interpreted.
> "Oh!" said Mr. Gradgrind, "that is tip, is it?" (23)

Certainly this exchange is carnivalesque; the normal social hierarchy is reversed, and Mr. Gradgrind is humiliated by having to speak the funny-sound-
ing circus slang. But the jargon is also a sign that the horse-riding is a regular
occupation, with its own professional vocabulary and standards of success and
failure that could be quite harshly imposed. Sissy's later description of her
father's humiliation implies that his fellow performers harassed him for his
incompetence.

The parallel thus suggested between Jupe's ostracism and eventual flight
and that of the novel's working-class hero, Stephen Blackpool, underlines the
similarities between Sleary's horse-riding and Bounderby's factory. Far from
being more imaginative and sympathetic than the cotton spinners, the workers
in Sleary's business seem more cruelly intent on protecting their master's
profits by driving out unproductive hands. The factory may realize larger
profits, but not because the circus performers are merely playing.[27]

---

[27] Others have argued that the Victorians generally justified play in terms of work. For example,
Peter Bailey, in *Leisure and Class in Victorian England* (New York: Methuen, 1987), gives a great deal
of evidence for the rationalization and disciplining of play in the period. J. Jeffrey Franklin, however,
argues convincingly, in *Serious Play: The Cultural Form of the Nineteenth-Century Realist Novel* (Phila-
delphia: University of Pennsylvania Press, 1999), that the Victorians simply had a different model of
play from that of their ancestors. He looks at theatricality as well as novel writing as forms of "serious
play" but unfortunately does not treat Dickens's novels. As Jeffrey points out, if the nineteenth century

Dickens, in short, is so intent on depicting the horse-riders as real workers that he sacrifices the work-versus-play opposition: the players are refigured as workers, and the contrast between the factory and the circus becomes a parallel. Since it is implausible that Dickens was trying, like Harriett Martineau, to illustrate a principle of political economy in this episode, and since he did not glorify work per se, why did he transform the circus performers into workers? The answer is easily given: he transformed them because he subscribed, like almost all other Victorians, to the proposition that value derives from labor, that work makes the wealth of nations. He probably did not reflect that this assumption mirrored a foundational tenet of the political economists. He draws on it spontaneously, as if it were a self-evident piece of common sense, to undergird his polemical purpose. Dickens wished to prove that the labor of amusers (like himself) is a positive contribution to, rather than a drain on, the wealth of England. To show that the products and services of this business are valuable, Dickens assumes he must demonstrate that they are the results of labor, just like the products and services of any other enterprise, and he therefore comes to rely on the most fundamental concept of its putative adversaries: the labor theory of value.

Recalling that work was thought to produce value not despite but because of its unpleasantness, we can see why *Hard Times* must penetrate behind the pleasant illusions of the horse-riding to its gritty reality. As I've noted in earlier chapters, the labor theory of value may seem indifferent to the laborer's subjective state, but it nevertheless assumes a calculus in which the pains of production are set against the pleasures of remuneration and consumption. If work were itself a pleasure, economic calculations would be unmotivated; producers would not care to be efficient or to record the hours of labor that go into a product because the telos of production—pleasure—would be achieved in the making itself.

In its attempt to make the amusement business respectable, *Hard Times* retraces this familiar logic. To be estimable, an enterprise must contribute to the wealth of the nation; to contribute, it must employ productive workers, whose labor is a source of value; to be working players, they must not only exert themselves but also register, as Mill noted, "all feelings of a disagreeable kind, all bodily inconvenience or mental annoyance, connected with the employment of [their] thoughts, or muscles, or both, in [their] particular occupation" (25). The diminutive performer Master Kidderminster, for example, works at representing a child at play; in his real leisure time, though, he does not go in for tumbling but for strutting about with a cigar in his mouth, dressing like a dandy, and betting on horse races. Kidderminster's unmasking

---

had a hard time with play, it was nevertheless the century in which play was "put into discourse" (19) and linked to art and culture by the likes of Schiller, Kant, Nietzsche, and Matthew Arnold, in a tradition that culminated in J. Huizinga's *Homo Ludens: A Study of the Play-Element in Culture* (1938).

as a hard-bitten and rather bellicose adult, who bears little resemblance to
the adorable, gamboling (as opposed to gambling) cupid he impersonates,
demonstrates that labor per se, no matter how seemingly joyous, is not a
pleasurable realization of one's nature.

By defending the circus's legitimacy through this invocation of the labor
theory of value, though, Dickens does more than merely repeat a lesson of
political economy; he extends it until its oddness and its paradoxes become
apparent. McCulloch had viewed amusers as productive laborers because their
exertions stimulated the industry of others, but Dickens goes further to spell
out the affective implications of classifying players as workers, and in the
process he reveals something about the labor theory of value that might otherwise have remained hidden. By viewing the circus at home, we can see that
work is defined circumstantially and has (despite emphasis on suffering) no
intrinsic attributes. The same activity is play under one set of circumstances
and work under another. Moreover, when the activity falls within those economic relations that make it work, its emotional valence changes, and it
crosses a boundary in the cultural imagination from a realm called freedom
to one called necessity. This line of thought gives an unexpected twist to the
theory. Instead of resting on a stable bedrock of sensations, the difference
between labor and leisure seems actually to produce those sensations in *Hard
Times*; any particular exertion would be pleasant or unpleasant depending on
its ambient economic relations. Pain and pleasure, the novel seems to hint,
are not the raw data of a felicific calculation, but instead lie dormant in activities and awaken in response to an economic context. Awareness of the productiveness of one's activity, in other words, intensifies the sensation of pain and
converts it to the emotion of unhappiness.

The uniqueness of the circus people in Coketown, therefore, stems not
from their playfulness but from the way they figure a special awareness of this
situational nature of work. If one of the things necessary to the unhappy
sensation of work is the understanding that one is working, the work of the
players demands a double dose of that consciousness; one must feel oneself to
be working in the first place, and then feel the need to control any outward
manifestation of the feeling. To put the same point less abstractly, what is
comic but nevertheless poignant about players is that, unlike other workers,
they must labor at seeming to play. Since their work provides the audience's
leisure, it must be presented under the aspect of fun. Master Kidderminster
panting and dripping with sweat could hardly constitute "the chief delight of
the maternal portion of the spectators." A competent entertainer's performance, the novel insists, will seem not only effortless but also felicitous. Only
failures like Signor Jupe appear to be working; only incompetent amusers
actually manifest the sure sign of labor: unhappiness. The miserable clown,
Sissy's father, whom we never directly encounter but who seems to haunt the
margins of the novel, is an apt emblem of the true but hidden state of he who

works to amuse. The crying clown—whose descendants, like Leoncavallo's Pagliacco, were to take on the status of existential heroes at the turn of the century—expresses the endemic, hidden and therefore deep, sadness of those who work to make people laugh. He manifests the weariness of imposed jollity and the affective dissonance that results from ceaselessly troping play into work and work into play. It is little wonder, then, that in *Hard Times*, the clown, like the metaphorical elephant in the factory, goes "melancholy mad."[28]

. . .

"I am three parts mad, and the fourth delirious, with perpetual rushing at Hard Times," Dickens wrote as he neared the end of the novel's composition. Could the sad, half-crazed clown be an emblem for some specific amuser who also haunts the margins of *Hard Times*?[29] In numerous letters from the first half of 1854, Dickens complains about the severe workfulness of his life. He is "crushed" at the very outset of the writing (February 1854), "stunned with work" as it continues (July 14, 1854), and "used up"(July 17, 1854) by the end. Even attempts at escape have a frightfully utilitarian purposiveness about them: "But let us go somewhere, say to the public [house] by the Thames where those performing dogs go at night. I think the travestie may be *useful* to me, and I may *make something* out of such an expedition" (June 1854; emphasis added).

However, the relentless unhappiness is, after all, a sign of productive labor; so, although Dickens's pity seems to have been reserved almost exclusively for himself during these months, his anger flares out against those who imply that his activity is not laborious. In a letter to Peter Cunningham, who had suggested in the *Illustrated London News* that Dickens got the idea of *Hard Times* while on a visit to Preston in late January, he indignantly insists that such a claim foreshortens the planning time of the novel: "[I]t encourages the public to believe in the impossibility that books are produced in that very sudden and cavalier manner (as poor Newton used to feign that he produced the elaborate drawings he made in his madness, by winking at his table)" (275). Whatever the process, planning takes time and effort. Even if it were done in a state of insane frenzy, Dickens's analogy insists, even if it later seemed inexplicable to the lucid, conscious mind, it was nevertheless work, bonafide work that makes one as authentically miserable as any other kind of

---

[28] We might conclude from evidence given by Paul Schlicke that the secretly miserable clown was already a traditional figure in the early nineteenth century: "Clowns are almost invariably described in their private lives as the most taciturn and sober of all performers, and John Ducrow, like Jupe, had two wholly distinct characters: the frolicsome zany of the ring was wracked with consumption and died prematurely" (167).

[29] In the Norton Critical Edition, the author's unhappiness is recorded in the letters appended to the novel. All of the following letters are quoted on 274–77.

labor: "I am in a dreary state," he attests in another letter, "planning and planning the story of Hard Times" (April 18, 1854). Between Newton's madness and Dickens's dreariness, it would seem that especially the creative work of the greatest geniuses was "alienated" labor, both in the archaic sense of lying beyond will and reason and in the more modern sense of being coerced.

As Dickens's allusion to Newton suggests, his own affiliation with the crying clown, his image of himself as a gloomy drudge in the entertainment business, was reinforced by a tradition of thought far older than political economy: a tradition dating back at least to Aristotle, which identified melancholy as the characteristic disease of authors. "Why is it," asked Aristotle, "that all men who have become outstanding in philosophy . . . poetry or the arts are melancholic?" That literary occupations result in unhappiness was also the refrain of Burton's satiric *Anatomy of Melancholy*, which was picked up and elaborated by numerous eighteenth-century doctors and writers. None of the major eighteenth-century male novelists escaped the diagnosis. "Fatigue of mind, and great exertion of its powers often give birth to this disease; and always tend to increase it. The finer spirits are wasted by the labour of the brain: the Philosopher rises from his study more exhausted than the Peasant leaves his drudgery; without the benefit that he has from exercise," explains one eighteenth-century physician.[30] Isaac D'Israeli's essay on "The Maladies of Authors" carried this tradition into the Victorian period, so it isn't surprising that when the weekly routine of *Household Words* began to seem oppressive to Dickens and melancholy ensued, he described his condition in eighteenth-century language: "Hypochondriacal whisperings tell me that I am rather overworked," he reported to his friend and biographer Forster at the end of 1853.[31]

Before the eighteenth century, the melancholy author was imagined to suffer from intellectual strain (intellectual activity not yet being identified as *labor*) and too much solitude. He was advised to engage in commerce with others in order to get his mind off of his own petty needs. But the conversion of authorship into widely recognized commercial labor (which took place slowly during the eighteenth century) and its further transformation into socially functional work destroyed this remedy. For Dickens authorship was still fatiguing, but since it was also a commercial enterprise surrounded by a web of social and economic considerations, sociability per se could not serve as its counterweight. Indeed, the weight of social and commercial responsibility, the new laboriousness of authorship, became an added misery, not a countervailing force. In *Hard Times*, thanks to the dismal science, melancholy is democratized and the author's malady thereby becomes incurable.

---

[30] John Hill, *Hypochondriasis, A Practical Treatise*, intro. G. S. Rousseau (Los Angeles: Williams Andrews Clark Memorial Library, 1969), 6. First published in 1766.

[31] *The Life of Charles Dickens* (London: Chapman and Hall, 1874), 443.

Dickens probably viewed his melancholy as at once a mark of intellectual distinction and a proof of his productivity; paradoxically it was both that which differentiated him from the mass of people and that which linked him to the great laboring bulk of the nation. The political-economic account of work and the older tradition of writerly melancholy meet in *Hard Times* to create a multiply virtuous and multiply miserable authorial persona. Our sense of an unhappy author is verified by Dickens's correspondence, but it is produced initially by the rhythms of the sentences, the pointless efficiency of the narrative, the repetitiveness of the allegories, the monotony of motivation, in short, by this novel's notorious *lack of play.* The lack is closely tied to the apologia for amusement that stresses its (failed) recreational objective. Dickens presents himself in this novel as one who has discovered, in dealing with the novel's themes, that he answers, not to the needs of his own imagination, but to those of others who "must be amused," and the pervasive melancholy both registers and resists the imposition. Some part of this usually exuberant author seems to be on strike in *Hard Times,* and yet the very signs of his rebellion are a revelation about Victorian sensations of labor.

· · ·

Even though this is not a typical Dickens novel, and Dickens is far from a typical Victorian author, *Hard Times* nevertheless allows us to gauge the distance between the premises the Romantics shared with the political economists they assailed and those that the early Victorians inhabited. The eudemonism of the earlier discourses was abandoned by some of the period's most influential writers, which made it difficult for either political economists or their adversaries to claim that they knew better how to make people happy. Dickens, to be sure, found no alternative to the greatest-happiness principle, and he certainly did not have the stomach to follow Carlyle to the ends of his logic, which were spelled out in the universally offensive essay "On the Negro Question" (1849).[32] There, in keeping with his declaration that the best we can do is seek suffering through labor, the sage went so far as to recommend a system of mass enslavement. Carlyle's hold over the minds of many Victorians was broken by that indication of where his disdain for happiness might lead, and though Dickens dedicated the one-volume edition of *Hard Times* to Carlyle ten years later, he clearly did not subscribe to the gospel of work. We see Dickens suspended, rather, between wanting to acknowledge the importance of happiness and being unable to imagine how it might proceed from work.

---

[32] This essay was first published in *Fraser's Magazine for Town and Country* in 1849, under the title "Occasional Discourse on the Negro Question." It only turned into "Occasional Discourse on the Nigger Question" when republished as a pamphlet in 1853.

The Victorian cult of work, however, also made the labor theory of value practically inescapable. Here we can see a movement bringing the literati closer to political economy from one perspective but moving further from the classical political economists from another perspective. The Romantics fostered utopian dreams of autonomous individuals who could support their families on a few hours of labor per day; although such visions obviously ignored the question of how a surplus could be generated to sustain intellectual life, they also seemed to register the basic assumption of the political economists that everyone naturally desires to spend as little time laboring as possible. Victorian writers, though, generally celebrated the increased endurance of their countrymen, confining their criticism of long hours to the cases of women and children. As we've seen, *Hard Times* is an instructive exception to this rule, but it does not entirely gainsay the period's dominant productivism; it merely displaces it onto the authorial persona, who becomes a hero of suffering.

Victorian writers generally tended to measure their own virtue by their capacity to produce, especially when the task seemed unpleasant. Sometimes, like Thackeray in *Pendennis*, they revived the ironic eighteenth-century rhetoric of Grub Street; sometimes, like Trollope in his *Autobiography*, they adopted a model of up-to-date industrial efficiency:

> When I have commenced a book, I have always prepared a diary, divided into weeks, and carried it on for the period which I have allowed myself for the completion of the work. In this I have entered, day by day, the number of pages I have written, so that if at any time I have slipped into idleness for a day or two, the record of that idleness has been there, staring me in the face, and demanding of me increased labour, so that the deficiency might be supplied.[33]

Such extreme measures were unusual, and there was little agreement about just what sort of laboriousness was required, but it was common to stress the virtue of the bread-winning author. For example, Marianne Evans, while still on her way to becoming George Eliot in 1856, reproachfully contrasted amateurish "lady novelists" with poor but industrious women writers:

> [T]here is something so antiseptic in the mere healthy fact of working for one's bread, that the most trashy and rotten kind of feminine literature is not likely to have been produced under such circumstances. "In all labour there is profit"; but ladies' silly novels, we imagine, are less the result of labour than of busy idleness.[34]

[33] *An Autobiography* (Berkeley: University of California Press, 1978), 100–101.
[34] "Silly Novels by Lady Novelists," in *Essays of George Eliot*, ed. Thomas Pinney (New York: Columbia University Press, 1963), 323.

Later, in the competition for authorial effort, George Eliot reported that her books went very slowly, to which Trollope blithely replied, "Yes, with imaginative work like yours that is quite natural; but with my mechanical stuff, it's a sheer matter of industry. It's not the head that does it—it's the cobbler's wax on the seat and the sticking to my chair!"[35] In his autobiography, though, he indicates that Eliot could have produced more, and better, novels if she had lavished less effort on each page: "[S]he struggles too hard to do work that shall be excellent. She lacks ease" (206). Of course, it is ease of style, the ability to conceal the struggle, that Trollope is recommending, and that he achieved, he brags, by simply demanding a certain number of pages from himself per day, never waiting for inspiration: "To me it would not be more absurd if the shoemaker were to wait for inspiration, or the tallow-chandler for the divine moment of melting" (102). Few Victorian writers followed the lead of the Romantics in presenting their own labor as an unalienated contrast to enforced drudgery, and it would have been quite out of keeping with the dominant tone to describe their works, in Shelley's terms, as records of "the happiest moments of the happiest men."[36] To be sure, Shelley's description cannot be taken to sum up the Romantics' view of authorship, since they had their own version of its perils, but they seldom focused as clearly as these Victorians on the sheer labor of it. The melancholy of the implied writer of *Hard Times*, therefore, is eccentric only in that it lets a common Victorian authorial self-understanding come unusually close to the experience of the novel reader. Most of the time, as Trollope implies, they pulled off the trick of the amuser, feigning the very thing Bentham contrasted with labor—"ease."

Finally, *Hard Times* gives us a perspective on the connection between pain and value that was not fully available to the Romantics but was in keeping with some developments in political economy during the 1830s and 1840s. In the largely unexamined assumption of political economy—that productive labor causes suffering and is, therefore, only exacted from us by the harsh requirements of our physical existence—the precise direction of causality had gone unspecified: is an activity labor by virtue of being painful, or is it painful by virtue of being labor? Political economists, even those who shunned eudemonism, generally avoided the issue by positing a primordial state of laziness, a Benthamite "natural aversion to labour," which made all exertion onerous. Before civilization stimulates insatiable desires, "necessity," writes McCulloch, first subdues our nature and gives "activity to indolence."[37] *Hard Times*, though, establishes a work versus play (not a work versus ease) dichotomy,

---

[35] In "Anthony Trollope's Place in Literature," *Forum* 19 (May 1895): 324–37, Frederic Harrison records the exchange as beginning with Eliot's complaint: " 'There are days and days together,' she groaned out, 'when I cannot write a line.' "

[36] *Shelley's Poetry and Prose*, eds. Donald H. Reiman and Sharon B. Powers (New York: Norton, 1977), 504.

[37] McCulloch, *Principles*, 11–12.

which several political economists also briefly considered as bearing on productive and unproductive labor. By then collapsing the very dichotomy it built, *Hard Times* opened the definition of labor to further scrutiny and implied that any activity performed to make a living becomes painful by virtue of its necessity.

When Marianne Evans, the proto–George Eliot, claims that there is something "antiseptic" about "working for one's bread," she makes a related claim, but adds a further twist. Necessity makes the difference between labor and "busy idleness"; necessity purges the product of the infection of "vanity," a word that, for Eliot, combines egoism with aimlessness. Writing under the pressure of necessity subdues the self; performing the same activity voluntarily is mere self-indulgence. Nothing internal to the act of authorship indicates this difference; indeed, the essayist admits that she is merely imagining the difference in authorial situations. Eliot seems to assume, in Benthamite fashion, the intrinsic unpleasantness of labor and the enjoyment of the busy idleness, else why would the former be self-renunciation and the latter self-indulgence? And yet she redeems the painful work as "healthy," while condemning the ladies' pleasurable but idle scribbling as "rotten," so that the moralized somatic valences seem reversed: a metaphorical body—the body of the reading public—benefits from the imposed discipline of labor but decays under the leniency of idleness. For Eliot, therefore, the laboring author is also compensated for her pains by a satisfying consciousness of moral superiority. In subsequent chapters, I will take a fuller measure of the gap between Dickens and Eliot in this regard, but for the time being, I would like to stress the similarity of their views in the 1850s: both took the labor/leisure divide to be contextual and presented the author's "powerful feeling" (to use Wordsworth's phrase), not as a "spontaneous overflow," but as the externally elicited sensations of economic life.

Chapter Four

The Bioeconomics of *Our Mutual Friend*

Wealth and Illth

Our Mutual Friend draws on an antithesis that John Ruskin had named in *Unto This Last* (1862) a few years before the novel appeared: that of wealth and illth. In developing this antithesis, Ruskin began with a question and an anecdote, both of which anticipated in striking detail the opening chapter of Dickens's novel. Ruskin's question was, "[I]f we may conclude generally that a dead body cannot possess property, what degree and period of animation in the body will render possession possible?"[1] In the first chapter of *Our Mutual Friend*, Gaffer Hexam also insists on the absurdity of the idea that a dead man can possess property. He raves, "Has a dead man any use for money? Is it possible for a dead man to have money? . . . How can money be a corpse's? Can a corpse own it, want it, spend it, claim it, miss it?"[2]

Gaffer seems to think that these questions automatically call for a negative reply: "No, a dead body cannot possess property." The novel, however, not only leaves this issue open but also goes on to ask Ruskin's more complicated question, the one that introduces the possibility of "illth": what degree of health, of life, of animation, is necessary before the body can no longer be properly said to possess something? Ruskin's question turns into an anecdote, like the one that opens *Our Mutual Friend*, of drowning and dredging up. Ruskin writes,

> [L]ately in a wreck of a California ship, one of the passengers fastened a belt about him with two hundred pounds of gold in it, with which he was found afterwards at the bottom. Now, as he was sinking—had he the gold? or had the gold him?
>
> And if, instead of sinking him in the sea by its weight, the gold had struck him on the forehead, and thereby caused incurable disease—suppose palsy or insanity, —would the gold in that case have been more a "possession" than in the first? Without pressing the inquiry up through instances of gradually

---

[1] *"Unto This Last" and Other Essays on Art and Political Economy,* ed. Ernest Rhys (New York: E. P. Dutton, 1932), 169. All quotations from Ruskin are from this edition, and subsequent page numbers are given in the text.

[2] *Our Mutual Friend* (London: Oxford University Press, 1974), 4. All subsequent quotations from the novel are from this Oxford University Press edition, and page numbers are given in the text.

increasingly vital power over the gold . . . I presume that the reader will see
that possession . . . is not an absolute, but a graduated power; and consists
not only in the . . . thing possessed, but also . . . in the possessor's vital power
to use it. (169–70)

Ruskin, then, begins his investigation into the nature of economic value
with death in order, it seems, to root wealth in bodily well-being. Wealth, he
concludes, is the possession of useful things by those who can use them. Useful
things are those that nurture life, and those who can use them are those who
are (at the very least) in a state of bodily animation. To the degree that possessions cause bodily harm, as in the story of the drowned man, to the degree
that they incapacitate or make people ill, they are "illth."

The hero of *Our Mutual Friend,* John Harmon, is closely identified with,
indeed, is identified as, the drowned body dredged up by Gaffer Hexam in
chapter 1. As a possessor of gold, he has also been killed by the action of illth
because he has been murdered for the sake of his money. We might say that
his story is Ruskin's retold, although in Dickens's version both the man and
the gold have surrogates. George Radfoot takes Harmon's place and, as Harmon later explains, is "murdered for the money" by "unknown hands," conceived merely as extensions of what Harmon calls "the fate that seemed to
have fallen on my father's riches—the fate that they should lead to nothing
but evil" (370). Thus, John Harmon is officially drowned and dredged up at
the novel's outset, a victim of illth. After being proclaimed dead, he staggers
dazed through the novel's opening episodes, as if, following the stages of Ruskin's inquiry, he had reached the state of merely being wounded in the head
by his would-be riches. The question that drives the plot is the same as that
asked by Ruskin: what degree of animation in the formerly dead man would
be necessary to render possible his possession of (instead of by) his money?
"Should John Harmon come to life again?" the hero keeps asking. If he were
to reanimate himself, gradually working his way from dead to ill to well, could
he change illth to wealth?

The point of remarking these parallels between *Unto This Last* and *Our
Mutual Friend* is to direct our attention to a pervasive pattern of mid-Victorian
thought, a widespread insistence that economic value can be determined only
in close relationship to vital power. In several key texts on economics, sanitation, social theory, and authorship, this way of structuring economic investigations around life and death took the dead body as a starting place and tried to
move toward reanimation. However, as I hope to show through an analysis of
Our Mutual Friend, this operation often resulted in the reseparation of value
(equated with Life) from any of its particular instantiations (or bodies). That
is, the attempt to put the human body at the center of economic concerns, to
rewrite economic discourse so that it constantly referred back to the body's
well-being, paradoxically itself tended to do what it accused unrecon-

structed political economists of doing: separating value from flesh and blood and relocating it in a state of suspended animation or apparent death.

Ruskin and Dickens were by no means pioneers in the attempt to pose the question of value in terms of bodily well-being. As we've seen, the effort had a long history within political economy, where Thomas Robert Malthus himself—whose *Essay on Population* (1797) was thought by Ruskin and Dickens to be the most outrageously hard-hearted book in the whole hard-hearted economic canon—had contended for a definition of productive labor that would attend closely to the discipline's implicit bioeconomics, that is to say, its underlying beliefs about the interactions between biological human life, its surrounding organic environment, and changing modes of economic production and exchange. In chapter 2 we examined Malthus's polemic against the abstracting tendencies of other political economists and noted that, although he certainly feared overpopulation, he gave (at least in the first edition of the *Essay*) no definition of value that can distinguish it from flesh. Hence Malthus was the originator of the very sentiments that Ruskin thought of as *anti*-Malthusian when rhetorically connecting economic and bodily health through etymology. Ruskin derives value from "*Valor* from *valere*, to be well, or strong . . . strong *in* life (if a man), or valiant; strong *for* life (if a thing), or valuable. To be 'valuable,' therefore, is to 'avail towards life' " (168). Ruskin faults the political economists for calculating the values of commodities without regard either to their potential for sustaining and enhancing life or to the ability and willingness of their possessors to activate that potential. Ruskin's own economic essays constantly return to this theme: the political economists have abstracted value, severed it from flesh and blood. "The true veins of wealth," he writes, " are purple—and not in Rock but in Flesh. . . . [T]he final outcome and consummation of all wealth is in the producing as many as possible full-breathed, bright-eyed, and happy-hearted human creatures" (144).

That contrast—blood veins in flesh versus metallic veins in rock—is at least as old as the Midas myth, but in the nineteenth century it had a new urgency and specificity. No longer directed simply against human greed or miserliness, it was used to censure especially those theorists who did not explain how the wealth of the nation would be converted into more abundant and healthier people. And, at the turn of the century, Malthus had been the first to deliver that challenge. It was he who initially deplored Adam Smith's failure to distinguish among commodities on the basis of their *biological* usefulness; indeed, Malthus in the early stages of his career seems an even more fanatical proponent than Ruskin of the idea that value is in flesh, for (as we've seen) he went so far as to suggest that the only productive labor is that which produces working-class food; that is, that the production of healthy laboring flesh is the sole proper outcome of labor. By that logic, purple veins would indeed be the only true measure of the wealth of nations. So when writers like Dickens and

Ruskin insisted that health and illness be introduced into the calculation of economic value, they were not adding ideas drawn from some moral discourse distinct from political economy but were, rather, unwittingly emphasizing one element—the often slighted but never wholly neglected bioeconomics—of that discipline.

The biological aspect of political economy, the emphasis on value derived from and returning to flesh, follows from its central premise, the labor theory of value. But this very theory, as we also saw in chapter 2, simultaneously dislodges considerations of physical well-being from calculations of value. Since labor was the source of exchange value, and, according to some, its own value could be calculated by the value of the commodities (primarily the food) necessary to replenish it, the exchange value of any commodity was rooted not only in the worker's body, the primary nexus of exchange, but also in the larger biosphere. The fertility of the soil, the weather conditions, the amount of land under pasture, and the presence of pests and blights were all, for Malthus, the basic productive circumstances surrounding the toiler. And yet these bioeconomic considerations, Malthus originally thought, could be too easily overlooked in Smith's formulations. Smith had also, as we've repeatedly noted, argued that the use of money wages merely conceals primary biological facts, which the discipline of political economy would be devoted to revealing: "What is bought with money or with goods is purchased by labour as much as what we acquire by the toil of our own body."[3] However, because the "toil of the body" is a universal equivalent determining exchange value, commodities can acquire abstract fungible values independent of their physiological utility. Malthus, we've seen, complained that the labor theory of value rendered a bushel of corn equivalent to a bit of lace, even though the corn has greater vital significance.

Ruskin's critique of political economy resembles that of the early Malthus in provisionally accepting the premise of the labor theory of value while rejecting its normal implications.[4] The value of a thing, he claims, is at least equivalent to, as he phrased it in *The Political Economy of Art* (echoing Smith),

[3] Adam Smith, *An Inquiry into the Nature and Causes of the Wealth of Nations* (Oxford: Clarendon Press, 1976), 1:47.

[4] James Clark Sherburne's invaluable study of Ruskin's economic thought, *John Ruskin or the Ambiguities of Abundance: A Study in Social and Economic Criticism* (Cambridge: Harvard University Press, 1972), also places Ruskin in the tradition of Malthus, noting that "In the history of economics, there is a close connection between a tendency to think in physiocratic or organic modes and a willingness to recognize the danger of crises due to a disproportion between production and consumption" (130). The reference to "physiocratic or organic modes" follows R. L. Meek's categorization in "Physiocracy and the Early Theories of Under-Consumption," *Economica* 71 (August 1951): 229–69. Perhaps the first economist to see Ruskin as the "legitimate continuator of the Physiocratic school" was Patrick Geddes in an article titled "John Ruskin" in *Economist* (1884): 35–42. For an account of the economists' reactions to Ruskin, see John Tyree Fain, *Ruskin and the Economists* (Nashville: Vanderbilt University Press, 1956).

the cost of keeping the artisan, for the length of time it takes to make the article, "in bread and water, fire and lodging" (25).[5] Biological regeneration is the foundation of all value for most of the critics as well as the proponents of political economy. But the critics, beginning with Malthus, assert that because the laboring body is the source of all value, commodities that immediately sustain more laboring bodies should be considered more desirable—indeed, more valuable—than those without direct physiological benefits. Thus the critics often accord a privileged position to the commodities that are most easily turned back into flesh. The early Malthus and Ruskin alike, then, required economic exchange to proceed from flesh back to flesh by the least circuitous route: life expended immediately converted into life replenished.

Viewed within this context, the emphasis on death in Ruskin's writings and *Our Mutual Friend* seems an extension of those very tendencies in political economy that claim to valorize life most fully. For those are the tendencies stressing the commodity's need to have a life-giving potential that makes up for its life-draining origins. In other words, the humane critics of political economy present the commodity, the bearer of value, as freighted with mortality, as a sign of spent vivacity, in order to demand all the more strenuously that it have a recuperative potential. In the second of the "Essays on Political Economy" that he published in *Fraser's Magazine* in 1862–63, and which he collected into the volume *Munera Pulveris* eight years later, Ruskin categorically states that the underlying cost of everything is life because labor is a form of dying:

> I have already [in *Unto This Last*] defined labour to be the Contest of the life of man with an opposite. Literally, it is the quantity of "Lapse," loss, or failure of human life caused by any effort. It is usually confused with effort itself, or the application of power (opera); but there is much effort which is merely a mode of recreation, or of pleasure. The most beautiful actions of the human body, and the highest results of the human intelligence, are conditions, or achievements, of quite unlaborious, nay, of recreative, effort. But labour is the suffering in effort. It is the negative quantity, or quantity of defeat which has to be counted against every Feat, and defect which has to be counted against every Fact, or Deed of men. In brief it is "that quantity of our toil which we die in."[6]

Although Ruskin had elsewhere objected to John Stuart Mill's definition of "labour"[7] ("all feelings of a disagreeable kind, all bodily inconvenience and mental annoyance"), he obviously follows the lead of the political economists

---

[5] *"Unto This Last" and Other Essays*, 25.

[6] Ibid., 231.

[7] Sherburne discusses Ruskin's earlier objections but does not emphasize that they are later contradicted by his own definition of "labour."

when he formulates his own definition, only making sure that "life and death" replace "pleasure and pain" as the relevant binary. Like most political economists, he then finds it necessary to posit a category of "effort" outside of "labour," and this he names "opera" (as others, we saw in chapter 2, sometimes called it "work").

His true break with the political economists, though, is not in his vitalism or his definition of labor, but in a disjunction between value and cost. Ruskin conceived of both in vitalist terms, but he notes that a commodity's life-expending "cost" may have little to do with its life-bearing "value." On very rare occasions, when "opera" is at work, the making might not deplete vitality at all and yet produce something highly valuable; far more frequently, Ruskin instances commodities that cost life in both production and consumption. Armaments are his favorite examples of purely morbid production, but he observes as well that anything accumulated rather than consumed would be a chunk of mortality. He consequently looks askance at the store of goods in a society, its "wealth," as an encumbrance, a dead weight. "*Munera Pulveris,*" "Gifts of the Dust," a phrase he takes from one of Horace's Odes, seems to signify the deathliness of mere accumulation.

Ruskin chose the title *Munera Pulveris* in 1871, the year after Dickens died and six years after *Our Mutual Friend* was completed. Dickens's death was a "great loss" for Ruskin,[8] and, although he claimed not to have felt a political kinship with the novelist, we might nevertheless surmise that the "*Pulveris*" of his title pays at least unconscious homage to the dust heaps of Dickens's last completed work, as surely as those heaps owe something to Ruskin's essays:

> For every hour of labour, however enthusiastic or well intended, which he spends for that which is not bread, so much possibility of life is lost to him. . . . Of all that he has laboured for, the eternal law of heaven and earth measures out to him for reward, to the utmost atom, that part which he ought to have laboured for, and withdraws from him (or enforces on him, it may be) inexorably that part which he ought not to have laboured for. The dust and chaff are all, to the last speck, winnowed away, and on his summer threshing-floor stands his heap of corn; little or much, not according to his labour, but to his discretion. (*Essays,* 201–202)

The main plot of *Our Mutual Friend* uncannily adheres to the outline of this little fable. To avoid having his father's dust mounds enforced on him, John Harmon feigns death while the piles are sifted and shifted, "winnowed away," and a heap of life-giving substance stands revealed.

Our first introduction to this plot insistently equates perishing and amassing. The solicitor Mortimer Lightwood regales a dinner party with a short description of old Harmon's so-called life, describing the dust mounds

---

[8] See Tim Hilton, *John Ruskin: The Later Years* (New Haven: Yale University Press, 2000), 193.

old Harmon collected as the assembled debris of a vast number of defunct lives. They also become, in Mortimer's highly metaphoric (and Ruskinian) narration, the spewed-forth life of old Harmon himself: "On his own small estate the growling old vagabond threw up his own mountain range, like an old volcano, and its geological formation was Dust. Coal-dust, vegetable dust, bone dust, crockery dust, rough dust and sifted dust,—all manner of Dust" (13). This is an image of peculiar fixity, seemingly ill assorted with the characterization of old Harmon as a "vagabond." It deemphasizes the circulation of debris in the scavenger trade and transforms the enterprise into Harmon's simultaneous expending and hoarding of his own substance. The expense of his life is a self-burying; dust erupts from him and settles on him, so that accumulation and interment are the same thing. The last we hear of old John Harmon makes his death seem the merest extension of the activity of his life: "He directs himself to be buried with certain eccentric ceremonies and precautions against coming to life" (15).

Old Harmon's whole existence seems to have consisted in "precautions against coming to life." He is the prototypically illthy individual, causing, in Ruskin's phrase, "various devastation and trouble around [him] in all directions" (171). He oppresses and anathematizes his own living flesh and blood, his son and daughter, while he builds up his geological formations of dust. The contrast between flesh and blood, and rock, echoes Ruskin's distinction between the true veins of wealth (purple and in flesh) and the false veins (gold and in rock). The conflation of gold and rock in mountains of dust turns both to death; Mortimer Lightwood, in telling old Harmon's story, makes this transformation explicit. But, at the same time, he calls attention to the clichéd nature of these associations: "[Harmon] chose a husband for [his daughter], entirely to his own satisfaction and not in the least to hers, and proceeded to settle upon her, as her marriage portion, I don't know how much Dust, but something immense. At this stage of the affair the poor girl respectfully intimated that she was secretly engaged to that popular character whom the novelists and versifiers call Another, and that such a marriage would make Dust of her heart and Dust of her life—in short, would set her up, on a very extensive scale, in her father's business" (13–14). Old Harmon was a death-dealer, both in the sense that he traded in the remains of life and in the sense that he converted life into those remains. His daughter, of course, dies after she is disowned.

The associations made here between dust, hoarded wealth, and death are presented by the blasé Mortimer as sentimental commonplaces, prompting us to take a closer look at them. Dickens's imagery mimics Ruskin's, but does his narrative really follow Ruskin's logic? Or does it, rather, veer off into a celebration of the transformative potential in drying out and storing up life's remains? Harmon's business emphasizes that value, as such, is always life expended and accumulated, stored up, and it can be stored for the long term only in inorganic form. Hence, Old Harmon's conversion of life into death, his death-dealing, is not different in principle from any other process of realizing value. Despite the death versus life metaphors in the passages that introduce us to the dustmen, the transmission of life into inorganic matter and thence into money is not consistently presented as life destroying in the novel. On the contrary, it is portrayed as a sanitizing process and one in which a pure potential called "Life" is released. This elongated circuit between life expended and life augmented is one of increasing abstraction in which a life-transmitting power finds itself outside of human bodies for a long period of time. And the liberation of such a vital potential turns out to be the novel's very means of making Life seem valuable. The curiously death-centered bioeconomics of *Our Mutual Friend,* therefore, may begin by echoing Ruskin, but it follows Ruskin's metaphor of winnowing into a paradox. In *Unto This Last* and *Munera Pulveris*, Ruskin's stated aim was to separate the grain of life-maintaining commodities from the dross of the rest, but Dickens seems to take the idea of a "grain" of life to signify a vital essence, from which the body itself all too easily falls away as "dust."

We have already seen that death from illth and the possibility of reanimation are at the core of the novel's main plot. But the book's obsession with the place of human bodies inside systems of economic accumulation and exchange goes far beyond John Harmon's story, and that story can best be illuminated by a view of the novel's overall bioeconomics. To begin once again at the beginning, our introduction to the theme shows us the dead body as a nexus of two kinds of economic exchange. John Harmon is not the only person interested in turning "his" dead body back into life. As one of the many kinds of garbage that Gaffer and Lizzie Hexam fish out of the river, the corpse forms a part of their livelihood. It is from this fact that Lizzie is trying to avert her own attention in the opening scene, as she and her father tow the putrefying corpse, which will later be identified as John Harmon's, to shore. In Lizzie's reluctant conversation with her father, the corpse and the river merge in the impersonal pronoun "it": "I—I do not like it, father." "As if it wasn't your living!" replies Hexam. "As if it wasn't meat and drink to you!" (3). The shocking power of this metaphor, which immediately turns Lizzie "deadly faint," is its removal of all mediations between the girl's "living," her sustenance, and the corpse's moldering flesh, which becomes, in this oddly literalizing image, her food; corpse and river are meat and drink. Lizzie's physical reaction is another literalizing metaphor of denial: she would rather turn her own body into the dead white thing than keep it alive on such carrion. This first suggestion of how death might be exchanged for life is the most primitive and horrific of bioeconomic possibilities encountered in the novel.

Gratefully, we move immediately on to another. We are relieved to learn, as the passage continues, that although the river has yielded many things that have directly nurtured Lizzie ("the fire that warmed you," "the basket you slept in," "the rockers I put upon it to make a cradle of it"), the dead bodies have been only *indirect* sources of life. They have been sources of money, and hence can be seen by Lizzie and the reader not as food itself but as the where-withal to purchase food. Gaffer robs the bodies before turning them over to the police and also collects inquest money for having found them. Hence the bodies are part of a seemingly thoroughly civilized, if a bit ghoulish, network of economic circulation. Lizzie is also disturbed by this exchange of the body for money; indeed, she claims that the sin of pilfering from the corpses is the root of her shame. However, coming to us as it does in the context of the primitive alternative presented in Gaffer's metaphor, the intervention of money has a double moral impact. On the one hand, it brings the Hexams' living inside the pale of civilization. But on the other hand, the intervention of money itself seems just a metaphor that would (but can't quite) cover over the reality of vulturism emphasized by Gaffer's and the narrator's insistent metaphorizing. The metaphors of the corpse as a living and of Gaffer as a bird of prey make the trope of economics—the mediation of money—seem to be a euphemism directing our attention from that which the explicit meta-phors reveal: the real exchange *is* life for life.

We are, then, given two ways in which a corpse can be a "living" in this passage, but the distinction between them is collapsible. The more acceptable account (in which the human body is an item of exchange in a money network that fails to distinguish it from other items) is disturbing. But the source of the disturbance, when sought, seems to be the open secret that money is always ultimately taken out of flesh. That is, the horror is not that human flesh becomes money, but that money is just a metaphor for human flesh. In this respect, the exchange made through the corpse is really not different from any other economic exchange, since all value is produced at the expense of life. So far, the novel follows the logic of both Ruskin and the political econo-mists. But the opening of *Our Mutual Friend*, while echoing *Unto This Last* and *Munera Pulveris*, also carries out the logic of the dream of a speedy transfer between life and death to a nightmarish extreme. If any commodity, qua com-modity, is expended life, and the dead body merely emphasizes this universal truth, it also renders the typical humanitarian suggestion that it should imme-diately become nutrition revolting, a revival of Swift's modest proposal. The opening pages of the novel reveal that the humanitarian critique, wishing as it does for the shortest possible circuit between expended and augmented life, conjures up as a reductio ad absurdum of itself, a fantastic, worse than cannibalistic bioeconomy.

Little wonder, then, that the revaluation of old Harmon's legacy, in the other main plot of this densely designed novel, is accomplished not simply by its attachment to a worthy body (as Ruskin would have it) but by its sustained suspension through the apparent death of young John Harmon. Apparent death is the structural principle of the narrative.[9] Young Harmon, as we have seen, describes himself as being dead but having the potential for reanimation. He is, like riches themselves, the possibility of embodied life in a state of suspended animation. And it is only in this state, when he has not claimed his money but has instead, by sloughing off his supposed body, achieved a kind of ontological oneness with the money as pure vital potential, that he can change illth into wealth. He is dead as its inheritor, and yet he manages the fortune as Mr. Boffin's secretary. "The living-dead man," as the narrator calls him, resolves to remain in this state of suspended animation until he has effaced even his function as manager, until he is a mere "method" by which the money manages itself: "[T]he method I am establishing through all the affairs . . . will be, I may hope, a machine in such working order as that [anyone] can keep it going" (373).

Apparent death becomes the only direct access to the essence and value of life. Apparent death is the condition of storytelling and regenerative change. It reveals the value of young Harmon's own story: "Dead, I have found the true friends of my lifetime still as true, as tender, and as faithful as when I was alive, and making my memory an incentive to good actions done in my name" (372). As John Harmon becomes merely a name, a memory, and a fortune, the nugget of value that the story of his life contained is scattered and proliferates. From this vantage point, John Harmon, like an omniscient narrator, can see the complete pattern and know its worth. Even better, like an omnipotent narrator, he can change the story to create more value. This he does by remaining apparently dead as John Harmon to win (disguised as a poor man) the love of the mercenary girl who would otherwise have married him simply for his money. Hence, although the final aim of the dust plot is to prevent the heroine Bella's reduction of herself to a commodity, its machinations all depend on Harmon's merger with the fortune, his organic death into it.

John Harmon's plot, then, demonstrates that value, even the value of Life itself, is only discoverable from some vantage point outside the body. And the novel, moreover, repeatedly relocates value outside the body through processes that resemble the substitution of inorganic wealth for live bodies, even though

---

[9] Critics have noted that *Our Mutual Friend* has more death in it than other Dickens novels. Patrick McCarthy explores the novel's treatment of one of Dickens's mythic themes, "how beleaguered life may make its way in the face of and by the use of death." See "Designs in Disorder: The Language of Death in *Our Mutual Friend*," *Dickens Studies Annual* 17 (1988): 129–44. In "'Come Back and Be Alive': Living and Dying in *Our Mutual Friend*" (*The Dickensian* 74 [1978]: 131–43), Andrew Sanders argues that in this novel "death becomes thematic and it is balanced by a parallel stress on rebirth" (134). Most recently, George Levine in *Dying to Know: Scientific Epistemology and Narrative in Victorian England* (Chicago: University of Chicago Press, 2002) takes the state of suspended animation in the novel to be the sine qua non of knowledge (148–70). Dickens's concerns, Levine argues in response to the article version of the present chapter, are as much espistemological as economic.

the origin of wealth in bodies is never effaced. Hence the fascination of the
novel with macabre commodities. If the organic "death" of young John Harmon and his merger with his fortune is one example of the connection between money and the release of vital power, the commodities of Mr. Venus,
a preserver of animals and birds and an articulator of human skeletons, recapitulate the same point in a grotesquely comic form. While the consciousness
of the living-dead John Harmon hovers around the Boffin residence as secretary, the mortal remains of the man whose death has enabled this suspended
animation are themselves suspended, it would seem, in Venus's shop. "I took
an interest in that discovery in the river," Venus tells Wegg. "I've got up
there—never mind, though" (84). Venus buys and sells body parts and also
labors on them to make them dry, stable, and hence valuable. Of course,
he also has a few fleshy organisms (various preserved babies), but most of his
trade is in turning bodies into inorganic representations of themselves. It is
this activity that not only releases value from the body and makes it a "living"
for Venus but also bizarrely restores a kind of life to the bodies themselves. As
he hands a stuffed canary to a customer, Venus triumphantly remarks,
"There's animation!" (81).

The same drawing out of value from the organic body and storing it up,
suspending it in inorganic forms, characterizes Jenny Wren's doll-making
trade. Jenny imagines that the great ladies, whose clothes she copies to make
her dolls' dresses, are working for her as models. She imagines that her own
effort of "scud[ding] about town at all hours" (435) to see these fashionable
clothes is matched by their owners' pains in trying on the dolls' dresses: "I am
making a perfect slave of her" (436), she says of one of her "models." And the
result of all this sweat is the thing of value, the inorganic body: "That's Lady
Belinda hanging up by the waist, much too near the gaslight for a wax one,
with her toes turned in" (436).

All of this metaphoric and imagistic insistence on the bodily origins of the
commodity and on its disembodiment, on its transcendence of its organic
origins and simultaneous conversion into vital potential, finds its culmination
in the explicit vitalism of a villain's, Rogue Riderhood's, revivification. In this
episode, Life takes on its pure reality and absolute value only because it has
been entirely disembodied. Rogue's body itself is merely a "dank carcase," and
no one (besides Rogue's pathetic daughter) has any interest in the fate of the
man himself. It is neither body nor spirit that is of concern in this scene, "but
the spark of life within him is curiously separable from himself now, and they
have a deep interest in it" (443). For the sake of this abstracted entity, "All
the best means are at once in action, and everybody present lends a hand, and
a heart and soul." But when that potential and hence essential Life begins to
instantiate itself in the particular body of Rogue Riderhood, its value dissolves:
"As he grows warm, the doctor and the four men cool. As his lineaments
soften with life, their faces and their hearts harden to him" (446). "The spark

of life," the narrator comments, "was deeply interesting while it was in abeyance" (446).

"Life in abeyance" characterizes not only the temporary condition of Rogue Riderhood but also the condition of John Harmon. As such, as we've seen, it is the condition underlying the narrative itself. Moreover, especially for those who insist most strenuously on the flesh and blood origins of economic value, "life in abeyance" is the definitive condition of commodities and the abstract representation of their value in money. As Rogue Riderhood's suspended animation shows clearly, the curious separation of Life from the body is the refinement and purification of vitality itself. Hence, the humanitarian attempt to place and hold the human body at the center of inquiries into the nature of value has a paradoxical result; it leaves the body suspended, apparently dead, while the newly valorized essence, Life, achieves ever more inorganic and even immaterial representations.[10]

This, then, was the destiny of the illth/wealth distinction and of the bioeconomy on which it relied in *Our Mutual Friend*: those transfers of vigor that were at the heart of a body-centered economy kept proving the dependence of vitality on the suspension of animation in the body, on its apparent death. In Dickens's novel, the illth/wealth duality cannot be said to collapse, but the two terms enter into a dynamic fluctuation that breaks their immediate, one-to-one pairing with their supposed physiological reference points, illness and health. The storytelling, value-creating consciousness, like the consciousness of love, like economic value and the vital force itself are all released from physical forms and exist only in their purity while they remain outside of bodies. In the name of Life itself, Dickens repeats the logical trajectory that Ruskin attributed to political economy and dislodges animate, flesh-and-blood people from the center of his discourse.

Wealth and Filth

Indeed, Dickens in this novel might be said to have given up embodiment more easily than the political economists did. Their theory of value may have resembled suspended animation, but other aspects of their thought evince a continuous concern with the problem of vitality and embodiment. We will turn now to a closer scrutiny of Malthusian-Ricardian bioeconomics and the reactions against it. While this turn requires attending to nonurban matters,

[10] For an overview and history of the concept of apparent death, or suspended animation, see Martin S. Pernick, "Back from the Grave: Recurring Controversies over Defining and Diagnosing Death in History," in *Death: Beyond Whole-Brain Criteria*, ed. Richard M. Zaner (Boston: Kluwer Academic Publishing, 1988), 17–74. For a longer look at Dickens's interest in the topic, see Catherine Gallagher and Stephen Greenblatt, *Practicing New Historicism* (Chicago: University of Chicago Press, 2000), 185–204.

it will give us a more comprehensive understanding of *Our Mutual Friend*'s vital morbidity.

When Malthus ultimately submitted to the orthodox view that making industrial goods was no less productive than raising food, he nevertheless continued to insist on the primacy of agriculture in the nation's economy because a plentiful supply of grain, he reasoned, was the basis of all other production. Moreover, one of the arguments he used to demonstrate the uniqueness of agricultural production, its natural difference from industrial endeavor, became a founding proposition of Ricardian economics: the theory of diminishing returns held that "agricultural skill remaining the same, additional Labour employed on the land within a given district produces in general a less proportionate return, or, in other words, that though with every increase of the labour bestowed, the aggregate return is increased, the increase of the return is not in proportion to the increase of the labour."[11] That particular formulation is Nassau Senior's, but, with few variations, it stood as a fundamental postulate of political economy from the 1810s until the 1870s, combined with Malthus's proposition that rents in general would be based on the cost of obtaining a crop from the least fertile lands, which were the last to be brought into cultivation. Higher rents and diminishing returns in agriculture would then lead to a greater share of the total national product going to wages and a proportionate fall in the rate of profit (that is, not an absolute drop in profits, but a drop in the share of the annual produce going to capitalists). The big difference between manufacturing and agriculture was that industrial improvement made the unit cost of each product cheaper to manufacture (all other things being equal), while in agriculture (given the relative infertility of the most recently cultivated lands) costs would tend to rise even if techniques of production improved. And eventually the higher costs in agriculture were bound to transfer into manufacturing. To quote Nassau Senior's compact explanation:

> [A]s the labourer consumes chiefly raw or slightly-manufactured produce, the increased facility of obtaining manufactures may not make up for an increased facility in obtaining raw produce. In an old Country, therefore, when the rate of profit has been reduced by an increase of capital [going to wages], it seldom can be fully restored by a proportionate increase of population [which would drive down wages again], unless either the labourer receives a smaller quantity of raw produce than before, or the necessity of cultivating lands of inferior productiveness is obviated . . . by permanent improvements . . . leaving as a general result, a constant tendency towards an increase of capital [going to wages] and population, and towards a fall in the rate of profits. (193)

[11] Nassau William Senior, *An Outline of the Science of Political Economy* (New York: Farrar and Rinehart, 1938 [first edition, 1836]), 26.

Therefore, despite the fact that the labor theory of value seemed indifferent to the biological significance of commodities, numerous other facets of political-economic theory continually raised the issue of the food supply. The theories of rent, of the wages fund, and of the falling rate of profit, in addition to the population principle, all demonstrate political economy's perennial preoccupation with the physiological preconditions of labor and with the extent to which commodity production and exchange are grounded in transfers of biological energy. To be sure, those issues were most urgent in the late 1830s and early 1840s, in the heat of the anti–Corn Law agitation, but they never entirely disappeared.[12]

So when Ruskin harps on grain in the early 1860s, he is echoing major themes of political economy. Imagining a society that increasingly diverts its efforts away from the production of life-sustaining yields toward the manufacture of gunpowder, for example, he asks us to suppose that

> an increasing number of labourers, giving what time they can spare to this branch of industry, bring increasing quantities of combustibles into the store, and use the general orders received in exchange to obtain such wine, wool, or corn as they may have need of. . . . But the corn and wine gradually vanish, and in their place, as gradually, appear sulphur and salt-petre; till at last, the labourers who have consumed corn and supplied nitre, presenting on a festal morning some of their currency to obtain materials for the feast, discover that no amount of currency will command anything Festive, except Fire. (224–25)

Ruskin's scenario certainly does not attempt to discover a general law by which the granary might be depleted in the normal course of a society's career; instead it attributes the dwindling of the supply to the mere folly that would prefer a particularly deadly dust to the life-giving grain. But it nevertheless resembles illustrative fables in the works of Senior and McCulloch, in which more and more labor goes into getting grain for working-class consumption, and less and less into augmenting the store "destined for the consumption [including reinvestment] of capitalists," resulting in dearth all around. As Mill summed up the theory in 1846, "This last is the condition of a country over-peopled in relation to its land; in which, food being dear, the poorness of the labourer's real reward does not prevent labour from costing much to the purchaser, and low [real] wages and low profits co-exist."[13] It was simply not

---

[12] Although Ricardo used Malthus's theory to formulate his view of the falling rate of profit, the two visions of the mechanism were quite different. For the sources of Malthus's as well as a description of its departures from the classical view, see Ronald L. Meek, "Physiocracy and the Early Theories of Under-Consumption," *Economica* 71 (August 1951): 229–69.

[13] J. S. Mill, *Principles of Political Economy* in *The Collected Works of John Stuart Mill* (Toronto: University of Toronto Press, 1963–91), 2:414.

the case, as Ruskin continually proclaimed, that he alone cared whether or not the nation's products were life-sustaining.

Moreover, political economists increasingly heeded advances in the biological sciences between 1848, when Mill published his *Principles*, and the early 1860s, when Ruskin launched his critique, for during those years the sanitary condition of Britain became one of their major concerns, starting a current of thought that ran counter to the orthodox belief in agricultural depletion, rising rents, and a falling rate of profit. The inquiry into "the health of towns," as is well known, grew directly out of the reform of the Poor Laws through the extraordinary efforts of the New Poor Law's main architect, who had previously been Jeremy Bentham's amanuensis, Edwin Chadwick.[14] Throughout the 1840s, 1850s, and 1860s, Chadwick and other sanitarians tried to integrate the study of the nation's wealth with that of its health, and Chadwick evidently hoped that the combination might acquit political economy of the charges Carlyle and Ruskin brought against it.[15]

In an 1862 address to the British Association for the Advancement of Science, for example, Chadwick reassured his listeners that political economy was no longer what Carlyle had dubbed it: a "dismal science."[16] For "the close scrutiny of particulars, by exhaustive collections of them, and wider inductions from them," have dissipated the bleak conclusion, "chiefly on the population question," that "reasoners of the abstract and geometric class" had previously reached. Turning from the deductive and theoretical speculations of the early Malthus and Ricardo to the inductive study of the lives of populations in their organic environments, he asserts, "that . . . conclusions . . . more in harmony with popular sentiments and instincts and with elevated views of human progress, are confidently indicated." Chadwick is here referring both to his claim that sanitary reform would produce a race of healthy, educated,

---

[14] Chadwick was the main author and principal agent behind the publication of the *Report to Her Majesty's Principal Secretary of State for the Home Department from the Poor Law Commissioners on an Inquiry into the Sanitary Condition of the Labouring Population of Great Britain* (London: Printed by W. Clowes and Sons for H. M. Stationery Off., 1842).

[15] The sanitarian's attempts to overcome the Malthusian dilemma seem to parallel the turn among Christian economic thinkers toward what Boyd Hilton has called "incarnational social thought," which he distinguishes from an earlier Evangelical emphasis on atonement. See *The Age of Atonement: The Influence of Evangelicalism on Social and Economic Thought, 1785–1865* (Oxford: Oxford University Press, 1988). Mary Poovey also makes a relevant but separate contrast between the Christian Malthusian Thomas Chalmers, with his charismatic individualism and emphasis on suffering for atonement, and the Benthamite Edwin Chadwick, with his bureaucratic individualism and emphasis on making rational and happy individuals; she sees both as moments in the consolidation of disciplinary individualism (*Making a Social Body: British Cultural Formation, 1830–1864*, Chicago: University of Chicago Press, 1995).

[16] Chadwick, "Opening Address of the President of Section F (Economic Science and Statistics) of the British Association for the Advancement of Science, at the Thirty-second Meeting, at Cambridge, in October, 1862," *Journal of the Statistical Society of London* 25 (December 1862): 502–3.

and self-disciplined workers, who would voluntarily put the "preventive check" into practice, and to his scheme—which we'll come back to shortly—for manuring the soil with urban organic waste to support a larger number of people. His hopeful conclusions, he declared, should ally him with Ruskin, and he even pledged allegiance to the main thesis of Ruskin's *Unto This Last*, "[a]dopting . . . this statement of the end of economical science, and adopting it not hypothetically but positively . . . 'that the true veins of wealth are purple, and not in rock but in flesh . . . that the final outcome and consummation of all wealth is in producing as many as possible of full-breathed, bright-eyed, and happy-hearted human creatures' " (504). Toward the end of his address, moreover, he returns to the same passage in *Unto This Last*, this time explicitly calling for the partnership of sanitation, physiology, political economy, and moral education: "Economic science, consulting sanitary science, would thus achieve Mr. Ruskin's aspiration, of which the success would be visibly denoted, by a well-formed and rosy-cheeked, as well as 'full-breathed, bright-eyed, and happy-hearted' population" (515).

Much that lies between these two invocations of him, however, would have outraged Ruskin, for Chadwick, trying to convince political economists that the waste of life caused by unsanitary living and working conditions is really a waste of capital, converts human lives into cash value without blinking an eye. How else to prove that wealth really is in flesh and blood than by doing the math?

> At 11 years of age, when the child can generally earn its own food and clothing, it may be taken as an investment of 130*l.*, or the value, say, of a team of four first-class farm horses, or of a hunter; or at 21 years of age it would be an investment of about 250*l.*, or about as much as two hunters. Economically he may be viewed as an amount of available productive power. (505)

Ruskin would consider the troping of these calculations, the very ease with which they convert the child into money and then into horses, to be proof that political economy is congenitally debasing, unable to fix on humanity any intrinsic, nonfungible value. Chadwick's rhetoric implies that the abstract "amount of available productive power" just happens to be stored in a human being; it might just as well be stored in the bank or in the horses. Once again, the focus on the body's "productive power" is precisely the thing that authorizes the extraction and relocation of value. To do Chadwick justice, we must recognize that he attempted to locate all kinds of value in human bodies, even exchange value. He insists that "moralists" (his word for Carlyle and Ruskin), must do their best to save lives, and so should political economists, by applying their own science, in conjunction with other life sciences, to the problem: "It may be set down as an economic axiom, that *whatsoever else they denote*,—filth and squalor in a class or population, denote loss of power and waste, and amongst other things, an immediate waste of food to produce a given amount of force" (514–15). He asserts both a division of labor between himself and Ruskin and an identity of goals.

But Ruskin was apparently having none of it; he wanted to exempt human life fully from the logic of capital. Once the economic motive for saving lives becomes dominant, once thinking of a child as an investment of capital becomes habitual, Ruskin implicitly replies in his *Essays on Political Economy,* one might also find economic motives for not saving them:

> Some years ago, a society formed at Geneva offered to embank the river for the ground which would have been recovered by the operation; but the offer was refused by the (then Sardinian) government. The capitalists saw that this expenditure would have "paid," if the ground saved from the river was to be theirs. But if, when the offer that had this aspect of profit was refused, they had nevertheless persisted in the plan, and merely taking security for the return of their outlay, lent the funds for the work, and thus saved a whole race of human souls from perishing in a pestiferous fen (as, I presume, some among them would, at personal risk, have dragged any one drowning creature out of the current of the stream, and not expected payment there for), such expenditure would have . . . been the king's, of grace, instead of the usurer's, for gain.[17]

The "king's" expenditure, government expenditure, must be unselfish and inspire similar private unselfishness; hence it should not be motivated by arguments like Chadwick's, which would encourage the state to see its responsibility toward the lives of its subjects as a matter of managing assets.

In fact, despite his confident economic rhetoric, by 1862 Chadwick himself had no great faith that capitalists would voluntarily seek their enlightened self-interest by sponsoring, or even tolerating, sanitary reform. He was fresh from a series of defeats, on sewage, water supply, and interment, which he attributed to the "vested interests" of privately owned water and burial companies, and his earlier attempt to attract investors into his own Towns Improvement Company had been a disaster.[18] His address to the British Association for the Advancement of Science might therefore be read, not as an uncompromising avowal of old-fashioned political-economic faith in the efficacy of the market, but as an attempt to win over the opposition by using the only form of reason they seemed to understand, that of profit and loss. Although he personally doubted the market's power to effect change single-handedly, he

---

[17] *"Unto This Last" and Other Essays,* 295.

[18] See Anthony Brundage, *England's "Prussian Minister": Edwin Chadwick and the Politics of Government Growth, 1832–1854* (University Park: Pennsylvania State University Press, 1988), and S. E. Finer, *The Life and Times of Sir Edwin Chadwick* (London: Methuen, 1952).

succeeded in foregrounding and augmenting the biological dimension of political economy, not only by figuring each healthy member of the population as so much invested capital and each sick or dying one as so much wasted capital, but also by reasserting the connection between the national economy and its organic environment, its life-supporting resources. As Mary Poovey has shown, Chadwick was a principal author of the peculiarly biological Victorian project that she calls "making the social body."[19] We can therefore identify Chadwick as an inheritor and perpetuator of Malthus's preoccupations, despite his departure from Malthus's recommendation to abolish (rather than reform) the Poor Laws[20] and from the older thinker's depressing insistence on the need for misery or vice to check population. Malthus's bioeconomic concerns were preserved in these very divergences, which fitted the basic premises to administrative realities and made them more palatable.

We should also recognize that, pace Ruskin's recalcitrance, Chadwick was correct to think that the prominent place he gave to physical vitality in his political economy might disarm its quondam opponents because, ironically, it *seemed* anti-Malthusian as well as anti-laissez-faire. Sanitary reform was a cause that appealed equally to Dickens, Ruskin, and the incipient bureaucracy represented by Chadwick, all of whom—for different reasons—wanted an increasingly active, interventionist government.[21] After a brief hesitation born of his distrust of the author of the New Poor Laws, Dickens became Chadwick's firmest public champion from the late 1840s through the 1860s.[22] The Health of Towns Association, where they met, comprehended a remarkably broad ideological and political spectrum, and Dickens might easily have viewed it as a continuation of the more radical "political medicine" that helped pass the factory legislation of the 1830s.[23] His support for Chadwick was based on their shared assertion of the need for a central authority, but he was

---

[19] See chapter 6 of Poovey (*Making a Social Body*), 98–131.

[20] For a discussion of the theoretical and practical roots of this change, see J. R. Poynter, *Society and Pauperism: English Ideas on Poor Relief, 1795–1834* (London: Routledge and Kegan Paul, 1969), 295–329.

[21] For the view that the growth in government, including public health administration, was driven less by the ideologies of individuals (e.g., Chadwick's Benthamism) than by "concrete day-to-day problems, pressed eventually to the surface by the sheer exigencies of the case," see Oliver MacDonagh, "The Nineteenth-Century Revolution in Government: A Reappraisal," in *The Victorian Revolution: Government and Society in Victoria's Britain*, ed. Peter Stansky (New York: Franklin Watts, 1973), 5–28. For recent counterarguments, see Poovey, *Making a Social Body*, 112–14, and Christopher Hamlin, *Public Health and Social Justice in the Age of Chadwick, 1800–1854* (Cambridge: Cambridge University Press, 1998), 335–41.

[22] Finer, *The Life and Times of Sir Edwin Chadwick*, 239.

[23] In *Public Health and Social Justice*, Hamlin distinguishes between the authority that medical men assumed over social issues in the first half of the century, often placing themselves against laissez-faire doctrine, and the more procapitalist, nonmedical reforms undertaken later by the sanitarians.

also drawn to the sanitarian's revision of the biological economy of the nation.[24] In the Malthusian model, production and consumption of food were clearly defined opposites; the energy spent on food production needed to be replaced by food consumption, but the labor became increasingly arduous while the yield became ever scantier. In the sanitarians' revision, though, consumption itself created by-products, human and other animal wastes, that could be used to grow more food. They intended not only to dispose of the waste that caused disease, but also to put it back into the soil, which would in turn become more fertile. Proposals abounded for returning the remains of spent human vitality—especially the organic waste of towns—to the earth for use in further rounds of production, many of them asserting that the tendency of food to become dearer and scarcer, the organic underpinning of the falling rate of profit tendency, could be overcome by the proper husbanding of human waste. One popular metaphor held that each nation had a God-given capital of fertilizing elements that generated its food as interest.[25] These fertilizing elements included human waste and decomposing human bodies. A way had to be found, sanitary reformers argued, to return this capital to the food-producing earth, for if it were not returned, it would not pay sufficient interest in food to keep the population alive. That is, a model of self-sustaining growth based on the continual recycling of the population's own remains (the more people, the more waste; the more waste, the more food; the more food, the more people; etc.) was imagined in response to the Malthusian-Ricardian theory of the falling rate of profits.

The sanitarians' determination to plow the remains of consumption back into the process of production seems to have inspired *Our Mutual Friend*. We have already seen that, in the novel, corpse commodities remind us of the life-draining nature of all commodities and hence contain in themselves the illth/wealth duality, and we have observed that the human body remains at the center of the novel's economy only in deanimated forms. Just as in the sanitarians' vision of recycling waste, bodily remains in *Our Mutual Friend* become the key, revivifying commodities, and their potency relies partly on their status as waste, as abundant, disposable by-products of spending. *Our Mutual Friend*, in other words, is interested not only in getting a living from dead or

[24] More evidence of Dickens's faith in Chadwick's ability to increase the food supply by retrieving waste can be found in a letter of 1866 to George Russell, in which Dickens's emphasis on sustaining the labor of poor children echoes Chadwick's own. Discussing a plan for a scrap-kitchen, he writes, "I have no doubt that an enormous quantity of good food is wasted in this town. . . . Also I have no doubt that if such food were well recooked and well-redistributed among poor children, it would soon prove itself to be so much labour-stamina." After noting many practical difficulties with the plan, he recommends Chadwick as the most likely man "to meet these difficulties." *The Letters of Charles Dickens*, eds. Madeline House, Graham Storey, Kathleen Tillotson, 11:285–86.

[25] See Christopher Hamlin's excellent "Providence and Putrefaction: Victorian Sanitarians and the Natural Theology of Health and Disease," *Victorian Studies* 28 (1985): 381–412.

apparently dead bodies but also in getting a living from them as *garbage*, as excess that is being at once disposed of and retrieved, salvaged.

Chadwick famously wanted to build sewers not only to carry off London's ordure but also to carry it down the river to manure large-scale agricultural endeavors. Given that London did not even have pressurized water or a rudimentary sewer network at the time, Chadwick's was a hugely ambitious scheme. As Christopher Hamlin notes, "[S]ewage recycling required building a new institution. That town wastes had value was uncontroversial; that sewage irrigation on a grand scale would vastly increase agricultural production, repaying the costs of sanitary improvement and overthrowing the Malthusian principle of population, seemed too much a political economist's bedtime fantasy."[26] Fantasy or not, the sanitarians who supported it set about making it seem like a practical necessity, largely by publicizing how much recycling of human and other forms of waste already took place in the capital and how much wealth it produced. Dickens's *Household Words* joined in the campaign, publishing numerous articles on sanitary matters."[27]

Viewing the novel's focus on London's scavengers from this perspective, we gain an additional insight into the waste's doubleness. For although there was considerable disagreement over how large concentrations of decomposing matter caused disease, everyone knew that they did. Life's remains had to be kept in productive circulation, not allowed to wash away in the river or to accumulate into stagnating pools and suffocating piles. Hence dead and decomposing human matter was organized into the sanitarians' bioeconomy as, to use Ruskin's terms again, both potential illth and wealth. Unlike the third-person narrator of *Bleak House*, *Our Mutual Friend*'s narrator shows little interest in the public health dangers of improperly buried, decomposing human bodies; corpses and body parts are instead, as I've already shown, placed in circulation as macabre commodities. Nevertheless, the sanitary imagination informs the novel's bioeconomics and further erodes the distinc-

---

[26] Hamlin, *Public Health and Social Justice*, 237.

[27] Several critics have noted Dickens's interest in sanitary matters. Michael Steig, in "Dickens's Excremental Vision" (*Victorian Studies* 13 [March 1970]: 339–54), writes of Dickens's "profound" artistic reaction to reading Chadwick's 1842 *Report on the Sanitary Conditions of the Labouring Population of Great Britain*, but he portrays "the implicit equation of excrement and wealth" as merely a widespread neurosis. Nancy Aycock Metz in "The Artistic Reclamation of Waste in *Our Mutual Friend*" (*Nineteenth-Century Fiction* 34 [June 1979]: 59–72), demonstrates that Dickens likens the power of the imagination to the natural regenerative processes that numerous *Household Words* articles described in the 1850s. She instances especially "Important Rubbish," and "Penny Wisdom," *Household Words*, 19 May 1855, and 16 October 1852, respectively. For other critical discussions of the novel's use of material on London's scavengers, see the following: Harland S. Nelson, "Dickens's *Our Mutual Friend* and Henry Mayhew's *London Labour and the London Poor*," *Nineteenth-Century Fiction* 20 (1966), 207–22; K. J. Fielding, "Nova Scotia Gardens and What Grew There," *Dickensian* 61 (1965), 112–19; and R. D. McMaster, "Birds of Prey: A Study of *Our Mutual Friend*," *Dalhousie Review* 40 (1960): 372–81.

tion between life and death, implying that "*munera*" and "*pulveris*" could be identical, that the dust, the dead husks and bodily remains, may, if properly handled, indeed be the gift of life.

By the late 1860s, the paradoxes flowing from the attempt to place all value on Life became apparent even to Ruskin. As the decade went on, he found Life suspended in all sorts of inanimate structures, including buildings and crystals, and he made it a property, as well, of the very matter that he had earlier used to symbolize death: dust.[28] His revaluation of dust began in *The Ethics of the Dust*, written, like most of *Our Mutual Friend*, in 1864, and it continued in one of his essays on Greek mythology, written a few years later and finally published in *The Queen of the Air*. Here the serpent is figured as animated dust, the earth itself made mobile through both its fatal and fertile potency: "[The serpent] is a divine hieroglyph of the demoniac power of the earth . . . of the grasp and sting of death. . . . [I]t is the strength of the base element that is so dreadful in the serpent; it is the very omnipotence of the earth."[29] A serpent "bites the dust with the ridges of its body," and is itself "a spectral procession of spotted dust, with dissolution in its fangs, dislocation in its coils" (363). And yet, "as the power of earth upon the seed—consuming it into new life ('that which thou sowest is not quickened except it die' [1 Cor. 15:36])—serpents sustain the chariot of the spirit of agriculture" (363). Primitive people, Ruskin writes, locate in the serpent a fitting symbol for the life-taking and life-giving of the dust, and they thereby anticipate the discoveries of the sanitarians, who have not only detected "the links between dead matter and animation" that "drift everywhere unseen" (362) but also recently discovered why "there is a power in the earth to take away corruption, and to purify, (hence the very fact of burial, and many uses of earth, only lately known); and in this sense, the serpent is a healing spirit,—the representative of Aesculapius, and of Hygieia" (364).

Ruskin made sanitary science into a continuation of an ancient symbolic system in order to keep his increasingly antimodern rhetoric consistent. In this passage, the hygienic serpent of Greek mythology foreshadows the very recent discoveries (alluded to as "uses of the earth, only lately known") of Henry Moule, who in 1860 had invented a new dry-earth system of sanitation. Moreover, Ruskin was thinking about launching an agricultural project of his own, to demonstrate (in defiance of Malthus) how much more food than had been previously calculated could be grown in a supposedly fully cultivated country, and this project, too, he conceived and presented in self-

[28] For a discussion of the wide array of writings that dealt with the doubleness of dust from the 1860s until the century's end, see Kate Flint, "'The Mote Within the Eye': Dust and Victorian Vision," in *Rethinking Victorian Culture*, eds. Juliet John and Alice Jenkins (New York: St. Martin's Press, 2000), 46–63.

[29] *Queen of the Air, Works*, 19, 362.

consciously anachronistic terms as a semireligious, medieval "Guild of St. George."

But the mystical eccentricities of Ruskin's agricultural and sanitary ruminations were only an exaggerated version of the flights of rhetoric made by many sanitarians and echoed in *Our Mutual Friend*'s allusions to resurrection, baptism, and sacrifice. Something in the oxymoronic structure of the ideas, which declared the foul to be fair and the cast-away to be precious, as well as in their cosmic resonances, seemed to appeal to the literary imagination. Over a decade before the publication of *Our Mutual Friend*, the hero of Charles Kingsley's novel *Yeast* (1850) sees the duality in organic remains as he looks down at the Thames,

> at that huge, black-mouthed sewer, vomiting its pestilential riches across the mud. There it runs ... hurrying to the sea vast stores of wealth, elaborated by Nature's chemistry into the ready materials of food; which proclaim, too, by their own foul smell God's will that they should be buried out of sight in the fruitful, all-regenerating grave of earth; there it runs; turning them all into the seeds of pestilence, filth, and drunkenness.[30]

As that last phrase indicates, not everyone agreed with Chadwick that the Thames should transport sewage to the countryside; there was a formidable controversy over dry versus wet manuring, but all parties to the debate concurred that death and fertility were contained in the same matter, which would only find its proper destination in the food-growing soil. To keep it from degenerating into mere urban foulness, the boundary between wet and dry in London should be made definite. Hence workaday civil engineering projects like the embankment of the Thames, under way when *Our Mutual Friend* was written, were recommended in language reverberating with solemn allusions to redemption.[31]

Closer to home, R. H. Horne's 1850 *Household Words* story, "Dust; or Ugliness Redeemed," long recognized as an inspiration for Dickens's novel,[32] not only stresses the identity of regeneration and decay—the decomposed vegetables, the dead animals, and the crushed bones, wool, soot, and fine ashes in the dust piles, Horne explains, will fertilize the next year's crop—but also anticipates the novel's use of apparent death and resurrection as a metaphor for the cycle. An impoverished gentleman drowns himself in the canal, is pulled out by cinder-shifters working in a dust yard, and buried in one of the dust mounds, for

---

[30] Charles Kingsley, *Yeast: A Problem* (New York: E. P. Dutton and Co., 1913), 223–24.

[31] For instances and analyses of this rhetoric, see Hamlin, "Providence and Putrefaction."

[32] Humphrey House first noted resemblances between the novel and story, but Frank Gibbon has given a fuller account, especially of the story's suggestion of the theme of suspended animation. See "R. H. Horne and *Our Mutual Friend*," *Dickensian* 81 (Fall 1985): 140–43.

[i]t is a fact well known to those who work in the vicinity of these great Dust-heaps, that when the ashes have been warmed by the sun, cats and kittens that have been taken out of the canal and buried a few inches beneath the surface, have usually revived; and the same has often occurred in the case of men. Accordingly the three [scavengers], without a moment's hesitation, dragged the body along to the Dust-heap, where they made a deep trench, in which they placed it, covering it all over up to the neck.[33]

The gentleman, of course, comes back to life.

It is not surprising, then, that the novel draws on these organizing concepts, imagining the river to be a potentially pestilential open sewer full of death, which can either work further destruction or become the stuff of new life. If political economy alone might have suggested the equation of commodity and life-drained body and further indicated that the out-of-body state was the most valuable of all, the merger of political economy with sanitation seems to have encouraged the novelist to imagine a world in which wealth was primarily drawn from the disposal of human remains. To be sure, Dickens's almost exclusive focus on London and its suburbs, combined with his desire to make a sensation and yet maintain his regard for "decency," led him away from the topic of manure and kept his attention on the corpses. Boffin's dust heaps are represented as inorganic and do not include "night soil," although, like the mounds in "Dust; or Ugliness Redeemed," they were thought to be replete with fertilizing agents. Hence, *Our Mutual Friend* does not need to show agricultural workers hauling dung out of the river in order to participate in the sanitarians' desire. As in R. H. Horne's story, the reviving corpses in the landscape of "dust" and river figure the revivifying potential of all of life's remains.

It is, moreover, only within the sanitarians' model that the division of the novel's world into wet and dry begins to make sense, and that the heroism and horror of dragging bodies out of the river comes into sharper focus. This is the discourse that allows us to understand why Bradley Headstone's internal rot expresses its essential sterility in images of churning water. It lets us understand, too, why the dust world is the place of transformations, why dryness and burial mounds would be the sites of regeneration. Further, it allows us to perceive the association between the river and the potential for tragedy. Characters in the river plot frequently undergo reductions; they have fewer and fewer options as the plot proceeds. On the other hand, the inhabitants of the dust world only apparently reduce themselves. In the cases of John Harmon, Boffin, and Bella, deathliness and insensibility are only stages in the process of preserving and releasing vital power, but in the river plot, more extreme action must be taken for regeneration. Hence, while political econ-

[33] R. H. Horne, "Dust; or Ugliness Redeemed," *Household Words*, 13 July 1850, 379–84, 383.

omy provided the metaphors that allow value to rest on suspended animation and even to require discardable bodies, the bioeconomics of the sanitarians' revisions to the science of wealth provides crucial insights into the novel's obsession with the disposal of the very bodies its own paradoxical logic keeps producing as waste products. The recycling of such garbage-bodies, their conversion from illth to wealth, is the prototypical act of value creation in this novel. In it, once again, the de-animated body, vitality, and value become indistinguishable, putting the terms illth and wealth, as well as death and life, into unstable fluctuation.

The whole richly contradictory and fertile mixture is perhaps best summed up in the novel's resolution of the love plot involving Lizzie Hexam and Eugene Wrayburn. Eugene resembles John Harmon and Rogue Riderhood in that he must undergo a period of apparent death, of suspended animation, and for Eugene this period follows Lizzie's retrieval of his garbage-body from the river, where it has been dumped, as John Harmon's was dumped, after a murder attempt. The two love plots work through a complicated series of parallels and inversions centering on images of suspended animation and discardable bodies; for both, the period of suspended animation, or apparent death, is the moment when life takes on value. Only then is Eugene able, as John Harmon was able during his tenure as "the dead man," to give and receive love. Thus the familiar pattern is repeated: suspending the body's animation allows the liberation of value.

But furthermore, since Eugene's apparent death is not accomplished with a surrogate body, the equation of the hero's own body first with floating refuse and then with a broken "thing," that is, the emphasis on the body as garbage, is far more pronounced in Eugene's story than it was in John Harmon's. Eugene, as a denizen of the river plot, must be agonizingly pulled from the water by his savior-wife, wound in cloth and placed in sepulchral darkness, for suspended animation, on which the release and transfer of vitality depend, requires removing the remains from the water and entombing them, as Eugene's body is entombed, in a dry place. In his speech to Lizzie as his body returns to a state of animation, he stresses the equality of garbage and wealth by turning her into both: " 'You have thrown yourself away,' said Eugene, shaking his head. 'But you have followed the treasure of your heart. . . . [Y]ou had thrown that away first, dear girl!' " (753). Hence Eugene and Lizzie are equally garbage and treasure to one another; indeed, they are treasure because they are garbage. And it is therefore perfectly rational for Eugene to fear the returning health of his body: "[I]n this maimed and broken state, you make so much of me." Lizzie can make much of him, add value to him, only while his body is thus broken. Only while the vitality is somewhere outside his body can he possess this treasure, which is the squandering of Lizzie's life.

And so we seem to be witnessing the regenerative inversion of the horrific life transfer suggested in the opening scene, for now Lizzie's life becomes the wealth of the cadaver; instead of getting a living off the garbage-body, she spends her life on it. But in *Our Mutual Friend* reversals are never so neat. The expense of Lizzie's life is experienced by Eugene as a heavy debt: "It would require a life, Lizzie, to pay all; more than a life" (753). Instead of inverting the novel's opening scene, Eugene's last words recapitulate it. There really is only one thing he can do to discharge his debt to Lizzie and keep himself in the condition of value he has achieved; we are put right back where we started when Eugene concludes, "I ought to die, my dear" (754).

Our Mutual Friend incessantly requires bodily suspension as a condition of the valuable Life; illness unto death brings wealth. Locating both mortality and vitality, both fatality and regeneration, in decomposition makes us acutely aware that illth and wealth are alike abstractions from the body's particularity. They are alike poised on the vanishing point of those "full-breathed, bright-eyed, and happy-hearted human creatures" that Ruskin had set out to vindicate.

The Apparent Death of the Author

We have so far looked at two locations for the storage of vital energy outside of bodies: commodities generally and the waste matter that results from their consumption. Chadwick suggested a third: literary texts. Indeed, he proposed that works by Carlyle, Dickens, and Ruskin should be read aloud, "In weaving shops and in places of semi-automatic" labor, where "works of imagination" and "matters of stirring interest" have already been "found to give to the hand, somewhat of the life energy and regularity of movement, which the band gives to the march" (514). Political economy, he claimed, could find something productive in the texts even of its critics, provided they were passionate enough to rouse and quicken their auditors: "[T]he 'dismal science,' to use Mr. Carlyle's phrase, may find a place for him, and for imaginative writers, like our friends Mr. Dickens . . . and Mr. Ruskin" in the very process of value extraction. For the army of industrial "hands" they could perform the part of the marching band, enlivening their listeners to work, "and [providing] . . . aid, which they may not have intended,—to capital and production."[34] Chadwick no doubt appreciated the irony of the proposal: it would be a fitting recompense for Carlyle and Ruskin to find their ringing denunciations of political economy put to use to increase capital accumulation.

The suggestion may be half facetious, but it calls our attention to the sort of energy transfer that texts were thought to effect. Regardless of what they might say about industrial production, Chadwick considered the writers we've been examining to be sources of animation, which lay dormant in their repre-

[34] Chadwick, "Opening Address to the President . . . of the British Association for the Advancement of Science," 514.

sented language. "Force" was contained in their words; it was placed there by their labor and genius and could be drawn out again by a reader, as if it were stored in a battery. A text, in short, was another form of suspended animation, holding not only ideas but also their animating motive power. Moreover, although the texts of Carlyle, Ruskin, and Dickens might originally have served some defined authorial purpose, they could be reused indefinitely for aims that the authors "may not have intended." Carlyle may be opposed to the dismal science, but his textual resting place, conveniently separated from his intentions, can be transferred into the productive process. To Chadwick, texts seem inexhaustible and fully appropriable; they can be recycled endlessly, and consequently, despite his irony, he presents them as ideal sources of energy. Almost literally "ideal"; Chadwick calls their "pleasurable mental excitement" a "metaphysical means" for sustaining productive human force. In contrast, what he calls the "physical means"—"food, clothing, housing"—can remain stubbornly external to production. No matter how good the physical means of reproducing force, Chadwick assures us, "the work, after a time, goes on heavily, wearily, slowly," and a "metaphysical means" must be employed to make the energy flow from the body of the worker to the product. The metaphysical means themselves, moreover, seem to expand almost infinitely, rather than to diminish, in their very consumption; the magic of textual dissemination amplifies the original force incomparably.

Chadwick's insistence on the need for "mental relief and stimuli to work"— he mentions hiring dancers, musicians, and "animating or sensation preachers," as well as reading Carlyle, Ruskin, and Dickens—reminds us of *Hard Times*. To be sure, Chadwick wants to *enliven*, rather than to *gladden* the workers, a distinction that indicates the differing emphases of soma- and bioeconomics, but his proposal nevertheless invites an inquiry, like the one undertaken in the last chapter, into the novel's reflections on itself as a component of the economic process it describes. Unlike *Hard Times*, *Our Mutual Friend* contains no advertisements for popular entertainment; instead of recommending its own power to revive the flagging energy of the people, the later novel apparently distrusts their very desire for literacy and breeds suspicion that readers, especially new readers, will be incapable of bringing the text back to life.[35] The schoolmaster Bradley Headstone's mechanical storage and lifeless retrieval of books aptly emblematizes the narrator's skepticism toward

---

[35] Discussions of Dickens's seeming pessimism regarding mass education in *Our Mutual Friend* include Richard D. Altick's "Education, Print, and Paper in *Our Mutual Friend*," in *Nineteenth-Century Literary Perspectives: Essays in Honor of Lionel Stevenson*, ed. Clyde Ryals (Durham, N.C.: Duke University Press, 1974), 237–54; and Pam Morris's "A Taste for Change in *Our Mutual Friend*: Cultivation or Education?" in *Rethinking Victorian Culture*, eds. Juliet John and Alice Jenkins (New York: St. Martin's Press, 2000), 180–95. See also Stanley Friedman, "The Motif of Reading in *Our Mutual Friend*," *Nineteenth-Century Fiction* 28 (1973): 38–61; and Robert S. Baker, "Imagination and Literacy in Dickens's *Our Mutual Friend*," *Criticism* 18 (1976): 57–72.

the newly literate: "From his early childhood up," we are told, "his mind had been a place of mechanical stowage" (217). And his careworn countenance is the result of the incessant stocktaking and "arrangement of his wholesale warehouse" of mental commodities, "so that it might be always ready to meet the demands of retail dealers—history here, geography there, astronomy to the right, political economy to the left—natural history, the physical sciences, figures, music, the lower mathematics, and what not, all in their several places" (217). He can store and transfer them—"do mental arithmetic mechanically, sing at sight mechanically, blow various wind instruments mechanically, even play the great church organ mechanically" (217)—but their forcefulness, their life, is inaccessible to him.

And yet, the novel also wants to assure us that vital reading is possible, that the author's force can be relayed and reused. Just as *Hard Times*'s suffering authorial persona supplements its thematic stress on labor's painful tedium, *Our Mutual Friend* proclaims the author as a hero of suspension, whose stored life force is available to readers only if they submit to his authority. That insistent authorial prerogative stamps itself on the many portraits of bad readers in *Our Mutual Friend*, almost as if Dickens were considering Chadwick's proposal and retorting that incapable readers can neither locate nor convey the Life in the text. Again, Ruskin's work on political economy makes a corresponding point, urging that the value inhering in any commodity depends on its capable use: "The production of effectual value, therefore, always involves two needs: first, the production of a thing essentially useful; then the production of the capacity to use it. Where the intrinsic value and acceptant capacity come together there is Effectual value, or wealth" (204). The reader without an "acceptant capacity" may, like Bradley Headstone, become a mere sepulcher for the works, or he may, like that same character, be injured by his mental burden—"Suppression of so much to make room for so much"—for, according to Ruskin, books, having the power "of exciting vital or noble emotion and intellectual action," also have the negative ability of "killing the noble emotions, or exciting base ones" (207).

Our Mutual Friend examines a variety of characters at the threshold of literacy, classifying them according to their "acceptant capacity." Charley Hexam, Lizzie's little brother and Headstone's student, for example, is characterized by the moral insufficiency of his desire to read; the narrator describes him as "coarse" and "stunted," a typical "figure" (18) of his class, set apart only by his represented relation to the very "figures" that convey him to the reader, letters: "[h]is writing, though large and round, was good; and he glanced at the backs of the books, with an awakened curiosity that went below the binding. No one who can read, ever looks at a book, even unopened on a shelf, like one who cannot" (18). This is no simple case of a deconstructive moment in which the reader is forced to acknowledge the textuality of the character under construction, for the passage gives the implied reader's self-awareness a specific class content, focusing attention not so much on the immediate act of reading as on the underlying condition of literacy. The implied reader's ability is not an anomaly but is rather his definitive and seemingly "natural" attribute, meriting no remark. But Charley's literacy, the unexpected skill of a riverman's son, invites immediate probing. Charley's intelligence, we are to understand, capably processes even the holiest of texts, giving him the biblical references for depicting the state of the drowned man identified as John Harmon as well as—ironically—the ultimate resurrection of that hero: "Pharaoh's multitude that were drowned in the Red Sea, ain't more beyond restoring to life. If Lazarus was only half as far gone, that was the greatest of all miracles" (19). These allusions raise Mortimer Lightwood's curiosity: "Halloa! . . . You seem at home in the Red Sea, my young friend?" The obvious pun on "Red" elicits Charley's proud proclamation: he has "read about it with teacher in school" so that he can navigate the biblical sea of words. But his reading has mainly produced social ambitions, and his soul might therefore be drowning in textuality despite his proficiency. Even his study of the good book, we are led to conclude, has failed to make him properly grateful, loving, and kind toward the sister, who supports his schooling: "She ain't half bad . . . but if she knows her letters it's the most she does— and them I learned her" (19). Charley's egoism is swiftly chastised by the very people he seeks to impress when, hearing him speak "slightingly of his sister, [Eugene] took him roughly enough by the chin, and turned up his face to look at it" (19). This act of sheer domination, punishing Charley for having the "face" to promote himself, admonishes both the boy's class and readerly insubordination. Selfishly appropriating the text, he has ignored its Author's intentions.

Compare our introduction to Noddy Boffin, who is no less carefully constructed against a background of print, although, as he puts it, "all print is shut to me" (50). Boffin is accordingly humble and submissive as he recalls having overheard Silas Wegg read ballads to the butcher's body: "[w]hen I listened that morning, I listened with hadmiration amounting to haw. I thought to myself, 'Here's a man with a wooden leg, a literary man . . . and all Print is open to him.' And it is, ain't it?" Wegg responds, "I believe you couldn't show me the piece of English print, that I wouldn't be equal to collaring and throwing." "On the spot?" persists Boffin; "On the spot," replies Wegg. To Wegg's mind, texts are things to be subdued; although he can collar and throw them by finding spoken sounds for the printed signs, he often cannot attach meanings to them. As if enacting a satire on Chadwick's faith in the energizing effect of employing "readers to read novels . . . histories, and matters of stirring interest," Boffin hires the incompetent Wegg to read *The Decline and Fall of the Roman Empire* aloud. Wegg marshals all of his antagonistic power against Gibbon, but far from conquering the volumes, he and his auditor "decline and fall" into an extended confusion.

The contrast between Charley's impudent reading (more intelligent but just as misguided as Wegg's) and Boffin's humble, guileless listening, combined with the repeated warnings that any book can be misread, that a lector without "acceptant power" can mangle, pervert, and destroy any text, point to a consistent conclusion: the "effectual value" of the text can only be realized by an obedient attention to authorial guidance. A text is not (as Chadwick implies) a reserve of energy that can be tapped and drawn off into any enterprise. Rather, it is a store that can only be tapped by a properly subordinate partner. Dickens seems to be developing here a fantasy of perpetual authorial control that would grant him a form of unlimited, recurrent reanimation. In his correspondence during the composition of the novel, Dickens frequently makes this same point. He is gratified when his readers wait patiently for the solutions to his mysteries, and hopes they won't anticipate the outcome: "It amuses me to find that you don't see your way with a certain Mutual Friend of ours. I have a horrible suspicion that you may begin to be fearfully knowing at somewhere about No. xii or xiii. But you shan't if I can help it."[36] He praises readers who notice the passages that most absorbed his own energy: "Your note delighted me, because it dwelt upon the places in the No. that *I* dwell on."[37] And he solicits approval for the total design even while ostensibly seeking advice from a fellow author:

> I hope you will find the purpose and the plot of my book very plain when you see it as a whole piece. I am looking forward to sending you the proofs complete, about the end of the month. It is all sketched out, and I am working hard at it, giving it all the pains possible to be bestowed on a labour of love. Your critical opinion two months in advance of the public will be invaluable to me. For you know what store I set by it, and how I think over a hint from you.[38]

Dickens's strong sense of the reader's receptive responsibility is perhaps clearest in the novel's "Postscript," where he chides critics of the early numbers for their distrust:

> When I devised this story, I foresaw the likelihood that a class of readers and commentators would suppose that I was at great pains to conceal exactly what I was at great pains to suggest: namely, that Mr. John Harmon was not slain, and that Mr. John Rokesmith was he. Pleasing myself with the idea that the supposition might in part arise out of some ingenuity in the story, and thinking it worth while, in the interests of art, to hint to an audience that an artist (of whatever denomination) may perhaps be trusted to know what he is about in his vocation, if they will concede him a little patience, I was not alarmed by the anticipation. (821)

[36] "To Charles Kent, 17 Jan., 1865." *The Letters of Charles Dickens*, 11:6.
[37] "To Charles Kent, 2 August 1865." Ibid., 77–78.
[38] "To Edward Bulwer Lytton, 20 July 1865." Ibid., 73.

The reader's duty to wait and trust, we also learn here, is especially necessary when the author is in his most suspended state, that of monthly serial publication:

> To keep for a long time unsuspected, yet always working itself out, another purpose [the secret that Boffin's degeneration to a miser was merely feigned] . . . was at once the most interesting and the most difficult part of my design. Its difficulty was much enhanced by the mode of publication; for, it would be very unreasonable to expect that many readers, pursuing a story in portions from month to month through nineteen months, will, until they have it before them complete, perceive the relations of its finer threads to the whole pattern which is always before the eyes of the story-weaver at his loom. (821)

The author who is willing to risk such a state will always meet with some doubting insubordination, but will also, heroically, chastise the unbelievers when he reveals the totality of his intention. And Dickens reminds his readers that he not only hazards that mode of publication, but indeed retrieved it from the literary dustheap: "[T]hat I hold the advantages of the mode of publication to outweigh its disadvantages, may be easily believed of one who revived it in the Pickwick Papers after long disuse." Hence, more than being merely the master of his own suspended authorship, Dickens brought that very mode of authorial suspension back to life from its long dormancy. He deserves able "acceptants" who will concede at the outset the artist's capacity to disguise, defer, and yet continuously build a single purpose. The good reader would be very much like the reformed Bella Wilfer at the novel's end, who waits patiently for the revelation of the mystery's solution: "I should dearly like to know, of course . . . but I wait until you can tell me of your own free will. You asked me if I could have perfect faith in you, and I said yes, and I meant it" (758).[39]

The gender division between those who maintain suspended continuity, even when their beings are interrupted, and those who merely receive the benefits of such continuity is too consistent to be accidental. In *Our Mutual Friend*, the power of suspension is given only to men. The commodity corpses, the discarded and suspended bodies, as well as the characters who can be retrieved from apparent death, are male. I would like very briefly, in conclusion, to sketch out an explanation of this fact and link it to the novel's presentation of the author. Although only male bodies go in and out of suspended animation, miming the condition of commodities, both the main plots, as well as several of the subplots, are driven by attempts to save women from becoming commodities. Bella, having escaped the fate of passively "being

---

[39] See Cathy Shuman's "Invigilating *Our Mutual Friend*: Gender and the Legitimation of Professional Authority" (*Novel* 28 [1995]: 154–72) for a more extended discussion of gender and authority in the novel.

made the property of others," must then be saved from offering herself on the marriage market. Lizzie is also vehemently opposed to being a passive item of exchange between her brother and Bradley Headstone and must be rescued from the fate of becoming Eugene's mistress, his "doll," and then presumably passing into the world of the common prostitute. The novel reworks this material in tragic, comic, sentimental, satirical, and farcical modes in many of the minor plots as well. Even Pleasant Riderhood, who is engaged to Mr. Venus, expresses a fear of being confused with one of her fiancé's skeletal commodities. She breaks off the engagement because "she does not wish to regard herself, nor yet to be regarded, in that boney light" (84).

Mr. Venus's solution to this problem, his plan for saving Pleasant from an identification with her body as commodity, is a humorous summary of the novel's operations: he promises to confine himself to the articulation of men. In this novel, then, women seem just naturally prone to commodification; but commodification is also the fate from which they must be rescued by men who preemptively enact the condition of suspended animation, the condition, as we've seen, of the commodity itself. Men are knocked out, drowned, dried out, stored up, and finally reanimated ("There's animation!") so that women need not undergo any such self-alienation. The state of suspended animation is thus exclusively masculine in *Our Mutual Friend* because it is so naturally feminine.

This masculinity that is achieved through the incorporation of the feminine differs from femininity in its ability to survive its apparent death. Only the men are capable of holding "Life in abeyance"; only they have extra bodies at their disposal. Bella and Lizzie have no such out-of-body possibilities, and hence they are debarred from the process of releasing value and being released as value, as pure vital potential, as *potency* itself. *Our Mutual Friend*, therefore, provides an example of how apparent lapses in identity, breaks in the continuity of the self, and moments of self-alienation associated with the marketplace, finally create the effect of an endlessly resilient, and in this case emphatically male, transcendent subject.[40]

Nowhere does this impression of broken, feminized, and hence enhanced male selfhood appear more overwhelmingly than at the end of the novel's postscript, in the author's final impression. The idea of Dickens as a principle of continuity suspended between the apparently discontinuous monthly parts of the novel is reinforced in the concluding anecdote, which tells of a train accident that befell him as he was taking a monthly part of *Our Mutual Friend*

[40] For other accounts of Dickens's desire to overwhelm his readers with his authorial energy, see John Kucich, *Excess and Restraint in the Novels of Charles Dickens* (Athens: University of Georgia Press, 1981), who draws on Bataille to analyze it as a "mechanical dissipation of energy," 221–35; and Andrew H. Miller, *Novels behind Glass: Commodity Culture and Victorian Narrative* (Cambridge: Cambridge University Press, 1995), who links it to the commodification of literature and calls it "a compensation for the increasing routinization of the author's task" (147).

to the printer. I'll close with this final paragraph of the completed works of Charles Dickens:

> On Friday the Ninth of June in the present year, Mr. and Mrs. Boffin (in their manuscript dress of receiving Mr. and Mrs. Lammle at breakfast) were on the South Eastern Railway with me, in a terribly destructive accident. When I had done what I could to help others, I climbed back into my carriage—nearly turned over a viaduct, and caught aslant upon the turn— to extricate the worthy couple. They were much soiled but otherwise unhurt. . . . I remember with devout thankfulness that I can never be much nearer parting company with my readers for ever, than I was then, until there shall be written against my life, the two words with which I have this day closed this book:—THE END. (822)

The author heroically risks his life to deliver his manuscript in this passage and then apparently dies into that commodity, where he remains immortally suspended.

Chapter Five

Daniel Deronda and the Too Much of Literature

When she began her last novel, George Eliot was in a funk. She had never been a truly self-confident novelist; in her private correspondence, she worried throughout her career about not pleasing her readership, about merely pleasing them, about having too little success, about having too much success, about dejection, and about egotistical elation. But the journals and correspondence of the mid-1870s betray an anxiety of authorship unusual even for her. At the apex of her career, after the triumphant reception of *Middlemarch*, she developed a horror of overproduction mixed with a dread of artistic depletion, which led to repeated condemnations of authorial repetition and excessive harping on excess:

> The fact is, I shrink from . . . sinking into an insistent echo of myself. That is a horrible destiny—and one cannot help seeing that many of the most powerful men fall into it.[1]

> • • •

> I have the conviction that excessive literary production is a social offense. (5:185)

> • • •

> I am haunted by the fear that I am only saying again what I have already said in better fashion. . . . Every one who contributes to the "too much" of literature is doing a grave social injury. (5:212)

What did she mean by the "too much" of literature? Not exactly what we would probably mean by it: for us the phrase tends to imply the supplemental nature of the signifier, the doubling of mimesis, the simulacra, imaginary annexes or multiple worlds of fiction—all the ways in which, we've convinced ourselves, literature is not only constitutionally but also proudly de trop. Eliot proceeded from the opposite bias: there should be *just enough* literature, which should be just sufficiently contained in books just adequate to express only the important thoughts of just those authors capable of genuine originality. When those authors repeat themselves, or when others make feebler imitations, Eliot complained, they bury even "the most carefully written books"

---

[1] *The George Eliot Letters*, ed. Gordon S. Haight (New Haven: Yale University Press, 1978), 5:76.

under "a heap of trash" (4:308–10).[2] A responsible author, she insisted, could only protect her achievement by quitting once she'd had her say; especially after *Middlemarch*, the thought threatened to strike her dumb.[3]

And yet, even as she propagandized for reticence, she also admitted that the conditions of literary production make self-repetition, the too-much of literature, almost inevitable. Over the course of a long and successful career, she explained in an unpublished note headed "Authorship," anyone trying to make a living as a writer will practically be forced "to do over again what has already been done, either by himself or others."[4] The odd materiality of the textual product encourages this duplication and reuse; moreover, it creates consumers who seem not to notice that they are buying the same things repeatedly. At first glance, this would seem to be a familiar complaint about the encroachments of marketplace values into the literary domain, but Eliot, in fact, draws the opposite conclusion: if people consumed books the way they consume other things, literature would *not* tend toward excess. The too-much of literature comes not from standard commodification, but from the abnormality of literary exchange. As Eliot explains,

> Here is the first grand difference between the capital which is turned into calico and the brain capital which is turned into literature. The calico scarcely varies in appropriateness of quality, [yet] no consumer is in danger of getting too much of it, and neglecting his boots, hats, and flannel-shirts in consequence. ... [T]he sameness is desirable, and nobody is likely to roll his person in so many folds of calico as to become a mere bale of cotton goods, and nullify his senses of hearing and touch, while his morbid passion for Manchester shirtings makes him still cry "More!" (*Essays*, 439)

[2] This letter to her publisher makes it clear that Eliot also thought the easy availability of cheap literature makes it more likely to be read than works of a higher caliber: "I suppose the reason my 6s editions are never on the railway stalls is partly of the same kind that hinders the free distribution of Felix [*Felix Holt*]. They are not so attractive to the majority as 'The Trail of *the* Serpent'; still a minority might sometimes buy them if they were there" (4:309–10). Nevertheless, she mainly feared repetition (not a marked decline in quality) in her own career.

[3] Rosemarie Bodenheimer has astutely explained these expressions of anxiety as functions of George Eliot's need to place herself above the literary marketplace by distinguishing between mere personal or financial ambition and true creative genius. The explanation is persuasive, and yet it does not quite account for Eliot's claim that the literary marketplace differs significantly from other areas of commerce. See *The Real Life of Mary Ann Evans: George Eliot, Her Letters and Fiction* (Ithaca, N.Y.: Cornell University Press, 1994), 174. For another discussion of her attitude toward the reception of her work, her fear of her audience, and her views on the marketplace in literature, see Alexander Welsh, *George Eliot and Blackmail* (Cambridge: Harvard University Press, 1985), 113–31. For a discussion of political economy and *Daniel Deronda*, see Jeff Nunokawa, *The Afterlife of Property: Domestic Security and the Victorian Novel* (Princeton: Princeton University Press, 1994), 77–99; and for a discussion of George Eliot and classical political economy, see Imraan Coovadia, "George Eliot's Realism and Adam Smith," *Studies in English Literature* 42 (2002): 819–35.

[4] "Authorship," in "Leaves from a Notebook," *Essays of George Eliot*, ed. Thomas Pinney (New York: Columbia University Press, 1963), 441.

But the buyers of literary commodities engage in such perverse behavior routinely, consuming the books of established authors even when they are already fully glutted by similar works from the same hand. In the literary marketplace, the laws of supply and demand simply do not work to prevent overproduction; it is a deviant market George Eliot imagines, in which readers (if we follow her metaphor) lose their senses rolling about in excess words.

Moreover, beneath that fear of rendering her consumers insensible through overproduction, there lurked another fantasy featuring readers who were yet more perverse than the mere overconsumers. This class of readers, Eliot imagines, are sensible of the repetitiousness of the literature they purchase, and they even discern degradations in the quality of the product, and yet they continue to buy it out of what Eliot calls "a habit of consumption," which overrides the healthy and normal tendency of consumers to reject inferior goods. The truly awful thing about these readers is that they [in Eliot's words] "complain, but pay, and *read while they complain*" (*Essays*, 440). What could be worse than readers who buy you without wanting you and disparage you while they consume you? In the literary market producers are all but destined to be purchased without desire and consumed without pleasure, and that disposition of indifference or negativity in the public, George Eliot tells us, will slowly degrade "the social vitality" (*Essays*, 438).

With this deranged commerce in mind, it is little wonder that she was having a hard time motivating herself to write her last novel, and yet that novel can be said to be motivated by just these concerns. How, you might ask, can I claim that George Eliot feared overproduction and that *Daniel Deronda* was the result? It certainly appears counterintuitive, since *Daniel Deronda* has famously seemed to be "too much" for most readers since its first publication. My task, then, is to explain how the fear of overwriting became an overwritten novel, and the first step in accomplishing it will be to tell you how Eliot's private anxieties about motivation intersected with contemporary economic and psychological thought on the subject. That is, I want to outline the models of motivation—and of its possible distortions—that shaped both the fears and the novel. I'll begin by explaining how a new trend in somaeconomics paralleled Eliot's authorial anxiety, summarizing as well the psychophysiological groundwork of that trend. I'll then go on to explain how the contemporary models of motivation underlying the somaeconomics of emergent marginal utility theory also provided the novel's framework, its thematic focus, and its ultimate formal surplus.

. . .

I'll try to summarize the parallels between George Eliot's concerns and those of contemporary economic innovators under four main points. First, the novelist's musings on motivation owed a great deal to the physiologist Alexander

Bain's claim that the desires normally motivating us arise from and follow certain rules of sensation. Maintaining that three functions of the central nervous system—sensation (that is, both physical and emotional feelings), intellection, and will—are brought into play in all motivation, Bain also claimed that sensation usually takes the lead. However, the motivating power of any feeling depends on our consciousness of it, and our consciousness depends on the feelings preceding it. This Bain called the "Law of Relativity": we become conscious of any sensation insofar as it *differs* from the sensation that preceded it; in Bain's own formulation, "Change of impression is necessary to our being conscious."[5] "The feeling of warmth" he illustrates, "is not an absolute, independent, or self-sustaining condition of mind, but the result of a transition from cold" (45). If we can experience pleasure only as an increase in pleasure (or pain only as an increase in pain), it follows, according to Bain, that only actual or anticipated *differential* changes in sensation can engage volition.

Second, although Bain credited the idea to a long line of earlier materialist thinkers, the law of relativity of sensation was certainly carried in new directions in the 1870s, especially by William Stanley Jevons, whose marginal utility theory recalls George Eliot's concerns about writing too much. Jevons drew on Bain and on an earlier political economist, Richard Jennings, who had also used Bain's law of relativity to explore the decay of desire. The marginal utilitarians noted that increments of a commodity are not equally valuable: the first bite of a loaf of bread has more value to a hungry person than the last bite has to the satisfied eater, just as small increments of money are always more valuable to poor people than they are to rich people. Like George Eliot, they insisted that the consumer's degree of satiety would (or should) determine his willingness to consume more and hence also would (or should) determine the producer's willingness to provide more.

Third, like George Eliot in 1874, the marginal utilitarians were interested in the *last* increments of a commodity that might be consumed. If the value of each piece is determined by the amount of it one has already consumed, and the pleasure in successive additions is found to taper off, when does the pleasure of having another piece become nugatory? That would be, in Jevons's durable phrase, the margin of utility, the moment when desire for the bread and desire for keeping its money equivalent or spending it on something else become almost equal. The overall pleasurable effect of a commodity (which,

---

[5] Alexander Bain, *Mind and Body: The Theories of the Relation* (New York: D. Appleton and Co., 1873), 45. For a discussion of Bain and Victorian ideas of relativity (with some references to Jevons), see Christopher Herbert, *Victorian Relativity: Radical Thought and Scientific Discovery* (Chicago: University of Chicago Press, 2001), 40–50. For other discussions of *Daniel Deronda* and psychophysiology, see Sally Shuttleworth, *George Eliot and Nineteenth-Century Science: The Make-Believe of a Beginning* (New York: Cambridge University Press, 1984), 188–95; and William Myers, *The Teaching of George Eliot* (Totowa, N.J.: Barnes and Noble, 1984), 5–8, 169–82.

once again, can only be felt as an *addition* to sensation) he called its "total utility": "Utility must be considered as measured by, or even as actually identical with the addition made to a person's happiness,"[6] and what he called the "final degree of utility" is "the last addition, or the next possible addition of a very small, or infinitely small, quantity to the existing stock" (110). Jevons formulated his general law as an inverse proportion between value and quantity—"the degree of utility varies with the quantity of commodity, and ultimately decreases as that quantity increases" (11), and he charted the inverse relation between quantity and pleasure as a curve, for there is no abrupt transition from want to surfeit: "[degrees of satisfaction] do not advance equally with each instalment of the commodity offered to the senses, and then suddenly stop; but diminish gradually, until they ultimately disappear, and further instalments can produce no further satisfaction" (114). In the normal course of things, the consumer, who always tries to maximize his pleasure by distributing "his resources as to render the final increments of each pleasure-giving commodity of equal utility for him" (Intro., 61), tries to avoid getting stuck with too much of anything.

Fourth, both Eliot and the marginal utility theorists were impressed by Alexander Bain's "rule of Novelty," a variation on the law of relativity which stressed that the first experience of any sensation will be the most keenly felt. To be sure, sensations can be refreshed in order to "maintain a state of pleasurable sensibility," and yet "[t]here is a certain amount of decay in the force of every impression, on the after-occasions when it is revived" (51), so that the same stimulus over time will lose its motivating force. Hence, the constant innovations of the marketplace that the "rule of Novelty" predicts: consumers instinctively seek the greatest "degree of transition" (to use Bain's phrase) in positive feelings and they find that intensity most readily in unfamiliar sensations. The rule of novelty explains how consumer economies avoid gluts and continue to grow: as the desire for one commodity naturally decays over time, the desire for another develops out of the constant motivation to add pleasure, for only by *adding* (again, according to the rule of relativity) can pleasure be maintained.

Bain repeatedly illustrated his rule of relativity and concomitant rule of novelty with aesthetic examples,[7] and George Eliot applied them with particular thoroughness at every level of *Daniel Deronda*, from the character systems I'll be analyzing in this chapter to the novel's many commentaries on the relativity of pain and pleasure in individual lives. Steep "degrees of transition" in the plot are generally accompanied by reminders of the rules. Thus we are

---

[6] W. Stanley Jevons, *The Theory of Political Economy* (Baltimore: Penguin, 1970), 160. Subsequent page numbers will be given in the text.

[7] "The principle of Relativity appears in all the Fine Arts under the name of Contrast" (*Mind and Body*, 46).

told that Mirah's previously troubled life makes a modestly quiet situation seem like heaven, whereas Gwendolen's preeminence in her small world makes any disappointment unbearable, and Daniel's pain at meeting his mother is caused by his expectation of maternal affection. And characters' reactions to each other are often in explicit conformity to these psychophysiological phenomena: "[Deronda's] voice, heard now for the first time, was to Grandcourt's toneless drawl, which had been in her ears every day, as the deep notes of a violoncello to the broken discourse of poultry and other lazy gentry in the afternoon sunshine."[8] George Eliot not only uses contrast (according to Bain, the manifestation of the rule of relativity in art) in passages like this, but also reflects on its aesthetic effect; Daniel's voice is strikingly musical to Gwendolen because she has been listening to Grandcourt's unvaried monotone. The constant sound of Daniel's voice would sink into neutrality. To take just one more instance, which highlights the sinister side of the manipulation of Bain's rule of novelty, Grandcourt, the tired epicurean, consciously seeks the most sensational degree of transition between states: "'Then I am not to ask for one kiss,' said Grandcourt, contented to pay a large price for this new kind of love-making, which introduced marriage by the finest contrast" (373).

Having given this schematic account of the parallels between George Eliot's concerns and techniques and the marginal utilitarians' premises, I want to explore briefly the genealogy of the latter. As their leading terms—"sensation," "pleasure," "pain," "happiness," "utility"—indicate, the marginal utility theorists revived Benthamite somaeconomics: a point I want to stress because historians have often been so intent on describing the marginalists' break with previous British economic thought that they have obscured the underlying continuities. In the next few pages, before returning to *Daniel Deronda*, I want to emphasize the physiological component of marginal utility theory both in order to establish its links with George Eliot's intellectual world and in order to complete the narrative of nineteenth-century somaeconomics, which culminated in marginal utility theory.

The publication in 1871 of Jevons's *The Theory of Political Economy*, the earliest full articulation of marginal utility theory, has often been said to have spelled the end of the "classical" phase of political economy and the beginning of its "neoclassical" phase.[9] Jevons inaugurated "the marginal revolution" by

[8] George Eliot, *Daniel Deronda*, ed. Barbara Hardy (New York: Penguin, 1995), 376. All quotations from the novel are from this edition, and page numbers are given in the text.

[9] Many histories deal with the shift in perspective created by this theory. I have relied especially on the following: R. D. Collison Black, "Introduction," *The Theory of Political Economy*, by W. Stanley Jevons (Baltimore: Penguin, 1970), 7–40; Mark Blaug, *Economic Theory in Retrospect* (New York: Cambridge University Press, 1997); and *Great Economists before Keynes* (Cambridge: Cambridge University Press, 1986); H. W. Spiegel, *The Growth of Economic Thought* (Durham, N.C.: Duke University Press, 1983). One literary historian who has dealt with this transition has judged Jevons quite harshly, accusing him of making economics inaccessible to most laypeople and of replacing its previous con-

denying Ricardo's claim that labor is the source of value and making the counterargument that value arises instead from the interactions of consumers trying to maximize their satisfaction and producers trying to maximize their profits. Prices—values—express these aggregated individual choices and tend toward equilibrium. In addition to redefining value, marginal utility theory also shifted the focus of the discipline from macroanalysis (analysis of such issues as the fund for the support of labor that we looked at in the last chapter) to microanalysis, or the treatment of individual variables; and it helped professionalize the discipline of economics by developing mathematical equations of exchange, which required an understanding of calculus, to model the operations of equilibrium.

In other ways, though, marginal utility theory continued to develop certain habits of thought that had been common in the classical phase, especially the somaeconomic tendencies. Indeed, Jevons and his precursor Richard Jennings (who published *Natural Elements of Political Economy* in 1855) explicated and strengthened the role of Jeremy Bentham's pain/pleasure calculus in economic thought.[10] I last visited that concept in chapter 3, when discussing the issue of happiness in Dickens's *Hard Times*, and I pointed out that political economists in the 1830s, 1840s, and 1850s often seemed unwilling to defend the greatest-happiness principle as an axiom, although they continued to assume that economic behavior tried to maximize pleasure and minimize pain, generally playing off the pains of labor against the pleasures of consumption. Jennings and Jevons raised that assumption into an explicit maxim: physiological stimuli as registered in the sensorium were asserted to be the primary motivators of economic activity.

Jennings, from whom Jevons took several key concepts, was determined to investigate the minutia of sensation in economic behavior. As he explained, when political economists looked only at the evidence of "external material Wealth," they were studying phenomena too "remote from the seat of our

cern with social production for a concern with mere individual consumption. See Regenia Gagnier, *The Insatiability of Human Wants: Economics and Aesthetics in Market Society* (Chicago: University of Chicago Press, 2000), 40–53. As the following argument will demonstrate, I disagree with this assessment.

[10] On the nature of Jevons's utilitarianism and his relation to others in that tradition, see John Bonner, *Economic Efficiency and Social Justice: The Development of Utilitarian Ideas in Economics from Bentham to Edgeworth* (Brookfield, Vt.: Edward Elgar, 1995); Robert B. Ekelund, Jr., and Yeugn-Nan Shieh, "Jevons on Utility, Exchange, and Demand Theory: A Reassessment," *The Manchester School* 57 (1989), 17–23; Sandra J. Peart, "Jevons's Applications of Utilitarian Theory to Economic Policy," *Utilitas* 2 (1990), 281–306. On the relation between his utilitarianism and his mathematical ambitions for economics, see Margaret Schabas, "The 'Worldly Philosophy' of William Stanley Jevons," *Victorian Studies* (Autumn 1984), 129–47; and for a discussion of other aspects of his moral thought and his humanism, see Bruce Mazlish, "Jevons' Science and His 'Second Nature,'" *Journal of the History of the Behavioral Sciences* 22 (1986): 140–49. See also Ross M. Robertson, "Jevons and His Precursors," *Econometrica* 19 (1951), 229–49.

ideas" to give reliable information about economic motivation, and if they tried to study the ideas themselves, they would be equally daunted by the "impalpability" of the phenomena. Jennings sought something between external material and strictly mental data: to understand economic behavior, he claimed, one must study "the intermediate field betwixt mind and external matter which is offered by the organization of the human body, as exhibited by the researches of anatomy and of physiology."[11] He then redefined the most important concepts of political economy in terms of the nervous system. "Consumption," for example, becomes "[t]hat action and reaction of matter and man, by which matter supplies the means of gratification to man, while man diminishes or annihilates the valuable properties of matter. . . . [D]uring its continuance, the operation of the *afferent* [conducting impulses to the central nervous system] trunks of nerve-fibre prevails" (73). And "[p]roduction" is "[t]hat action and reaction of man and matter, by which valuable properties are imparted to matter, whilst reflex impressions of resistence are felt and sustained by man . . . denoted, physiologically, by the fact that, during its continuance, the operation of the *efferent* [conducting impulses from the central nervous system] trunks of nerve-fibre prevails" (73). The difference between mental and physical labor was given an equally precise physiological location: in mental labor "the actions performed originate in the brain," whereas in physical labor, the actions "originate in the spinal column" (74). And commodities are divided into "primary commodities," which affect "common sensation," and "secondary commodities," which affect "special sensation" through the "nerves of the organs of the five senses" (88).

Jevons did not use Jennings's elaborate physiological language, but he took the earlier writer's premises about sensation and economics to serve as the basis of his own *Theory of Political Economy,* and he imported wholesale Jennings's main contention that value changes depending on the amount of the commodity already consumed. Jennings had made it clear that the insight came from his methodological insistence on sensation:

> If it be borne in mind that the feeling to which we are here adverting is *sensation*—the first effect of matter on mind, not the complex conception of Value, and still less the ideas of unpriced dignity and power usually associated with the idea of large possessions—it will be quite evident how different are the effects produced on the senses by different quantities of a Commodity. These effects require to be closely observed, because they are the foundation of the changes of money price, which valuable objects command in times of varied scarcity and abundance; we shall therefore here direct our attention to them for the purpose of ascertaining the nature of the law ac-

---

[11] Richard Jennings, *Natural Elements of Political Economy* (London: Longman, Brown, Green, and Longmans, 1855), 27. Subsequent page numbers given in the text.

cording to which the sensations that attend on Consumption vary in degree with changes in the quantity of the Commodity consumed. (97)

This underscoring of bodily sensation followed, as I've already mentioned, from a new psychophysiology, which in the 1840s began to supplant the vaguer associationist accounts of the mind-body connection. Associationism had, of course, dominated British psychology since Locke, and it was assumed by the somaeconomic tradition we've been exploring. Psychophysiologists added a close-up of the mechanics of the nervous substance, which helped shift the focus of economic thought further into the sensorium as a physiological space.[12] Jennings quoted W. B. Carpenter (*Principles of Human Physiology*, 1853), who had used Bain's ideas prior to Bain's own publication of them; Jevons quoted directly from Bain. For his part, Bain illustrated his theories with utilitarian economic examples:

> The blessings of leisure, retirement, and rest, are pleasant only by contrast to previous toil and excitement. The incessant demand for novelty and change, for constant advances in wealth . . . attest the existence and the power of the law of Relativity in all the provisions for enjoyment. It is a law that greatly neutralizes one part of the advantages of superior fortune, the sense of the superiority itself; but leaves another part untouched, namely the range, variety, and alternation of pleasures. (46)

The centrality of this line of thinking to the marginal revolution can hardly be exaggerated. Like Jennings, Jevons declined to speculate on individual mental phenomena (ideas), but looked instead to sensation as the key to economic action. Political economy, he insisted, can be put on the right track by returning to Bentham's sensationalist wisdom as modified by recent physiology; he praised both the substance and the quasi-mathematical method of the felicific calculus. But even as he insisted that "it is the amount of these feelings which is continually prompting us to buying and selling, borrowing and lending, labouring and resting, producing and consuming," he also noted the difficulty of measuring changes of increases in pleasure and pain. His solution (foreshadowed in the passage above from Jennings) was to study "the quantitative effects of the feelings" in order to "estimate their comparative amounts" (83), and he considered the most available "quantitative effects" to be market

[12] On psychophysiology, see Edwin G. Boring, *A History of Experimental Psychology* (New York: Appleton-Century-Crofts, 1957), 211–45; K. Danzinger, "Mid-Nineteenth-Century British Psycho-Physiology: A Neglected Chapter in the History of Psychology," in *The Problematic Science: Psychology in Nineteenth-Century Thought*, eds. W. R. Woodward and M. G. Ash (New York: Praeger, 1982), 119–46; and L. J. Daston, "British Responses to Psycho-Physiology, 1860–1900," *Isis* 69 (247): 192–208. On the connections between psychophysiology and marginal utility theory, see Michael V. White, "The Moment of Richard Jennings: The Production of Jevons's Marginalist Economic Agent," in *Natural Images in Economic Thought*, ed. Philip Mirowski (New York: Cambridge University Press, 1994), 197–230.

prices. He believed prices were the objective data recording psychophysiological phenomena, and hence his mathematical program extrapolated from somaeconomics even as it radically revised the earlier tradition.

Jevons, moreover, was eager to stress his filiation with Jeremy Bentham as the founder of that tradition. While acknowledging Jennings as his most immediate forerunner and Alexander Bain as the expert on the underlying physiology of sensation, Jevons was careful to trace this line of thought back to Bentham's contention that pleasures and pains differ according to their intensity and duration. Hence, Jevons's denial that value is stable and intrinsic to commodities, and that its source was simply the amount of labor expended, was not a retreat from physiological universals to subjectivist consumerism but an incorporation of a different set of biological facts.[13] Moreover, labor was an important part of his theory, and he did not hesitate to call Adam Smith's famous formulation—"The real price of everything . . . is the toil and trouble of obtaining it"—substantially, but not entirely, true. In keeping with his explicit Benthamite sensationalism, he is more adamant than many of his classical predecessors in flatly declaring labor to be pain, or disutility: "Labour is the painful exertion which we undergo to ward off pains of greater amount, or to procure pleasures which leave a balance in our favour" (188). So the older somaeconomics of the Ricardian school persists to some extent in marginal utility theory, but the idea that a commodity carries the value of the pain (or spent life) poured into it by the producer is contravened, for value is not sedimented in objects but is negotiated in the marketplace. To be sure, the body that receives the most attention in Jevons's *Theory* is that of the consumer, but the "disutility" of labor is by no means absent from his calculations. Just as consumers try to avoid getting stuck with a surfeit of anything, producers also reckon what loss of money would be preferable to continued "painful exertions."

Moreover, Jennings and Jevons encountered some of the same contradictions in utilitarianism that had driven previous political economists to deemphasize it. For example, their hedonics forced them to ask why very rich people, who already have more than they can possibly consume, continue to accumulate. Alexander Bain had noticed the problem glancingly when, after arguing that we are sensible only of changes in the amount of pleasure or pain we experience and cannot sustain the pleasurable sensation "as the memory of the previous condition fades away" (46), he remarks that this "Law of Relativity" "greatly neutralizes one part of the advantages of superior fortune, the sense of superiority itself" (46). In other words, when one gets used to riches they become merely the neutral ground of existence, and hence it might be expected that the desire to amass more of the same would abate.

---

[13] For the view of Jevons as a subjectivist, see Gagnier. My view is that the labor theory of value relies as much on "subjective" sensation as does marginal utility theory.

The motivation of the wealthy is difficult to explain in purely Benthamite terms once the law of relativity is in place, and since marginal utilitarians emphasized their Benthamism and their relativism, they were under a peculiar necessity to reconcile the two. Jennings began by admitting that "they who possess the largest share of Wealth often exhibit the greatest disregard for pleasurable sensations" (189); precisely because they have had too much, insensibility has set in. Jennings is here adverting not only to wealthy consumers but also to the theoretical problem of explaining the behavior of capitalists themselves, who must (as we've seen in previous chapters) learn to prefer stockpiling the means of enjoyment to indulging in further pleasures. Although Benthamism implies that sensation is the key to our actions, in fact societies only become rich because numerous people amass much more wealth than they intend to enjoy, supplying "Labour with Capital," and enriching "successive generations with the accumulated production of bygone Industry" (192). Jennings reconciles the surplus that makes capitalism possible with the adage that we seek to avoid having too much of anything by exempting value in the abstract (as represented by money, for example) from the category of things one could have too much of, and by invoking what he called one "of the strangest anomalies of human character": "a transference of affection from Sensations [enjoyment] or Ideas to their *material causes* [means of enjoyment] takes place, and in consequence of this transference, a desire to attain the former ceases to be, and a desire to attain the latter becomes an efficient motive of conduct" (191). Jevons took the tautological route out of this difficulty by asserting that we are always motivated by the prospect of maximizing pleasure, and hence anything we seek ipso facto should be called pleasurable. Jennings, though, speculated that the wealthiest have undergone a transformation of the usual pain/pleasure perceptions, and in their minds, "the objects that were originally valued, only because they afforded pleasure, have ultimately been valued for themselves, independently of, or *in opposition to, pleasure*" (emphasis added, 191).

The somaeconomics of marginal utility theory, therefore, differed in important ways from its labor-centered predecessor, but in other ways it extended similar lines of thought. Most importantly for the purposes of this chapter, it shifted the physiological basis of value and turned theoretical attention toward the decrease of pleasure that accompanies satiety, building its system up from that crucial insight, and it put further pressure on the already problematic question of what motivates people when increased pleasurable sensation is not a reasonable prospect. During the same years that Jevons was spreading his ideas about the effect of surfeit on value, George Eliot, we've seen, was worrying about the sheer "too-much" of literature and maintaining that each addition to the pile of books was somehow less valuable than the previous addition. She probably had not read Jevons by the mid-1870s, although it is highly likely that she knew about him; friends of hers had reviewed his *Theory,* often negatively, but they did not severely criticize the concepts I've been describing. Indeed, they tended to think that those ideas were the common property of the age, even if they were not sure how to incorporate them into economic thought. Unlike Dickens's, George Eliot's intellectual milieu was friendly to political economy; she herself read widely in the subject and was knowledgeable about its central debates. In her career, we can see the waning of that overt enmity between literary culture and political economy that had characterized the first half of the century. She began publishing in an intellectual London very different from the one that had shaped Dickens's mind in the 1830s; her milieu was permeated by radical scepticism, "developmentalism," and materialist positivisim. Political economy seemed a normal and worthy endeavor among her acquaintances, and every well-informed person was expected to have a knowledge of its latest episodes.

So even if George Eliot never read Jevons, the similarities between his theories of the role of surfeit in economic value and her theories of the decline of aesthetic value through repetition should not surprise us, for they were conceived in overlapping intellectual circles. In particular, they might be thought of as parallel modes of receiving the psychophysiological innovations of Alexander Bain. Indeed, while she was writing *Daniel Deronda*, in another room of their house George Henry Lewes was occupied by his last work, *The Physiological Basis of Mind*, which drew heavily on Bain's models of sensation, will, and intellect. Always interested in physiology and psychology, therefore, George Eliot, in the mid-1870s, was unusually close to the same developments in those disciplines that also inspired Jevons. The novelist, however, used those concepts in ways that often problematize the marginal utilitarians' conclusions. George Eliot and Jevons assembled the same elements, and may even have posited the same normal dynamics among them, but the novelist is far more interested than the political economist in the forces that operate against the norm. If Jevons wanted to tautologize away the question of why people continue to accumulate once they have crossed the margins of pleasure, Eliot wanted to explore that very question. She readily took up Alexander Bain's numerous excursions into those realms of psychophysiology that lead beyond "the ordinary action of the will," which is "to gain our own pleasures and remove our own pains" (350). "This," Bain persists, "is all that can, strictly speaking, interest us. Each organization is more or less formed to work for conserving itself; and it would seem, at first sight, an irrelevance to go beyond this."[14] And yet Bain and George Eliot try to explain what lies beyond "first sight," whereas Jevons modestly attempted to limit his inquiry to what he called the "lowest" forms of motivation: "Motives and feelings are certainly of the same kind to the extent that we are able to weight them against each other; but they are, nevertheless, almost incomparable in power and authority."

[14] Alexander Bain, *The Senses and the Intellect* (London: Longman, 1864), 350.

... It is the lowest rank of feelings which we here treat" (93). The distance between the parallel tracks of Jevons and Eliot, however, was not always very great. As we have seen and will continue to see, the novelist's insights into these issues seem to have been gained from brooding not only on aesthetic value but also on artistic *marketplaces.* And, as we have seen, the marginal utilitarians found it difficult to explain the actual workings of the psychophysiology of capitalism while adhering to a simple calculus of utility; they were therefore themselves led to speculate on the murkier byways of human motivation.

· · ·

When we look specifically at *Daniel Deronda* within this conceptual framework, we can see both why Eliot feared to write that final increment and why she wrote the sort of novel she did. On the one hand, she dreaded giving her readers just one more George Eliot novel—the too much of self-repetition; on the other hand, she knew that all sensation is *additional* sensation, so she was obliged to give more of something and consequently (just as the law of novelty would predict) turned her efforts toward the representation of realms of experience beyond those she had previously explored. In the view of many critics, this straining beyond produced an outré novel, but that does not negate the strong possibility that George Eliot *thought* she was counteracting the effect of satiety in her readers.

As her persona in one of the *Theophrastus Such* essays (titled "The Too-Ready Writer") explains, even great artists become wearying: "I begin with a liking for an estimable master," declares Theophrastus, "but by the time he has stretched his interpretation of the world unbrokenly along a palatial gallery, I have had what the cautious Scotch mind would call 'enough' of him."[15] The picture-gallery metaphor recalls the "[t]wo rows of [Hugues le Malingre's] descendants," who "looked down in the gallery over the cloisters on the nephew Daniel [Deronda] as he walked there" (204). The narrator tells us that "in the nephew Daniel Deronda the family faces of various types, seen on the walls of the gallery, found no reflex" (205), and although Daniel may take such dissimilarity to be a sign that he is no legitimate member of the family, the reader should take it as a promise that his story will be something new, that it will not be merely another installment of the same old thing, the English novel of marriage and inheritance of which we already have "enough." That kind of novel will, to be sure, find a species of "final increment" in the plot of Sir Hugo Mallinger's real nephew, whose portrait (the syntax is unclear) may already hang in the gallery: "Happily the appropriate nose of the family [the narrator continues] reappeared in his younger brother, and was to

<hr />

[15] *Impressions of Theophrastus Such*, ed. Nancy Henry (Iowa City: University of Iowa Press, 1994), 112. First published in 1879.

be seen in all its refined regularity in his nephew Mallinger Grandcourt" (205). Mallinger Grandcourt is the final installment of some old story; Daniel Deronda the promise of the new.

And yet George Eliot seems not thereby to have dispelled the menacing fantasy of that dreadful reader who pays and complains. If the invention of Daniel partially solved (in her mind) the problem of motivation, judging by the novel itself, worries about the oddities of the literary marketplace persisted. And just as Dickens, in his last completed novel, had identified his authorial state with the suspended animation of the commodity, Eliot wrote her fears of being an undesirable but nevertheless bought commodity into the plot of *Daniel Deronda*. The difference between these two authorial allegories is instructive. Dickens, I argued in the last chapter, puts his men in suspended animation to enact and thereby ward off female commodification; the distinctiveness of this maneuver lies not only in the substitution of genders that allows for heroic self-exchange but also in the figuration of the state of mind and body thus achieved. Suspended animation—placing life and identity in abeyance, indeed, outside of the body—is the novel's way of imagining the release of value in exchange. George Eliot's equally bizarre figuration is in a completely different register. Far from imagining the shelved "life"of the commodity to be a state of passive suspension, in which consciousness is either blank or remote from active life, *Daniel Deronda* depicts agonies of exchange, states of intense subjective suffering. I'm not referring here simply to the obvious humiliations of self-sale: for example, Gwendolen's mortification that Grandcourt's check for £500 arrives with the engagement ring, that she knows she is marrying for money, that she does not love her husband and he knows it—in short, all of the obvious ways in which "Harleth" rhymes with "harlot." I'm referring as well to the fact that Eliot repeatedly creates scenarios in which a "consumer," for example Grandcourt, has no real appetite for what he purchases. Such a husband, who will "complain, but pay," bears an obvious resemblance to the reader with "a habit of consumption" but no enjoyment of what he reads. Gwendolen, like an author who cannot stop publishing even though she does not think anyone really wants her next book, must appeal to a reflex in her audience even as her self-commodification becomes decreasingly successful, hopeful, or comprehensible, and increasingly faltering, desperate, and incoherent. The suspensions of life, conversions from animate to inanimate matter, and transfers of energy characterizing *Our Mutual Friend*'s bioeconomics conformed to the productivist orthodoxies of classical political economy; labor remained the primary source of value, placed in commodities through the expenditure of life, and even though value as abstraction must float free of embodiment, realizing the potential value of a commodity is often figured as reanimation. In contrast, the drama of exchange in *Daniel Deronda* resembles marginal utility theory's radical departures from the classical school, departures that denied the labor theory of value and emphasized instead the choices of individuals in the market, the determinations of demand, and the way value varies according to the decrease of desire as the commodity is consumed.

Gwendolen's, moreover, is not the only plot organized around the agony of being "too much," for questions about motivation—especially about how an excess of something kills desire—are refracted at every level of the novel. Think, to take an obvious contrast, of *Middlemarch*, another novel consisting of two main plots, which remain quite separate, one organized around a young man's vocation and the other around a young woman's marriage choice. In both novels, the relation between the male and female protagonists, destined not to marry, is the main juncture of the two plots and forms their metonymic bridge, while the metaphoric relation between the pair (their characterization as variations on a single motif) carries the thematic unity of the novel. The structural similarity between *Middlemarch* and *Daniel Deronda* makes the thematic contrast obvious: whereas its predecessor featured the chastening of youthful ambition, the latter stresses the overcoming of aimlessness.

Daniel Deronda's central character system is insistently organized around the problem of impaired motivation. I want to explain not only how that "character system" keeps the problem of motivation before our minds, but also how it embodies the psychophysiologists' schemata of motivation. Moreover, it is primarily through this character system that Eliot's worries stay alive, for its three cases of impaired motivation continually refer to the economics of art. I also want to suggest, though, that by the time of its reception she had convinced herself that this novel, far from being simply another novel, was the beginning of a national epic.

The three figures in the novel's central conjunction are arranged around a single malady: an inability to feel strong desires or to act on them. Their lack of motivation, and the consequent possibility that their narratives might falter altogether or at least fail to rise to the level of novelistic plot, create uncertainty about the novel's sources of propulsion. For example, Henleigh Grandcourt is characterized as a man who has so exhausted his small funds of feeling that he has no "motive" even for acts of violence or cruelty. Through enervation he has become a "chancy personage," causing, in himself as well as those around him, "an uncertainty about what he may do next" (364). Gwendolen at first has no difficulty desiring pleasures, but she is too capricious to pursue them consistently. An incapacity of the will, in each phase of her career, prevents the translation of specific desires into purposeful actions; at first she has a tendency to act impulsively against her own intentions and later is overcome with "numbness"—a word repeated often to describe the main characters. Deronda practically requires a summons from God to awaken him from his own "meditative numbness," in which he glides [we are told] "farther and farther from that life of practical energetic sentiment which he would have proclaimed (if he had been inclined to proclaim anything) to be the best of all life, and for himself the only life worth living" (414). If Grandcourt and Gwendolyn suffer, respectively, from disconnections between willing and feeling, Deronda is incapacitated (the narrator explicitly tells us) by hypertrophy of the intellect: "He wanted a way of keeping emotion and its progeny of sentiments . . . substantial and strong in the face of a reflectiveness that threatened to nullify all differences. To pound the objects of sentiment into small dust, yet keep sentiment alive and active, was something like the famous recipe for making cannon—to first take a round hole and then enclose it with iron; whatever you do keeping fast hold of your round hole" (414).[16]

This unmotivated, benumbed trio hardly promises a meaningful and eventful plot; at best, as the similes used to describe Grandcourt and Deronda indicate, we can expect violent explosions to arise from emptiness. The characters are imaged as a set of psychological cases; they present permutations on the condition of impaired motivation arising from the predominance—the excess—of a single mental function in each character. As numerous critics have noticed, this is the Eliot novel most interested in abnormality, but its deviances are hardly random. They are tightly structured around Alexander Bain's outline of the basic elements of human consciousness: "Sensation" or emotion, "Volition" or will, and "Intellect" or thought.[17] In normal human motivation, the three functions are aligned: Feeling, according to Bain, informs us of our interests by connecting pleasurable sensation "with an increase in Vital Power, Pain with the diminution of Vital Power";[18] this stimulates Volition, which "starts forth at any time when pleasure is to be secured, or pain to be banished" (77); and Thought overlays this "groundwork of Volition" with a large superstructure of "acquired connexions between feelings and specific movements" (79) and allows for the operation of the will in the absence of immediate sensations and in pursuit of remote goals, as well as for the correction of faulty associations.

That's the way motivation is supposed to work; but Bain also paid considerable attention to abnormalities of each of these major divisions of the nervous substance, abnormalities in which one function is hyperactive and overwhelms the others. The deviances can be easily mapped onto our trio: Gwendolen is frequently overpowered by emotions that find a vent in precipitous, incoherent actions or altogether paralyze her; Grandcourt has an autonomous and arbitrary will that exercises itself in the absence of both feelings and thought; and Deronda's relentless intellection attenuates his emotions and neutralizes

[16] Neil Herz also notes and analyzes the "numbness" of this trio in *George Eliot's Pulse* (Stanford: Stanford University Press, 2003), 128–37.

[17] Myers sees a different pattern in the Grandcourt-Gwendolen-Deronda triangle; he relates it to Auguste Comte's concept of Submission. Myers, *The Teaching of George Eliot*, 181–82. Shuttleworth concentrates on the ways in which Gwendolen illustrates certain ideas of the unconscious in the works of George Henry Lewes. Shuttleworth, *George Eliot and Nineteenth-Century Science*, 192–97.

[18] *Mind and Body: The Theories of Their Relation* (New York: D. Appleton and Co., 1873), 78.

his will. In splitting the functions and isolating them in different characters, we should further note, Eliot was also following one of the offshoots of Bain's rule of relativity: that all sensation and hence all knowledge originates in contrast: "[I]n every kind of knowledge there should be a real negative to every real notion or real proposition. . . . [I]n short, knowledge is never single but always double or two-sided, though the two sides are not always both stated" (42). To know human motivation, one must parse it and oppose the elements; in Eliot's often-noted habit of contrast, therefore, characters will always have exaggerated traits in relation to each other.[19] In this regard, Bain explained, science and art are based on the same "principle of Relativity," which "appears in all the Fine Arts under the name of Contrast" (46). In her earlier novels, though, Eliot was able to develop the same sorts of "typological" contrasts without straying into the territory of actual perversion: think, again, of *Middlemarch*, in which Lydgate, Dorothea, and Ladislaw obviously represent various modes of dissociated sensibility, due to the almost exclusive exercise of, respectively, scientific, ethical, and aesthetic habits of mind. The isolation and hypertrophy of the psychophysiological functions in *Daniel Deronda*, though, unavoidable as it seems to their very representation, lead into those excesses of abnormal function where motivation stalls and characters become unlikely to initiate any action.

I will take up the novel's invitation to look at each character as a case study while simultaneously analyzing their systematic configuration, the combined psychological and economic dynamics that hold the structure in place. Moreover, I will display the consistent figuration of these cases as perversions and impairments of motivation that especially afflict artists, their audiences, and their patrons.

· · ·

Case 1: Grandcourt's Arbitrary Will

In the characterization of Grandcourt, we can see most clearly the problem posed for the novelist by trying to incarnate a single function of the tripartite motivational system. It is relatively easy to imagine immobilizing feeling or thinking, but how does the will, which is always described as stimulus-driven, "start-forth," to use Bain's term, in their absence? The first answer to that question seems inadequate: Grandcourt, we are originally told, acts on whims. For example, following a caprice rather than a settled intention, he finds himself

---

[19] For example, Barbara Hardy called these characterizations, according to parallels and contrasts, Eliot's "habit of antithesis" in *The Novels of George Eliot: A Study in Form* (Fairlawn, N.J.: Essential Books, 1959), 84–88. For a new interpretation of the method, see Herz's discussions of "double surrogation."

inclined toward Gwendolen Harleth; at first sight, this would seem to be the intervention of a drive toward immediate enjoyment and away from his mediated interests (represented by the heiress Catherine Arrowpoint), but closer inspection shows that the case is more complicated, for it would be inaccurate to say that Grandcourt anticipates *enjoying* Gwendolen. He wants, more precisely, to keep her at his disposal; any more robust or active desire would violate his carefully maintained indifference, the sign and consequence of satiety. He is, the narrator tells us, in a state of "lotus-eater stupor" even as he feels himself drawn to her, a lukewarm consumer responding out of habit to things that once would have attracted him. Glutting has so spoiled his appetites that the outside world makes few distinct impressions on him and affords little incentive for action. In one of the narrator's descriptions of his mental processes, the challenge that such a character poses to normal novelistic representation is obvious: "The need for action lapses into a mere image of what has been, is, and may or might be; where impulse is born and dies in a phantasmal world, pausing in rejection even of shadowy fulfillment" (364). The very temporal and modal shifts in the sentence—it is all one to Grandcourt whether an object "has been, is, or may or might be"—indicate a suspension of the sequencing necessary for the accomplishment of any goal. We might liken Grandcourt to Jennings's description of the very wealthy person who seems least driven by a desire for pleasurable sensation and who can no longer tell the difference between enjoying things and having means of enjoyment around him, which he has no intention of consuming in any normal sense. Indeed, at the time this portrait of Grandcourt's interiority is taken, the narrator tells us, he sits "with various new publications on the table, of the kind a gentleman may like to have at hand without touching" (363–64).

And yet Grandcourt is not without will—quite the opposite—and in the course of the novel another explanation of the appearance of an arbitrary volition emerges. His sated condition has concentrated his remaining pleasurable sensations in the exercise of willing alone—and only, it seems, in opposition to the will of another. The impairment of the organs of desire—the inability to seek "fulfillment"—lies at the heart of Grandcourt's sadism, for the only way he has left to assert a self is through the sensation of imposing his will against someone else's inclination.[20] Hence, his languid pursuit of Gwendolen Harleth, who originally piques his interest by not meeting his advances, results in a proposal only when he realizes how completely he can undermine her own intentions by pressing her solely on the grounds of her economic need. In marked contrast to the previously quoted passage, Grandcourt's rare moment of "satisfaction" is captured by the cold triumph

---

[20] Myers points out that Alexander Bain had described this motivation in *The Emotions and the Will* as the "love of power," which he called, "the deepest fountain of general corruption." See Myers, *The Teaching*, 181.

of his suddenly distinct mental image: "She had been brought to accept him in spite of everything—brought to kneel down like a horse under training for the arena, though she might have an objection to it all the while." The narrator assures us that Grandcourt "got more pleasure out of this notion than he could have done out of winning a girl of whom he was sure that she had a strong inclination for him personally" (365).[21]

That image of the horse "under training for the arena" recalls the figure of the unhappy performer, which we last encountered in *Hard Times*. I noted, in discussing that figure, Dickens's tendency to present the labor of players as particularly onerous because they must take pains to represent feelings of enjoyment. *Daniel Deronda* gives us a far deeper exploration of the misery of enforced performance by figuring the relation between performer and audience as sadistic domination tainted with sexual perversion. That is, Grandcourt wills not only to see a performance but also to perceive the performer's wretched sensation of being coerced. The sadistic spectator, unlike the presumably naive spectators at Sleary's horse-riding, does not want to enter into the illusion that the performers are happily playful; instead he wants to savor the effortful, unhappy consciousness beneath the show, and he revels in penetrating the gap between what is seen and what is felt; indeed, he exults in the idea that he causes the mortifying travail. Whereas the crying clown figured the hidden unhappiness of laboring to amuse others and a self-pitying phase in Dickens's authorial self-consciousness, Gwendolen-the-performing-horse represents a more perverse relation between entertainer and audience—and, by extension, between writer and reader—in which the audience realizes and even relishes the unwillingness of the performance. The blasé spectator who has seen everything can only be enticed by the exhilaration of exercising his will to create unpleasant emotions that the performer must learn to hide. The Grandcourt who buys books but "abstains from literature" is a figure for the reader who buys the author only to remain indifferent to her, but Grandcourt the performer's torturer is an extreme allegory of the reader who buys only to find fault. The performing horse figures the artist at her most abject, and her abjection is her incomplete success in hiding her lack of motivation.

CASE 2: GWENDOLEN'S PREDOMINANT EMOTIONS

I do not mean to imply that we should read Gwendolen's misery merely as an allegory of the author's faltering will, but I do want to point out that the question of artistic motivation resonates through the various plot lines of this vast novel and that it finds its most dismal echo in the utter disconnection

---

[21] For other discussions of the perversity of the relation between Grandcourt and Gwendolen, see Jerome Thale, *The Novels of George Eliot* (Columbia University Press, 1959), 126–30, as well as Myers and Shuttleworth.

between Gwendolen's feelings and actions. Grandcourt, we are told, appreciates Gwendolen's "natural acting" but seeks to make it a more effortful and therefore—from his perspective—entertaining show. The images of enforced performance are in Gwendolen's consciousness as well Grandcourt's: "It is all like a dance set beforehand" (507), she complains to Deronda.

The coerced performance, therefore, serves as the metaphorical groundwork for the case study in hyperactive emotions. The narrator emphasizes that those two functions had never been integrated in Gwendolen:

> Gwendolen's will had seemed imperious in its small girlish sway; but it was the will of a creature with a large discourse of imaginative fears: a shadow would have been enough to relax its hold. And she had found [in Grandcourt] a will like that of a crab or a boa-constrictor which goes on pinching or crushing without alarm at thunder. (477)

After her marriage, we are to understand, she devotes what's left of her little determination to concealing her torment: "She fancied that his eyes showed a delight in torturing her. How could she be defiant? She had nothing to say that would touch him—nothing but what would give him a more painful grasp on her consciousness" (481). Thus, Eliot constructs the plot so that the character who has a will but no feeling—Grandcourt—inflames the already overly emotional condition of the character he dominates—Gwendolen—while simultaneously depriving her of volition; the dissociation of the two functions is rendered complete, and they become antagonistic principles.

By transforming her natural acting into a coerced performance, the novelist at once produces Gwendolen as a case of emotional hypertrophy and places her among those characters in the novel who make a living as artists and constitute a character system representing variations on the recurrent theme of artistic motivation. I'll refer to that configuration of characters frequently in the following discussion, but for now I want to note that Gwendolen's allegorical status as a figure for "emotion" in a state of helpless isolation coincides with her function as the novel's most debased, dominated, and prostituted performer. Moreover, her debasement stems from the fact that she is, paradoxically, superannuated even at the start of her career. As an erotic article she is, to use the marginal utilitarians' terms, the final increment of a commodity already sufficiently consumed by Grandcourt. Indeed, Grandcourt's romantic ennui is precisely what shifts Gwendolen's role from that of a "normal" erotic object to that of a sadistically coerced performer. Even during their courtship, the narrator emphasizes, it is Gwendolen's resistance to his will and her natural acting that has the charm of "novelty" for Grandcourt, and he later takes pleasure only in making her feel new humiliations, so he does manage to "refresh" his sensations by making unfamiliar uses of her. But, in an excruciating twist, he takes the richest enjoyment in forcing her to understand that she has entered his romantic life belatedly, after his appetite

has diminished, by constantly reminding her of her equivalence with his discarded mistress, Lydia Glasher. Gwendolen, of course, struggles to hide her
knowledge of his past and the fact that she met Lydia and promised her she
would not marry Grandcourt, but Grandcourt's pleasure is in knowing the
secret, watching Gwendolen conceal it, and thrusting reminders of it into her
consciousness. Indeed, he assumes that she is pained by Lydia's priority in his
affections, and he is partly right in that conjecture, which Lydia also insists
on in the note she sends to Gwendolen with Grandcourt's family diamonds
on the couple's wedding night: "The man you have married has a withered
heart. His best young love was mine; you could not take that from me when
you took the rest. It is dead; but I am the grave in which your chance of
happiness is buried as well as mine" (406). This declaration forces Gwendolen
to see that she is already redundant, that she will never excite normal affection
and admiration because the man she must try to attract has already spent his
little fund of love. She becomes aware of herself at this moment as a final
increment who can never be as valuable to her husband as his mistress was.
Noting, but not fully understanding, the pain this consciousness causes,
Grandcourt picks up the instrument of torture and continues to apply it until
he has made Gwendolen completely change places with Lydia: he makes a
new will specifying that Gwendolyn be moved, in the event of his death, to
the out-of-the-way house in which the illegitimate family has been living,
while Lydia's son will be legitimated and inherit the fortune and title. And as
an ultimate insult, he indicates that he is growing tired even of the spectacle
of her performance by letting her know that he had fathomed her shameful
secret from the outset, and consequently her performance of innocence, which
he enjoyed merely as a spirited show, had all along been futile. In short, Gwendolen's excessive emotional state and her absence of motivation result from
her consciousness of being a redundant item, slipping constantly toward the
margins of the disdainful consumer's desire.

In all of these particulars, the etiology and progress of Gwendolen's case
subtly indicates the healthy psychophysiological norm from which it departs,
and if we need more evidence that Alexander Bain's model informs the novel's
exploration of motivation, we can look at those occasional passages in which
the narrator resorts to the psychophysiologist's vocabulary. Commenting on
Gwendolen's developing lack of hedonistic motivation, for example, the narrator explains that "to solace ourselves with imagining any course beforehand,
there must be some foretaste of pleasure in the shape of appetite; and Gwendolen's appetite had sickened" (484). A decrease in pleasurable feelings usually
stimulates ideas about how to overcome the hedonistic deficit, which would
in turn inform resolve and lead to action. However, thrust back into the
medium of her predominant sensation—the sensation of fear—and with all
outlets for action shut, the very ability to imagine pleasure atrophies: "If she
could only feel a keen appetite for those pleasures—could only believe in

pleasure as she used to do!" Her sensations cannot be refreshed in thought because her mental images themselves come "clad in [the sufferer's] own weariness and disgust" (484). In a diagram of motivation, Bain had shown emotion stimulating thought and thereby inciting the will to action, but in Gwendolen's case, the flow of energy has backed up like a faulty hydraulic system: the thwarting of action causes a negation of will that reverses the nervous impulses, flooding thought with negativity and swamping the emotional function. So despite the fact that she has hardly had enough pleasure in her life to feel sated, Gwendolen nevertheless prematurely enters that state of acedia inhabited by her husband, where their plot stalls.

Deronda, too, echoes Bain when he tells Gwendolen to use her fear as a means of avoiding further wrongdoing. According to Bain, the mind-body nexus is created to facilitate self-preservation, so that, even in the absence of reasoning, we know by our gut feelings when we have begun to put ourselves in danger, and we retrace our steps. But Gwendolen cannot retrace her steps and hence becomes paralyzed by dread in a dynamic that adheres closely to Bain's description of emotional dysfunction:

> The healthy and regular action of the will, aiming at the suppression of pain and the procuring of pleasure, would work for subduing the state of panic, so as to leave the mind in a cool and collected condition, able to estimate the danger at its exact amount and with reference to all other interests. But the passion of fear is too much for the will. The idea [of danger] rules the situation like a despot. (349)

Right down to the transformation of the dangerous object into a despotic mental principle, this passage recalls the description of Gwendolen's "large discourse of imaginative fears" that constantly breaks down her will.

My point, however, is not that Gwendolen's characterization is textbookish but rather that her case, like Grandcourt's, tends toward stasis and inactivity and thereby seems to obviate the possibility of a plot arising from the struggle of characters' purposes, of narrative "motivation" in Viktor Shklovsky's sense of a meaningful movement from one state to another.[22] Indeed, the novel takes some pains to create a sense of stalemate by revealing the feeble operations of Gwendolen's will in rebellion against her husband only retrospectively. We learn of her plans—that she has been contemplating killing her husband by stabbing him with a knife that she keeps locked in her jewel box, and that she had thrown away the key, and that she had planned to have the box opened

---

[22] Shklovsky was himself very close to the psychophysiologists in his theories of how art works on the sensorium. Although he argues with Herbert Spencer (who draws on Bain) about the purpose of rhythm, he mainly reverses the values Spencer gives to certain efforts of the nervous system, but the underlying psychophysiology informs his own theories as well. See *Theory of Prose*, trans. Benjamin Sher (Elmwood Park, Ill.: Dalkey Archive Press, 1991), 3–4, 13–14.

again at Genoa when they disembark from the yacht, and that she changed her mind when she saw Daniel there, and that she then planned instead to give Daniel the box for safe-keeping—only when she confesses them to Daniel after her husband is drowned. Our ignorance of all this, maintained even though the narrator seems to be entering the deepest recesses of the character's cloudy consciousness, sustains the separation of emotion from will and thought that defines Gwendolen's predicament: the representation of Gwendolen's homicidal planning would dilute the isolation of living predominantly in the medium of paralyzing sensations. But narratively suppressing the deranged plan yields a plot that sometimes seems as static, uneventful, and repetitious as the Grandcourts' yachting excursion.

Case 2a: Gwendolen's Artistic Double

Although Gwendolen's plot seems stalled, the second half of the novel builds a series of analogies around her, which continue to keep her metaphoric associations with failing performers before the reader's mind. The syntagmatic character system I've been examining functions at the level of plot interactions, but the paradigmatic pattern I'll be looking at now operates across plots and between figures who have no, or very few, diegetic interactions. The density of these cross-references is no doubt another formal reason for our sense of the novel's excess: the forward movement of the plot's chronology seems stymied while significance emerges from side plots that develop variations on the same themes: repetitions with differences. Gwendolen is refracted and multiplied through other stories in Daniel's plot, especially those of Mirah, the reluctant performer who nevertheless makes an honest living by her talent, and the Alcharisi, Daniel's mother, who sacrifices him for her genius. The parallels and contrasts between Mirah and Gwendolen are obvious: the moral integrity of the former is a foil for the mercenary guilt of the latter, and the correspondences in their stories establish a relation of equivalent opposition between being a performer and commodifying one's sexuality: Mirah's father tries to sell her into prostitution, and Gwendolen makes a mercenary marriage, which Grandcourt ratifies by sending checks to her mother.[23]

The analogies between Gwendolen and the Alcharisi are subtler and more complex, but they tell us more about the miseries of superannuation with which the author was struggling. Until the end of the novel, Daniel's unnamed mother is an explicitly imaginary personage who forms the center of a nexus of

---

[23] For a discussion of the relation between prostitution and performance in *Daniel Deronda*, see Catherine Gallagher, "George Eliot and *Daniel Deronda*: The Prostitute and the Jewish Question" in *Sex, Politics, and Science in the Nineteenth-Century Novel*, Selected Papers of the English Institute, 1983–84, n.s. 10 (Baltimore: Johns Hopkins University Press, 1986), 39–62.

analogies and serves as a primary template for female misery. Because Daniel imagines that his mother must have suffered in the way that Mirah and Lydia Glasher (Grandcourt's former mistress and the mother of his children) suffer, that she must have been the victim of sexual exploitation, he embraces them in his sympathetic imagination. And because Gwendolen similarly imagines that Lydia Glasher is a double for Daniel's mother, she is drawn to confess her guilt to him, and he is moved by her displays of remorse. The careful and explicit structuring of this web of analogies encourages us to imagine an open sexual secret where a surprising artistic secret ultimately emerges: whereas everyone thinks Daniel's mother was Sir Hugo's mistress, who left her child in the care of his father, we finally learn that the hero is the legitimate son of a woman who left him to become the greatest lyric actress of her time. The shame that Daniel feels, and from which his ethos springs, is groundless, as is Gwendolen's fixation on him as a placeholder for those she has wronged. But at the moment one set of analogies collapses, another set, linking Gwendolen and the Alcharisi, comes into view and allows a glimpse of the author's heroic struggle with dread and her claim to have vanquished it.

A slew of parallels shadow Gwendolen's story with the Alcharisi's as the novel draws to a climax and the two women arrive at the same Italian hotel, both asking Daniel to hear their confessions. Both are haunted by dead men who threaten to impose their wills even from beyond the grave; unable to oppose those men while they were alive, both women desire the deaths of their oppressors but are afterward (the Alcharisi eventually and Gwendolen immediately) overwhelmed by guilt; both women, at the time of their confessions, which are made only hours apart, are unable to enjoy the freedom for which they longed; and each woman wants Daniel to relieve her of a burden—symbolized by a box, or casket—associated with her crime toward her husband or father. Moreover, they behave in tellingly opposite ways: the Alcharisi remorselessly reveals her reasons for leaving her son in the care of Sir Hugo Mallinger, refusing to feel any shame for having followed the dictates of her artistic ambition and repulsing Daniel's proffered filial devotion; Gwendolen, on the other hand, exaggerates her crime, indulges in extreme self-recrimination and begs Daniel not to abandon her. In both cases, Daniel, whom the narrator uses only intermittently as the focalizer in these interviews, registers the disproportion between the facts of the stories and the characters' emotional apprehensions of them.

Like Gwendolen, however, the Alcharisi is often overwhelmed by extreme fears and other painful passions, that offset her conscious intentions. Indeed, her career ended because she dreaded the mere possibility of failure, as she explains to Daniel in her only expression of regret:

> "But something befell me. It was like a fit of forgetfulness. I began to sing out of tune. They told me of it. Another woman was thrusting herself in my

place. I could not endure the prospect of failure and decline. It was horrible to me." She started up again, with a shudder, and lifted screening hands like one who dreads missiles. "It drove me to marry. I made believe that I preferred being the wife of a Russian noble to being the greatest lyric actress of Europe; I made believe—I acted that part. It was because I felt my greatness sinking away from me, as I feel my life sinking now. I would not wait till men said, 'She had better go.' "(702–3)

The denouement of this little drama links it closely to Gwendolen's agony: "I repented. It was a resolve taken in desperation. That singing out of tune was only like a fit of illness; it went away. I repented; but it was too late. I could not go back. All things hindered me—all things" (703).

This curious, almost gratuitous, twist in the Alcharisi's story not only sharpens the resemblance between the suffering of the two women but also emphasizes their common fate. We've heard that refrain—"I could not go back"— before, in Gwendolen's earlier confessions of her remorse at having married Grandcourt: "I can't alter it. I am punished, but I can't alter it. . . . And I must go on" (506). To be sure, the two women have quite different reasons for regretting their marriages, but they share the sense that they are obliged to perform, mechanically and perpetually, in a pantomime of domestic life ("I acted that part"; "It is all like a dance set beforehand" [507]). Their marriages require Gwendolen and the Alcharisi to go on acting—powerlessly, unwillingly—after the kinds of performances they had either reveled in (the Alcharisi) or hoped for (Gwendolen) have become impossible. Indeed, the author incessantly connects Gwendolen's acting ambitions and her ultimate position; for example, Klesmer, in explaining how arduous and unpleasant her training for the stage would be, is the first to foresee Gwendolen's future in exactly the terms that later excite Grandcourt: she must be "trained to bear [herself] on the stage, as a horse, however beautiful, must be trained for the circus" (302).

Gwendolen and the Alcharisi are not, however, punished so much for their original ambitions as for their failures of nerve, for letting their fearful emotions, the signs of mere egoism, dictate their actions. The Alcharisi's confession recalls the interview between Gwendolen and Herr Klesmer, every deprecating word of which, we are told, "seemed to have been branded into her memory" (306):

> Too old—should have begun seven years ago—you will not, at best, achieve more than mediocrity—hard, incessant work, uncertain praise—bread coming slowly, scantily, perhaps not at all—mortifications, people no longer feigning not to see your blunders—glaring insignificance. (307)

Klesmer's more emboldening words are ignored: "I have not said—I will not say—you will do wrong to choose the hard, climbing path of an endeavouring artist. . . . If you take that more courageous resolve I will ask leave to shake hands with you on the strength of our freemasonry, where we are all vowed to the service of Art, and to serve her by helping every fellow-servant" (304). Indeed, the author takes care to give Gwendolen the wherewithal for training to become an actress by having Klesmer offer to support her and her family while she studies; but her feelings, the narrator stresses in a particularly excruciating metaphor, are too painful to allow her to accept his help: "His words had really bitten into her self-confidence and turned it into the pain of a bleeding wound; and the idea of presenting herself before other judges was now poisoned with the dread that they also might be harsh: they also would not recognize the talent she was conscious of" (305). So despite the vast differences between the natural endowments and training of Gwendolen and the Alcharisi, despite the superior gravitas of the older woman, and despite our understanding that Gwendolen's career, if undertaken, would not thrive, the characters are linked by their overpowering dread of harsh judgment. Fear of failure on the stage so thoroughly unnerves them both that they sell themselves as wives instead.

Their inability to summon the will necessary to persevere, their surrender to dread, ironically leads them both into the very kind of domestic yoke that they had hoped to escape. One of the chapter epigrams might be taken as a comment on the characters' inability to overcome the servitude they despise:

> We please our fancy with ideal webs
> Of innovation, but our life meanwhile
> Is in the loom, where busy passion plies
> The shuttle to and fro, and gives our deeds
> The accustomed pattern. (278)

Passion in these women's lives is not an all-conquering love, as it was in the life of *Middlemarch*'s Dorothea Brooke, but a vehement horror that triumphs over volition and thought and dictates self-repetition. The Alcharisi ends in the "accustomed pattern" because, as she explains, "I never would risk failure" (695).

The fear of negative judgment links both characters to their creator, but, ironically, their fear, instead of impelling them toward innovation, prevents them from reinventing themselves. Thus, an implicit contrast also comes into view; these women, who cannot conquer their feelings and persevere in the face of failure, are the opposite of the implied author, who can use the fear to generate novelty.[24] Indeed, George Eliot seems anxious to imagine thoroughly the potentially debilitating effect of her personal emotions by incarnating them in these two women. The Alcharisi's staccato sentences, for example, and the melodramatic pantomime of screening herself with her hands—the whole performance of the horror of losing her powers as a performer and being subjected to the disapproval of an audience—may express the very dread

---

[24] For another discussion of the women artists in *Daniel Deronda* in relation to their maker, see Gillian Beer, *George Eliot* (Bloomington: Indiana University Press, 1986), 200–228.

the author herself was suffering, and yet the exaggerated affect also disavows it as an abnormal symptom of the Alcharisi's much remarked emotionalism. The very existence of *Daniel Deronda*, in contrast, proves that the author could overcome her own dread of failure; instead of retiring from her chosen profession, she tries to offer her audience something new: the beginnings of a national epic. She demonstrates that she can take risks, that she need not merely repeat herself, producing just one more increment of her usual fare. The "Jewish plot" surrounding Daniel has been controversial since its publication; many have thought it a failure, but no one doubts its novelty. We'll shortly look further into that attempt at innovation; suffice it to say for now that George Eliot showcases its artistic bravery by the contrasting collapse of the Alcharisi, who acts not only as a link between her own anxiety of becoming passé and Gwendolen's misery, but also as a way of chastising her professional fear, exposing its egoism, and amplifying its dangers. Through these figures of insufficient perseverance, she attempts to create a fear of the fear that can disable one's self-confidence and bar the way to success.

Even political economists like Jevons, who claimed to be taking emotions seriously as the bedrock of exchange, had not let such fears enter into their calculations; they had instead assumed that buyers and sellers would meet in the marketplace feeling neither intimidated nor ambivalent. But *Daniel Deronda* demonstrates that the artist, especially the female artist, is peculiarly vulnerable to such emotions because she is herself the commodity under scrutiny and is peculiarly mortified by being judged like any other kind of goods: "Ah, my dear Miss Harleth, that is the easy criticism of the buyer," Klesmer tells Gwendolen when she declares that she has seen "actresses who seemed to me to act not at all well and who were quite plain." Klesmer elaborates: "We who buy slippers toss away this pair and the other as clumsy; but there went an apprenticeship to the making of them" (302). To strengthen the will against the fear of being tossed away like a pair of clumsy slippers, Klesmer explains, an aspiring artist needs to be emboldened by an indomitable sense of vocation, a countervailing passionate devotion to a higher purpose than merely earning one's bread, and the easy triumph of Gwendolen's fear proves that she, unlike the author, has no such vocation. But if even the Alcharisi's resolve might falter, vocation and apprenticeship must not be enough; persisting in the face of fears would seem to require a sublime selflessness. Hence, in a reversal of her earlier apprehensions, Eliot seemed to have turned the existence of her last novel into proof of the *suppression*, rather than the expression, of her egoism.

Case 3: Daniel's Disabling Thoughtfulness

As the third term in the novel's central character system and its primary protagonist, Daniel functions both metonymically as Gwendolen's potential savior and metaphorically as her dispassionate antithesis. Just as she suffers from overwhelmingly strong emotions, Daniel lacks, as the passage quoted earlier explicitly states, "a way of keeping emotion and its progeny of sentiments . . . substantial and strong in the face of a reflectiveness that threatened to nullify all differences" (414). We are led to expect that a sympathetic connection between Gwendolen and Daniel will at least partially heal the dissociation of sensibility that organizes the novel, but their interactions instead often seem designed to demonstrate the comparative weakness of mere thought when confronted with an obstinate will, an excessive emotion, or even just the drift of events. If the dynamic between Grandcourt and Gwendolen divorces Will from Feeling, the dynamic between Daniel and Gwendolen illustrates the powerlessness of Thought to reconnect them.[25]

When Deronda counsels the penitent Gwendolen to break out of her co-erced performance, for example, his words echo ironically: "Is there any single occupation of mind that you care about with passionate delight or even inde-pendent interest?" he asks, and yet we know that Daniel has so far failed in the quest for a "single occupation." "What sort of earth or heaven would hold any spiritual wealth in it for souls pauperised by inaction?" (507), demands the young hero whose own inaction is already well-remarked. The narrator overtly draws our attention to Daniel's need to apply these prescriptions for passion and activity to himself: "The half-indignant remonstrance that vi-brated in Deronda's voice came, as often happens, from the habit of inward argument with himself rather than from severity toward Gwendolen" (508). To be sure, we are meant to see that Gwendolen needs some of Daniel's wide-angled, all-inclusive imagination, just as he needs some of her ability to feel injuries done to himself. But Gwendolen responds more to Daniel's mere responsiveness—to his ability to enter into others' emotions instead of having his own—than to his actual ideas. As an antidote to her feelings, he also prescribes many of the sorts of "sympathetic" reflections that keep his emo-tions from "coming to life," as the narrator puts it, but the tepid affective results obviously carry very little motive force for his interlocutor. His ideas, the narrator insists, are powerless against her recurring negative passions ("there are some feelings—hatred and anger—how can I be good when they keep rising?"). She might want to "be good" in some general sense, but the abstract wish, the novel insists, is no match for the opposite concrete sensa-

[25] Critics have long debated whether we are to think Daniel's effect on Gwendolen to be a success-fully therapeutic one. See two articles in *American Journal of Psychoanalysis* 59 (1999): Margot Wad-dell, "On Ideas of 'the Good' and 'the Ideal' in George Eliot's Novels and Post-Kleinian Psychoanalytic Thought," 271–86; and Carl Rotenberg, "George Eliot—Proto-Psychoanalyst," 257–70. See also Eliz-abeth Daniels, "A Meredithian Glance at Gwendolen Harleth," in *George Eliot: A Centenary Tribute*, ed. G. S. Haight and R. T. Van Arsdel (Totowa, N.J.: Barnes and Noble, 1982); Mary Ellen Doyle, *The Sympathetic Response: George Eliot's Fictional Rhetoric* (Rutherford, N.J.: Dickinson University Press, 1981). And see Bernard J. Paris, *Reading George Eliot: Changing Responses to Her Experiments in Life* (Albany: SUNY Press, 2003), 157–208, for a contribution to and a discussion of this debate.

tions: "[Deronda] was under the baffling difficulty of discerning, that what he had been urging on her was thrown into the pallid distance of mere thought before the outburst of her habitual emotion" (509).

And yet pointing to this somewhat banal opposition between Thought and Feeling does not tell the whole story, for Daniel and Gwendolen are actually two versions of what Alexander Bain theorized as a single derangement of motivation. Looking at his account of the hypertrophy of the emotions and of thought, we might be struck by its similarities to *Daniel Deronda* and by the intimacy it suggests between the two characters' pathologies. Bain explicitly lumps fears like Gwendolen's and seeming virtues like Daniel's under the category of "fixed ideas" that disable the normal functioning of the will. After analyzing obsessive dread (in a passage already quoted) as his first instance of a dysfunctional idée fixe, he immediately moves on to pathologize sympathy:

> But for some such domination of an idea, I see nothing in the constitution of the human mind that would make us sympathise with other men's pleasures and pains. The ordinary action of the will is to gain our own pleasures and remove our own pains. . . . But the intellect, which can form ideas of the mental condition of other sensitive beings, urges us to make those ideas actualities. (349)

Indeed, in this section on the unhealthy dominance of idées fixes, Bain even goes on to pathologize the sorts of aspiration Daniel develops in the course of his supposed cure: his heroic national ambition:

> Much of the ambition and the aspiration of human beings belongs rather to the sphere of fixed ideas, than to the sphere of volition prompted by pleasures. It is true that the things that we aspire after, are calculated to give us pleasure, but very often we indulge in ideal aspirations that are utterly impracticable, and that, if we were masters of ourselves, we would utterly disregard and repress. Unfortunately, however, a certain notion, say of power, wealth, grandeur, has fixed itself in our mind and keeps a persistent hold there, perverting the regular operation of the will, which would lead us to renounce whatever is hopeless or not worth the cost. (350)

In Bain's judgment, Daniel's story might be merely the replacement of one dominant idea by another, neither of which has healthy roots in "the sphere of volition prompted by pleasures."

Bain's view is by no means the overt judgment of the novel; we're obviously intended to admire Daniel's selflessness, and his ultimate goal, if not the generic stuff of novels, is presented as the condition of historical change. But the straining created by bringing Bain's diagnosis to Daniel's malady actually allows us to complicate what might otherwise appear to be a simple binary contrast between the functions the two main characters are supposed to embody. Bain's description of the tendency of an idea saturated with strong feeling to "take forcible possession" of a mind, predominating "over every other idea that seeks for admittance," and finally "act[ing] itself out in opposition to the will" (348–49), has obvious echoes in Gwendolen's story: "the evil longings, the evil prayers came again and blotted everything else dim, till, in the midst of them—I don't know how it was—he was turning the sail—there was a gust—he was struck—I know nothing—I only know that I saw my wish outside me" (761). But the kinship between this state and Daniel's overextended sympathy, which keeps him from willing his own pleasure, may be less obvious. Even after his cure, Daniel remains fixated on the idea of others' pleasures: "He watched the sober gladness which gave new beauty to [Mirah's] movements and her habitual attitudes of repose, with a delight which made him say to himself that it was enough of personal joy for him to save her from pain" (880). In Bain's analysis, where ideational fixation is the common root, we can see the similarity between "the infection of particular crimes, and . . . the operation of sympathy generally" (349).

Unlike Bain, Eliot places opposite moral values on these two deviations from normal motivation: crime and sympathy are not just instances of a single ailment, even though "diffusive sympathy" is the pathology from which Daniel must recover.[26] To be sure, by identifying a mistaken idea of his mother's suffering as the source of Daniel's debilitating thoughts, Eliot does at times come close to Bain's diagnosis: "We become possessed with the mere idea of pain, there being no reality corresponding" (350). And yet this pathologization does not seem to undermine Daniel's ability to carry positive values in the novel, a fact that is most evident when we analyze the hero's role in the novel's economy of art. Indeed, one might argue that his relation to that economy is a source of the novel's equivocal judgment of his "sympathy." Like all the main characters, Daniel is linked to the economy of art, but in peculiarly conflicted ways. As a mere child, he had made the refusal he recommends to Gwendolen: that she should stop acting. Instead of letting himself be scripted into the role of performer, he insisted on being a patron. Perceiving with childish alarm that Sir Hugo expected him to want a career on the stage, Daniel pleads with the man he thinks sired him to let him be an English gentleman. And when he becomes an English gentleman, Daniel's main economic activity seems to be that of supporting artists: he serves as the benefactor of the painter Hans Meyrick (and thereby of the entire Meyrick family), as well as the singer Mirah. The activity links him to Catherine Arrowpoint

---

[26] For discussions of Eliot's problematization of sympathy in the person of Daniel Deronda, see Welsh, 302ff; Audrey Jaffe, *Scenes of Sympathy* (Ithaca, N.Y.: Cornell University Press, 2000), 130–33; Garrett Stewart, *Dear Reader: The Conscripted Audience in Nineteenth-Century British Fiction* (Baltimore: Johns Hopkins University Press, 1996), 305–22; Elizabeth Deeds Ermarth, "George Eliot's Conception of Sympathy," *Nineteenth-Century Fiction* 40 (June 1985): 23–42. For analyses relating Daniel's sympathy to his inaction, see Stefanie Markovits, "George Eliot's Problem with Action," *Studies in English Literature 1500–1900* 41 (Autumn 2001): 785–803.

and Herr Klesmer, who spend Catherine's much larger disposable income in similar ways, and it recalls the original intention of Sir Hugo in offering to do anything Daniel's mother, the Alcharisi, requested of him. The economics of art thus provide yet another paradigmatic character system like the one containing Gwendolen as a performer. Daniel is one of several characters who are known by their modes of supporting performers. In this configuration, a beneficent and enabling patronage is contrasted with a malevolent and disabling compulsion. Daniel, the Klesmers, and Sir Hugo are counterbalanced by Grandcourt and Mirah's father, Lapidoth, the coercers. Daniel, the patron-consumer, derives his pleasure partly from Mirah's performances and partly from perceiving her pleasure and relief. In contrast, Grandcourt, the coercive consumer, is gratified by the performance in conjunction with the unhappy emotion in the performer. In the benevolent art economy, the consumer Daniel buys the intellectual satisfaction of reflecting on the pleasures of others; in the malevolent art economy, the consumer Grandcourt buys the sense of exerting his will in response to opposition. Just as Grandcourt is George Eliot's nightmare of a reader, Daniel seems to be the reader created by what she called the "aesthetic effect": "the rousing of the nobler emotions, which make mankind desire the social right" (7:44).

And yet even as the novelist indulges the dream of the perfect reader, underlined by the contrast between extremes of good and bad treatment of "artists," she repeatedly demonstrates that Daniel's aesthetic disposition equals contemplative passivity. Obviously, Daniel is no advertisement for indulging in vicarious pleasures, and his patronage is certainly not presented as a fulfilling career. Indeed, giving others the wherewithal for a life instead of having one himself is *the* symptom of Daniel's abnormal condition. By highlighting the problematic nature of Daniel's motivation, moreover, the novel creates a perspective on the "too-much" of its narrative practices. The Daniel who patronizes others has long been recognized by critics as only partly a character and partly a figure for novelistic functions. In him, some critics maintain, George Eliot tried to incarnate her narrative persona by imagining the sort of life experience and psychology that might lead one to become a floating sympathizer.[27] Who, after all, could make a more appreciative reader than someone with her narrator's breadth and depth of empathetic understanding? Characterizing such a consciousness, it has also been noted, entailed problematizing it by making it mindful of its own deracinated state, its lack of immanence: "But how and whence was the needed event to come?—the influence that would justify partiality, and making him what he longed to be yet was unable to make himself—an organic part of social life, instead of roaming in it like a yearning

---

[27] See, for example, Janice Carlisle, *The Sense of Audience: Dickens, Thackeray and George Eliot at Mid-Century* (Athens: University of Georgia Press, 1981), 216–19; Jaffe, *Scenes*, 153–54; Herz, *Pulse*, 122–37; Stewart, *Dear Reader*, 305ff.

disembodied spirit, stirred with a vague social passion, but without a fixed local habitation to render fellowship real?" (413). The mobile, detached condition that goes unremarked in an omniscient third-person narrator becomes a psychological abnormality, rather than a literary device, when attributed to a *character.*

Moreover, passages like this direct our attention to the creative labor of fiction, what Eliot thought of as "incarnation," in which types becomes individuals, ideas become concrete, and transcendence turns into immanence. As the Wordsworthian echo emphasizes, Daniel is at first the designation of an "airy nothing" that as yet lacks "a local habitation." In no other incarnation plot, however, does George Eliot explicitly define the very virtues that her narrators had been recommending for the past two decades as the highest moral achievement and accuse them of undermining ethical action: "A too reflective and diffusive sympathy was in danger of paralyzing in him that indignation against wrong and that selectness of fellowship which are the conditions of moral force" (413). Giving character to a combination of readerly and narrative operations, in short, implicitly denigrates them as psychological quirks, as "too-much" thoughtful consideration, which diffuses regard, erodes personal desire, and undermines the will.

No wonder, then, that Daniel's cure is effected by the traumatic subversion of the mistaken "fixed idea" of his mother's suffering, which had formed the basis of his "diffusive sympathy." The psychophysiological understanding of motivation permeates the first interview between Daniel and his mother, in which strong *sensation* disrupts the son's thought and breaks through his "numbness." The narrator explicitly tells us that he loses the ability to hear her story with his accustomed "dispassionate" empathetic understanding. Intending, in his habitual cerebral way, to contemplate and admire the life of this woman, "whose errors lay along high pathways," as he would "if, instead of being his mother, she had been a stranger who had appealed to his sympathy" (695), Daniel is instead overwhelmed by a "repugnance" that he cannot tame by reflection. The narrator emphasizes that strong painful *sensation*—not exactly even a mental emotion, let alone a thought process—breaks Daniel's sympathetic bond with his formerly spectral mother: "Deronda turned pale with what seems always more of a sensation than an emotion—the pain of repulsed tenderness" (697). Daniel only learns to feel strongly on his own behalf, in other words, when raw pain triumphs over sympathetic reflection, engaging the will to reverse the trajectory his mother had set for his life.

Significantly, the episode also breaks through Daniel's aesthetic disposition; he cannot appreciate the tragic artist in his mother; he knows that he should at least admire her for seeking "high pathways," but the sense of his personal loss destroys the effect. He is no longer the good reader or the enabling patron; instead he is acutely conscious that her art had already cost him too much. Finally, Daniel confronts a performance—the narrator mentions several times that the Alcharisi is always acting—that he cannot stomach. When Daniel learns that his mother left him to pursue her career, he must confront his kinship with the performer while also acknowledging that his absence, rather than his sympathetic presence, has been the condition of her success. He therefore not only loses his habitual dispassion and comes to feel something akin to Gwendolen's hatred, but also finds himself repelled by the economy of art, in which he is far more deeply steeped than he had realized. For art is partly the foundation of the very fortune he spends as a patron; he was grati-fied by the dependency of artists on him, but his dependency on an artist—and one who seems not to care about him personally—is deeply humiliating. We could see this as part of the allegory of incarnation, for Daniel must step down from the disembodied ideality where readers and narrators dwell into the world of dramatis personae, where no one is truly above the action. But that wouldn't account for Daniel's rebellion against the economy he unwit-tingly inhabited, which is clearly signaled by his repudiation of his mother's will and then reprised for emphasis in the parallel dismissal of Mirah and Mordecai's actor-father. Only by shifting the use of his fortune from art pa-tronage to national establishment can Daniel take on motivation. Thus it would seem that one cannot become real inside the economy of art.

The "readerly" disposition has a deleterious effect on motivation: this seems to be the point reiterated in large and little ways throughout Daniel's plot. Making her protagonists "real" by forcing them out of impersonal transcen-dence into dutiful immanence was nothing new for George Eliot, and even the transformation of Daniel Deronda from a dispassionate, impartial cosmo-politan intellectual into a proponent of Jewish statehood through the *shrinkage* of his capacity to identify has subtler precedents in the earlier novels. But the contracting of Daniel's sympathy to accommodate his vocation causes a momentous break between the protagonist and the narrative consciousness in this novel, which is genuinely new. Daniel's repulsion from his mother—presented as his most "organic" and uncontrolled sensation—is so fully partic-ular to him that we feel the loss of the narrator's grip on it.

Consider, for example, the tortured syntax of the sentence partially quoted above:

> [A]ll these busy elements of [emotional] collision between them were subsid-ing for a time, and making more and more room for that effort at just allowance and that admiration of a forcible nature whose errors lay along high pathways, which he would have felt if, instead of being his mother, she had been a stranger who had appealed to his sympathy. (695)

Daniel at this point must defect from the effort of "just allowance"—"Still it was impossible"—whereas the narrator continues to make "room" for the compassion Daniel *would have felt* if the Alcharisi had not been his mother and to mark the appropriateness of such feelings in those of us who are not her abandoned children. We are impressed with the understanding that we cannot simultaneously feel Daniel's repugnance and feel *as Daniel would if he were us*. And in the oddly unoccupied "room" opened by this breach, the transactions of sympathetic identification seem peculiarly empty and left over from some prior state of being. We may inhabit this breach, but only with the sensation that we are floating outside, as Daniel previously did, in unattached narrative space. Such floating, to be sure, usually seems appropriate for readers and narrators who know the ontological difference between themselves and fictional characters. But the thematic stress this novel places on sympathy as a dysfunctional excess enforces an uncomfortable self-consciousness in the reader. The novelistic disposition Eliot normally sought appears, in this new light, to be a luxurious excess, which should only be experienced in a world where one's will is properly disengaged—that is, a fictional world—but cannot fuel action in the real world. The pathologization of Daniel, in short, signals that a certain phase of Eliot's career has come to an end. And although it might be tempting to say that Daniel's pathology reveals that fiction could never be adequately motivated in psychophysiological terms and hence just is ipso facto excessive, such a truism would not explain his cure, which points to a reorientation between the novel and the world outside the text. The cure signals that this novel should not be read as the last in a series, but as the first of a new kind of writing with a different bearing toward reality, and hence it indicates a fresh novelistic program that saves the author from her own motivational entropy.[28]

. . .

For some readers, the initiative was successful; they reacted exactly as Jevons's "Rule of Novelty" would have predicted: "[*Daniel Deronda*] is as much a first novel, from a fresh hand and mind, as if no scene of clerical life had ever been penned,"[29] wrote the reviewer for the *Gentleman's Magazine*, explaining that it "lies far outside George Eliot's other works." Even the negative judgments of other reviewers became evidence in the *Gentleman's Magazine* for Eliot's successful solution to the problem of the final increment:

> When a great artist, whose very name has become a sure note of excellence, produces a work that the great fame-giving majority refuses to accept on the sole ground that it is his, or hers, there is a matter for dull congratulation. Such an event shows that past triumphs have been neither decreed blindly on the one hand, nor on the other accepted as a dispensation from the duty

---

[28] See Stewart, *Dear Reader*, 312–22, for an analysis of the Mordecai-Daniel relationship as one that models Eliot's injunction to her readers to act beyond the text, to complete this novel in the world.

[29] David Carroll, *George Eliot, The Critical Heritage* (London: Routledge and Kegan Paul, 1971), 383.

of making every new work a new and original title to future laurels. And
such an event is the production of *Daniel Deronda*. (382)

But this friendliest reviewer—uncannily in tune with both the marginalists'
theories of value and George Eliot's own terms of self-judgment—admitted
that the majority had bought the product because it was Eliot's, and then,
just as the author had feared, turned out to be the sort who "read while they
complain." Eliot's diagnosis of the literary market's motivational neuroses, in
short, seems to have been born out in the disconnection between sales and
reception.

Indeed, the great irony was that the novel's innovations—Daniel's cure, and
the entire unprecedented "Jewish element" in which it takes place—seemed
especially *un*motivated to most of its first readers: unmotivated in a couple of
ways. First, it seemed an abrupt departure from Eliot's normal realism, and
thus it failed the formal test of plot "motivation" described in the next century
by Viktor Shklovsky. The Deronda plot, full of coincidences and mystical
encounters, was judged to follow an implausible pattern of cause and effect.
Those who liked it noted the change just as frequently as those who scorned
it. The reviewer for the *Spectator* thought the new pattern of causation belonged to a higher form of Art, "that at times resembles that of the Hebrew
Prophet's belief in the Eternal purposes, and at times that of the Greek tragedi-
an's" (367). The *Gentleman's Magazine* reviewer was just as careful to label
Deronda a *formal* break in Eliot's career, insisting that it was her first "romance." Hitherto, the critic continued, "If George Eliot can be said to have
shown any serious fault as an artist, it is that she has . . . almost timidly kept
to the safe ground of probability" (384). Precisely by the improbabilities of
"meeting a Hebrew prophet in a second-hand book-stall or hearing from a
Frankfort banker the legacies of wisdom bequeathed by a Daniel Charisi,"
according to this review, "George Eliot has paid us a higher compliment than
if she had given us another Silas Marner. She has practically refused to believe
the common libel, upon us who read fiction, that we only care to look at our
own photograph and to be told what we already know" (385). This was one
reader who clearly perceived and appreciated Eliot's application of the rule of
novelty, even though it entailed certain "wonderful" and inexplicable
conjunctions.

But many other reviewers thought the novel was an intolerable formal hy-
brid, in which Gwendolen's plot adhered to Eliot's previous mode of plausible
progression occasionally interrupted by fluky coincidences while Deronda's
plot—especially the events surrounding his relation with Mordecai—verged
on mystical supernaturalism. Daniel, complained the reviewer for the *Saturday
Review*, too often suggests "the idea of Providence . . . is a Being with a capital
B, and is foretold by his grandfather as Deliverer with a capital D" (381). No
wonder, he maintains, that readers have simply split the book in half: "The

ordinary reader indeed ignores these mystic persons, and in family circles Gwendolen has been as much the heroine . . . as if there were no Mirah" (379). And in the most famous review of the novel, Henry James's "Daniel Deronda: A Conversation," which appeared in the *Atlantic Monthly*, Constantius admits that he "began to feel an occasional temptation to skip. Roughly speaking, all the Jewish burden of the story tended to weary me" (422). Later, he also attaches generic language to the split in narrative logic, pronouncing Daniel's materialization at Mordecai's bidding "romantic" (although not "vulgar romance"). Almost all reviewers, in short, found *Daniel Deronda*'s motive force to be the main feature distinguishing it from her earlier works; none of them fails to notice the innovation, but most of them fail to appreciate it.

Reviewers complained as well about what they considered the disproportion of analysis over action in the novel, about sententious moralizing and motto-making, especially about psychological and physiological jargon (the word "emotive," a favorite of Alexander Bain's, comes in for heaps of abuse). They speculated on the author's motive for including all of the psychophysiological minutiae I have been pointing out in this chapter, and generally concluded that the stylistic echoes of the psychologists were unseemly exhibitions of her knowledge: "No doubt the truths of science, mental and physical, are here, as elsewhere in our author's works, rendered with astonishing correctness and facility," wrote George Saintsbury in the *Academy*. "But," he continued, "the technical language of psychology is as much out of place in prose fiction as illustration of its facts is appropriate. . . . [A] novelist, when he speaks in his own person, should have no opinion, should be of no sect, should indulge in no *argot*" (374). Surprisingly, the narrator's self-presentation as something of a scientist reduces her universal appeal and makes her seem partial. Novels, the reviewer assumes, should never include other discourses, and if they do, the novelist's motivation comes into question.

The specific charge against technical psychophysiological language tends to merge in other reviews with more general complaints about repetitive "authorial" discourse predominating over the narratorial function: "Reflection prevails over description, and . . . threatens to throw into the shade the author's creative power," wrote the reviewer for the *Nation* (399). The judgment that the book is spoiled by a shift in authorial motivation from the earlier works is frequently repeated, and it blends as well into the allegation that the plot has no strong pulsation of forward motion; Saintsbury accused Eliot of "repressing" her gift of narrative and shoving her characters into the background, "in order that the author may talk about them while the action stands still" (374). Henry James's Pulcheria remarks, "I never read a story with less current. It is not a river; it is a series of lakes" (418). And these grievances against the author's unaccountable new discursiveness were multiplied when the reviewers turned to her handling of the Jewish plot, which led to even more perplexity about her motives. "What," asks the *Saturday Review*, "can have encouraged the unwinding of Mordecai's mazy, husky sentences, with their false air of prophecy without foretelling anything? She must know her public too well to have allowed herself any delusion here" (379). Even her friendly reviewers wondered why she did it: "The author herself can have looked for no immediate fortune but that of battle" (382).

If Eliot was trying to refresh her readers' appetite for her, the strategy was lost on them; she may have motivated herself by reflecting on motivation and insisting on innovation, but her readers (or at least her reviewers) found those very moves utterly inscrutable. As the negative reviews sank in, however, she began to claim that her intention was never to keep up her market or even to win her readers' favor with novelty. In an often quoted letter to Harriet Beecher Stowe, Eliot maintained that she had never expected her readers to like "the Jewish element in *Deronda*" and that she had been able to create it only because of her financial independence: "I was happily independent in material things and felt no temptation to accommodate my writing to any standard except that of trying to do my best in what seemed to me most needful to be done."[30] What was "most needful to be done," explained the author was "to rouse the imagination of men and women to a vision of human claims in those races of their fellow-men who most differ from them in customs and beliefs" (301). She might have been prompted to give this version of her motivation by a desire to seem like her correspondent, for no novelist of the nineteenth century could be credited with having "roused the imagination" on behalf of a downtrodden race more effectively than Harriet Beecher Stowe, but we should also note that this account of her motivation neatly reversed the power relation that had seemed to oppress her previously—the fantasy of facing the disapproving reader. Following the negative reception, she came to fashion herself the independent judge, the disapproving author who faults her readers for failing to meet *her* high expectations of *them*: their aversion to the Jewish plot is merely "an inability to find interest in any form of life that is not clad in the same coat-tails and flounces as our own." Thus when her publisher, John Blackwood, told her that the sales of the novel testified to her extraordinary popularity, for "Anti-Jews grumbled but went on" (282),[31] she was prepared to attribute their unappreciative reading to their own "intellectual narrowness" and "stupidity" (302).

It is at this point, too, that she begins to console herself with the idea that *Daniel Deronda* has a different orientation to the world outside its pages than did any of her other novels. She has reached for a "good" beyond her usual

[30] *Letters*, 6:301.

[31] For Eliot's relation to Blackwood, see Donald Gray, "George Eliot and Her Publishers," in *The Cambridge Companion to George Eliot*, ed. George Levine (Cambridge: Cambridge University Press, 2001), 181–201.

conclusions, and she proudly recorded in her journals and letters that the book was producing a "spiritual effect" on its Jewish readers. She carefully assembled "signs" of its real-world effectiveness, anticipating that future event—an attempt to establish a Jewish homeland—that would "confirm" the novel's role in reshaping reality (316). She writes hopefully of her novel's "fulfillment" in secular time, an incarnational ambition like none she had indulged before. We might say, therefore, that she solved the problem of the final increment with two strategies: she pretended she was not writing for a market, and she refused to think of her novel as finished. It was merely the beginning of a story, but its completion was left to those oncoming forces the narrator summons after Gwendolen learns of Daniel's plans, explicitly (if bathetically) imitating the Psalmist: "Then is it as if the Invisible Power that has been the object of lip-worship and lip-resignation became visible, according to the imagery of the Hebrew poet, making the flames of his chariot and riding the wings of the wind, till the mountains smoke and the plains shudder under the rolling, fiery visitation," and so on (875). Prophecy takes over from narration at moments like this so that conclusions, final increments, are indefinitely deferred. Instead of ending, George Eliot's career, like Mordecai's life, will flow into the tide of history.

In the meantime, she still clung to another measure of the novel's success: "the sale both in America and England has been an unmistakeable guarantee that the public [as opposed to the reviewers] has been touched. Words of gratitude have come from Jews and Jewesses, and there are certain signs that I may have contributed my mite to a good result. The sale hitherto has exceeded that of Middlemarch as to the £2.2s four-volumed form."[32] By 1879 she was pleased to calculate that, although *Middlemarch* had sold more copies (33,000 as opposed to *Daniel Deronda*'s 22,000), she had made £9,200 from *Daniel Deronda* as opposed to £8,700 from the earlier novel (vii:364). So even though she anticipates its role in the retrieval of the promised land and views it as the first installment in a living national romance, she ultimately turns to exactly the data Jevons would have used to convince herself of the novel's value: its sales figures.

[32] *Letters*, 6:314.

Chapter Six

Malthusian Anthropology and the Aesthetics
of Sacrifice in *Scenes of Clerical Life*

Not too long ago, it would have seemed implausible to link the Victorian concepts of *culture* with the name of Thomas Robert Malthus. Although the impact of his thought on a variety of developing disciplines was widely recognized—think, for example, of demographics and evolutionary biology—until quite recently we regarded Malthus's influence on the nineteenth century's *cultural* discourses as almost nil. During the last twenty years, though, scholars in various fields have reassessed Malthus's impact on nineteenth-century anthropological and literary discourses, discovering (as several earlier chapters of this book corroborate) the unwitting conformity of many of his severest critics to the fundamentals of his vision. It has become commonplace to view Malthusianism as an integral component of several interlocking discourses that include not only political economy but also speculative history, moral philosophy, nascent anthropology, linguistics, and aesthetics;[1] consequently, it no longer seems surprising to think of Malthus as a pioneer of cultural theory.

Nevertheless, it is one of the ironies of intellectual history that Malthus's writings nourished ideas that were so thoroughly intertwined with Victorian "developmentalism." Culture came into focus for the British primarily as an evolutionary concept, and in the second half of the century it was laden with the issues already linked to developmentalism, one of which was the role of population growth in stimulating cultural change. The culture idea took the shape it still recognizably holds for us alongside its evolutionary diacritical term: the "nature" that lacked it but out of which it must have emerged. This was the case, moreover, in both of the contexts in which the word was most often used: (1) the study of the whole way of life and collective consciousness of a specified people (the protoanthropological context); and (2) the study of the singular, inward processes that result in unusual achievements of individual consciousness (for my purposes, the literary context). In the first half of

---

[1] For example, in *Romanticism and the Human Sciences: Poetry, Population, and the Discourse of the Species* (Cambridge: Cambridge University Press, 2000), Maureen McLane traces Malthusian concepts of Man in the works of Mary Shelley, Percy Bysshe Shelley, and Wordsworth. Christopher Herbert's *Culture and Anomie: Ethnographic Imagination in the Nineteenth Century* (Chicago: University of Chicago Press, 1991) details numerous ways in which "Malthus's population theory moves decisively into the field of cultural theory" (111). See also Philip Connell, *Romanticism, Economics and the Question of "Culture"* (Oxford: Oxford University Press, 2001), 13–18.

the nineteenth century, though, Malthus's writings seemed mainly to pose problems rather than solutions for progressive evolutionary thinkers: how could progressively higher forms of human civilization be generated if nature in the form of population pressure constantly created cycles of plenty and want and if our sexual instincts could only be overcome by vice or misery?[2] It was only when the Malthusian dilemma was integrated into various developmental narratives that the culture idea explicitly and suddenly came into its own, almost simultaneously, in adjacent but discrete disciplines.

This chapter will analyze how Malthus became culture-friendly. I'll begin by describing his inroads into evolutionary anthropology, which are easier to trace than the path that his ideas traveled toward an account of the origin of art. In the second half of the chapter, we will take the more circuitous and obscure route into the aesthetic realm, but much of what I say about the Malthusian body in anthropology will carry over into the discussion of Victorian and early modernist aesthetics. Indeed, it is because I want to show the extent of the bioeconomic and somaeconomic overlap in the two discourses of culture that I am pursuing this line of thought in the first place. We can probably agree at the outset that traces of Malthus can be detected in places where we hadn't previously expected to find them, but I would additionally like to identify and analyze certain common features of British ideas about culture that were born from the body of economic thought. In particular, I'll be examining the potent combination of Malthusian treatments of sexuality, the origins of religion, and life-giving sacrifice. I'll sketch three lines of thought: two in the anthropological context, linking primitive culture to the population principal, and one in the literary context connecting religious and artistic expression to heightened states of consciousness engendered by procreative casualties. Instead of treating a moment in the history of the body economic, this chapter traces three intersecting trajectories of thought that start at the beginning of the nineteenth century and wind their way into twentieth-century modernism. Nevertheless, it does have a work of fiction—George Eliot's *Scenes of Clerical Life* (1857)—at its center. In relation to the last chapter, therefore, we may appear to be merely regressing to the beginning of Eliot's career, but we'll actually be stepping backward and reorienting ourselves toward the anthropological use of bioeconomics so that we can jump forward to modernist aesthetics at the end of the century.

Malthusian Plots Among the Anthropologists

The most obvious and undeniable link between Malthus and the evolutionary anthropological culture concept is that connecting Malthus to Darwin.

[2] For a discussion of the problems Malthus presented to evolutionary progressives, see George W. Stocking, *Victorian Anthropology* (New York: The Free Press, 1987), 220ff.

In his autobiography, Darwin acknowledged the magnitude of his debt to Malthus:

> In October 1838 [he tells us] . . . I happened to read for amusement Malthus on *Population*, and being well prepared to appreciate the struggle for existence which everywhere goes on from long-continued observation of the habits of animals and plants, it at once struck me that under these circumstances favorable variations would tend to be preserved, and unfavorable ones to be destroyed. The result of this would be the formation of new species. Here, then, I at last got a theory by which to work.[3]

Darwin thus avowed that he applied the population principle—that reproduction will always outstrip the food supply unless preventively or positively checked—to all living things and came up with the theory of natural selection: any organism that varies in such a way as to produce even a slight advantage in the competition for scarce resources will be more likely to survive to maturity and hence more likely to pass on the variation to its offspring. Without, in other words, the chronic tendency toward overpopulation that Malthus described, natural selection would be impossible.[4] More specifically apropos early humans and their culture, Darwin cites Malthus repeatedly in *The Descent of Man*, on the relative fertility of "savages" and on their mating habits. Malthus is also behind Darwin's claim that the population principle is the engine, not just of change, but of something resembling progress: "Man . . . has no doubt advanced to his present high condition through a struggle for existence consequent on his rapid multiplication" (403). Even more fundamentally, Darwin's *Origin of Species* incorporated Malthus's axioms that the basic, implacable necessities of animal existence are food and sex, and he thereby inherited the scandal that still attached to viewing mankind as an animal species and analyzing our behavior accordingly. Even Darwin's methodological insistence that the real, deepest springs of interaction, although omnipresent and uniform, hide themselves from our civilized eyes, revealing themselves only among more "primitive" creatures, might be said to echo Malthus.

---

[3] *The Autobiography of Charles Darwin, 1809–1882*, ed. Nora Barlow (New York: W. W. Norton, 1958), 120.

[4] There is an ongoing debate over the Malthus-Darwin connection. See Michael Mogie, "Malthus and Darwin: World Views Apart," *Evolution* 50 (October 1996): 2086–88; Peter Bowler, "Malthus, Darwin, and the Concept of Struggle," *Journal of the History of Ideas* 37 (October 1976): 631–50; Peter Vorzimmer, "Darwin, Malthus, and the Theory of Natural Selection," *Journal of the History of Ideas* 30 (October 1969): 527–42. See also Robert M. Young, *Darwin's Metaphor* (New York: Cambridge University Press, 1985) and "Malthus and the Evolutionists: The Common Context of Biological and Social Theory," *Past and Present* 43 (May 1969): 109–45; S. S. Schweber, "Darwin and the Political Economists: Divergence of Character," *Journal of the History of Biology* 13 (Fall 1980): 195–289. For a consideration of Darwin's impact on political economy, see Margaret Schabas, "The Greyhound and the Mastiff: Darwinian Themes in Mill and Marshall," in *Natural Images in Economic Thought*, ed. Philip Mirowski (Cambridge: Cambridge University Press, 1994), 322–35.

The links that Darwin made between evolutionary science—including evolutionary anthropology—and Malthus are clear, but their very obviousness may be deceptive if they encourage us to think that all Victorian anthropologists followed Darwin's lead in his later Malthusian account of human culture. Darwin showed how to make a general evolutionary use of the population principle, but in the specifically anthropological discourse that followed, the field, I believe, quickly bifurcated into two distinct and competing Malthusian modes of analysis. By the time Darwin wrote his *Descent of Man* (published in 1870), he was already faced with an anthropological account quite different from his own, although no less Malthusian. John McLennan's *Primitive Marriage* (published in 1865) had begun to develop a picture of primitive culture organized primarily around a single side of the Malthusian tension between reproduction and resources; Darwin was to develop, primarily, the other side. That is, one view of primitive culture, McLennan's, emphasized the organization of sexuality, while the other view, Darwin's, emphasized the organization of food.[5] This argument about which side of the Malthusian dilemma should be privileged spread beyond McLennan and Darwin. I'll be showing how the emphasis on sexuality was continued in the works of W. Robertson Smith as well as how the Darwinian view was upheld in the work of E. B. Tylor, and finally, I'll end my analysis of Malthusian anthropology by describing how James G. Frazer's *The Golden Bough* succeeded in integrating these different Malthusian tendencies in a synthesis that helped shape literary modernism.

As I argued in the first two chapters of this book, the sexual side of Malthusianism, which McLennan developed into a theory of primitive culture, was certainly the most shocking and original side. No one before Malthus contended that the sexual instinct was at the very core of our human nature or that it was as permanent and intractable as the instinct for self-preservation. To be sure, some eighteenth-century writers, especially those associated with Scottish "conjectural history," had stressed the role of population pressure in the progress from hunting to pastoralism to agriculture, and on to commercial society: for example, Lord Kames named "Hunger" the "overbearing cause" that drives civilization forward, "overcoming indolence and idleness."[6] And hunger, he knew, resulted from the increases in population that each new

---

[5] I depart here from the usual way of organizing the debate between McLennan and his adversaries, which has tended to focus on the distinction between matriarchalists (McLennan and [later] Bachofen) and patriarchalists (Henry Maine and Darwin). For other accounts of this debate, see George Stocking, 176ff, and Adam Kuper, *The Invention of Primitive Society: Transformations of an Illusion* (New York: Routledge, 1988), 1–42. For McLennan's use of Malthus, see Stocking, 221ff. For a particularly rich analysis of the emergence of the concept of culture, see Christopher Herbert, *Culture and Anomie: Ethnographic Imagination in the Nineteenth Century* (Chicago: University of Chicago Press, 1991).

[6] Henry Home, Lord Kames, *Sketches of the History of Man*, 2nd ed. (Edinburgh: W. Creech, 1778), 1:98.

mode of production allowed. But he did not imply that there was a sexual appetite, comparable to hunger, whose denial was a form of misery. When Malthus made the claim in 1798, reacting to Godwin's speculation that the sexual instinct would fade as civilization proceeded, it created a scandal. The story of his attempts to bring his thinking more into line with Anglican orthodoxy on this issue is well known;[7] whereas he first classified the voluntary renunciation of sexual activity (the preventive check of moral restraint) as "misery," he later put it in a separate category of its own, belonging to neither misery (like war or famine) nor vice (like birth control or prostitution). Nevertheless, he persisted in pointing out that even moral restraint causes "at least temporary unhappiness," and the successive editions of his *Essay on Population*, if outwardly more orthodox, did little to mollify those who thought his analysis of the moral condition of mankind depended too heavily on sexual activity as an individual biological need.

In chapter 1, we looked at Robert Southey's outraged review of the second edition, and part of it bears repeating: "There lives not a wretch corrupt enough of heart, and shameless enough of front to say that this [doctrine of a need for copulation] is so: there lives not a man who can look upon his wife and his daughter, who can think upon his sister, and remember her who bore him, without feeling indignation and resentment that he should be insulted by so infamous an assertion." [8] The incest taboo, the taboo on taking a sexual view of every member of the opposite sex, leaps to Southey's mind as a defense against Malthus's impious assertion of sexual exigency because it indicates the difference between our animal nature and our higher, human attributes. But Malthus busied himself with demonstrating that much of what was "higher," because distinctively human, was vicious because it divorced sexuality from procreation. The armchair ethnography he undertook in those later versions of the *Essay*—the survey of the often covert customs and mores governing how people actually lived, especially how they lived in ancient times, in "savage" states, or among the poor and in foreign lands—not only augmented the proportion of the *Essay* devoted to detailing the demoralizing consequences of the population principle, but also analyzed them as the customary reactions (what we would call the cultural reactions) to the omnipresence of the sexual impulse and the fear of its consequences. And in time, John McLennan, following Malthus into the exploration of sexual behavior, would even work out

---

[7] See, for example, Patricia James, *Population Malthus: His Life and Times* (London: Routledge and Kegan Paul, 1979), 116–21. For an account of the Evangelical economic thought that the subtly sexually revised Malthusianism stimulated, see Boyd Hilton, *The Age of Atonement: The Influence of Evangelicalism on Social and Economic Thought, 1785–1865* (Oxford: Clarendon Press, 1986), chapters 3 and 4.

[8] Rev. of *An Essay on the Principles* [sic] *of Population,* in *The Annual Review and History of Literature for 1803,* 2:296.

a Malthusian account of the very thing Southey called into evidence against Malthus, the incest taboo.

McLennan (1827–1881), who began as an Edinburgh lawyer closely allied (as J. R. McCulloch's son-in-law) to political economy, thought that the natural process leading to human culture was obviously population pressure. Primitive culture, he argued, began when humans developed the foresight to limit their numbers. Malthus was the obvious inspiration for this claim; indeed, early in the *Essay on Population* he pointed out that only humans try to prevent their own fertility:

> The preventive check is peculiar to man, and arises from that distinctive superiority in his reasoning faculties, which enables him to calculate distant consequences. Plants and animals have apparently no doubts about the future support of their offspring. The checks to their indefinite increase, therefore, are all positive.[9]

All creatures feel population pressure, in other words, but only humans anticipate it and try to avoid it by limiting their numbers. Among the conscious attempts to prevent increase, Malthus listed prostitution and all other forms of promiscuity, birth control, vast inequalities of wealth that enable only a few to have families, infanticide (including abortion), and homosexuality. In the future, he hoped, these might be superseded by moral restraint, but the preventive check for Malthus consisted mainly in a catalogue of sexual misbehavior or miserable abstinence. The preventive check was certainly the offspring of superior human intelligence, but it was also largely unnatural in the negative sense of the term.

Consequently, McLennan's installation of not only sexual need but also some of the most obnoxious preventive checks at the very foundation of culture was a bold and risky move. He claimed that the most primitive people organized their tribes into a sexual hierarchy and imposed rules of mating that would severely restrict births. The first cultural act in McLennan's history is female infanticide:

> Foremost among the results of this early struggle for food and security, must have been an effect upon the balance of the sexes. As braves and hunters were required and valued, it would be the interest of every horde to rear, when possible, its healthy male children. It would be less its interest to rear females, as they would be less capable of self-support, and of contributing, by their exertions, to the common good. In this lies the only explanation which can be accepted of the origin of those systems of female infanticide

---

[9] *Essay on the Principle of Population, Works of Thomas Malthus*, 2:14. The essay printed in the *Works* is the 1826 version, which gives variations from the 1803 edition. I have used the 1803 variation, given in fn. 4 in the volume cited here.

still existing, the discovery of which from time to time, in out of the way places, so shocks our humanity.[10]

It was, of course, Malthus who first assiduously sought out those systems as evidence of the continuous pressure of population and who pointed as well to promiscuity and polyandry as forms of sexuality that inhibited fertility. In these regards, too, McLennan followed in Malthus's footsteps, but he also made a radical departure: whereas Malthus had labeled all such practices vice, virtuous procreative sexuality being their antithesis, McLennan withheld moral judgment and derived exogamy (and finally the incest taboo, the foundation of sexual virtue) from these primitive sexual arrangements:

> We may predicate of the primitive groups that they were all . . . marked by a want of balance between the sexes—the males being in the majority. The reader will have little difficulty in granting that we may do so when he reflects on the prevalence of exogamy, the origin of which must be referred to that want of balance. (68)

To explain just how McLennan derived exogamy (a word he invented) from female infanticide, I must say a few words about his style and method. The rhetorical insistence of the last sentence—"exogamy . . . *must be referred*" to the shortage of females—is typical of his style, which is designed to support his heavily deductive reasoning. Rather than try to assemble large amounts of archaeological evidence for his claims, he admits the lack of direct confirmation, noting that by "primitive" he means the earliest humans at the inception of the species, about whom we can only speculate. He ransacks the existing ethnographies of "savage" groups and other tribal peoples for instances of preventive checks to population growth, and he arranges the scattered particulars into a causal chain of events as well as a coherent, synchronic cultural system. In some of the literature, he finds evidence of significant sexual imbalances among the most undeveloped tribes, in other places he finds accounts of female infanticide, and he links the two. In yet other ethnographies, he encounters polyandry, or rules against marrying inside the tribe (which he calls "exogamy"), or marriage ceremonies that contain ritual vestiges of bride capture. All of these he takes as evidence of a much earlier primal stage of development in which the individual elements fit together thus: first, female infanticide led to a shortage of women in the tribe; second, the shortage of women necessitated stealing them from other tribes; third, the difficulty of bride capture meant there was still an imbalance between the sexes, which led to promiscuous coupling and, later, polyandry; fourth, promiscuity and polyandry led to matrilineal kinship. Eventually, the existence of the outsider

---

[10] *Primitive Marriage: An Inquiry into the Origin of the Form of Capture in Marriage Ceremonies*, ed. and intro. Peter Rivière (Chicago: University of Chicago Press, 1970; first published, 1865 by Adam and Charles Black, Edinburgh), 68.

women and their outsider children in the group, he reasoned, would create an "other" inside the tribe, with which one could mate, and tribal exogamy would gradually diminish into the incest taboo as applied to families. But the formation of families, he reasoned, was a later stage that did not belong to primitive culture.

The coherence of McLennan's primitive culture was, therefore, partly a function of his deductive and conjectural methods, and he went on to extend his system so that it would encompass not only kinship and sexuality but also intragroup solidarity, intergroup hostility, and even ritual observance. Having demolished the time-honored belief that the patriarchal family lay at the origin of human social structure, McLennan then went on to argue that his version of primitive mating could also account for the primitive religion known as totemism. Totemism, he proposed, originated as an attempt to solve the problems of group identity created by the system of matrilineal descent. It strengthened the cohesion of separate matrilineal groups and organized the exogamous raids; before patriarchy, totemic identification supplied the group with something like a "spiritual" identity.

McLennan's assimilation of totemism into his thesis yielded an even more highly satisfying, because remarkably coherent, set of connections radiating outward from the exigencies of the preventive checks to the formation of the "cult," both etymologically and developmentally the acknowledged seed of culture. He arrived at the complex wholeness that the word "culture" indicated by picking up the reproduction side of the Malthusian dilemma and placing it at the core of a tight little social organism complete with a rudimentary religion. The construction of such a whole seemed to require a center, and an evolutionary succession of wholes required an unstable center that would constantly yield new and more elaborate forms for containing or displacing its contradictions. The relentless threat of an imbalance between the food supply and the power of reproduction was just such a productive instability; the engine of cultural evolution, it acted perpetually, just as it did in the process of biological evolution. Because the instability was basic to our organic nature, it would never go away, but it also spawned a variety of unexpected forms out of its own internal dynamic. McLennan's strong suit was his extraordinary facility as a dialectician, his ability to imagine how one form had followed another to contain some developing incoherence. We might even say that the appeal of McLennan's work was largely formal, indeed, aesthetic, for it repeatedly foregrounds the elegant economy of its derivation of an entire culture from a few methods of preventing fertility. And its formal appeal reinforced the pleasure of contemplating the wholeness that the study of primitive culture seemed to promise. These attractions may help explain the tenacity of McLennan's ideas, for they remained strong contenders against other accounts of primitive social organization until the last decade of the century,

despite the opposition of Tylor, and Darwin's rejection of McLennan's fundamental postulate—the existence of primeval attempts to limit population.

Before recounting Darwin's objections, I want to highlight one further
advantage of McLennan's approach to primitive culture, one more feature
that might have counterbalanced its scandalous implications. Although
McLennan was by no means always clear about his objectives, an interest in
the origin of the incest taboo was just under the surface of his writing, and
consequently he seemed to be formulating a natural explanation (that is,
pointing to a process operating in all organic life), of the break with nature,
the onset of modes of behavior that are distinguished by their human social
conditioning. In contrast, as we're about to see, the Darwinian thinkers, including Darwin himself, were reluctant to pursue the idea of any sharp discon-
tinuity between animal and human adaptation, so in emphasizing the maximization of the food supply, they kept the focus on developmental continuities.
Looking at sexual relations instead, McLennan immediately saw a developmental break—the incest taboo—which seemed to be a human universal
without any animal analogues. Victorians did not doubt that this was a phenomenon limited to humans, perpetuated by social rules, and varying in its
local details in both time and space—that is to say, no one doubted that it is
a *cultural* phenomenon—and yet its ubiquity in one form or another pointed
toward a natural exigency. McLennan, in short, performed the magic trick of
conjuring culture out of nature more successfully than the Darwinians to
whom we now turn.

In *The Descent of Man* Darwin's disagreement with McLennan stems not
from any neglect of the Malthusian dilemma but from a differing assessment
of its operation, one that emphasized the expansion of the food supply instead
of the limitation of the tribe. Whereas McLennan started with Malthus and
derived a culture built on population limitation, Darwin started with Malthus
and derived one built on population growth. As is well known, Darwin
wanted to describe not just the descent of man but also his ascent, and so his
interest was in how population pressure, always assumed in his analyses, drove
the cultural inventiveness that increased individual and species survival. It has
also been noted that his use of Malthus reversed the earlier writer's emphasis
(and that of McLennan) on human reproductive control. Darwin's primitive
people needed to multiply as fast as possible in order to create the greatest
probability of variation and to increase beyond the food supply so that the
most adaptive variations, biologically and culturally, could be naturally selected. The apelike progenitors of human beings, he therefore reminds us,

> would not have practiced infanticide, for the instincts of the lower animals
> are never so perverted as to lead them regularly to destroy their own off-
> spring. There would have been no prudential restraint from marriage, and
> the sexes would have freely united at an early age. Hence the progenitors of

man would have tended to increase rapidly, but checks of some kind, either periodical or constant, must have kept down their numbers, even more severely than with existing savages.[11]

The "checks," of course, are the various modes of deselection through which natural selection occurs, but these, according to Darwin, must have been Malthus's positive checks, such as famine, pestilence, disease, and war. Darwin conceded that in later stages of human history, infanticide was probably widely used, even more widely than Malthus had thought, but he balked at McLennan's hypothesis of a chronic, artificially induced primitive shortage of women leading to a communal, nonpatriarchal form of mating. Although Darwin does not expressly say so, a culture so intently focused on the prevention of fertility might check population growth effectively enough to interfere with natural selection itself.

His most clearly stated objection to McLennan's hypothesis, however, was that it would obviate *sexual* selection, that second evolutionary motor that regulated not who survived to procreative age but who actually procreated. Darwin by no means ignored the topics of sexuality and culture in *The Descent of Man*, but his treatment of the topic runs counter to McLennan's at every point. Sexual selection, Darwin thought, was driven only by aesthetic-erotic pleasure, not reproductive stringency. Darwin's sexual selection required an abundance of women, whereas McLennan's population restriction was based on a dearth of them. If the proportion of women in a population were small, Darwin reasoned, they would be equally likely to produce the same number of offspring, regardless of their possession of the attributes considered sexually attractive, such as lack of body hair or enlarged mammary glands. Under those conditions, Darwin's explanation of many secondary sexual characteristics and of human sexual dimorphism generally would be disabled. Moreover, if primitive man mated indiscriminately with all of the available women because they were scarce instead of choosing the most desirable from an ample supply, Darwin would no longer have an explanation for the visual and aural aesthetic faculties that he linked to sexual selection. Allowing that the social form McLennan describes might have been a temporary stage in human development, Darwin's entire theory forces him to conclude that the earliest groups were patriarchal and polygamous:

> [I]t is extremely improbable that primeval men and women lived promiscuously together. Judging from the social habits of man as he now exists, and from most savages being polygamists, the most probable view is that primeval man aboriginally lived in small communities, each with as many wives as he could support and obtain, whom he would have jealously guarded against

[11] *The Descent of Man, and Selection in Relation to Sex* (Princeton: Princeton University Press, 1981), 134–35. Page numbers for other quotations given in the text.

all other men. Or he may have lived with several wives by himself, like the
Gorilla. (362)

As that last sentence indicates, Darwin's primitive marriage was thus a cultural arrangement that hardly distinguishes itself from nature; his gorilla-like
men are not, like McLennan's early humans, "perverted" enough to destroy
their offspring. However, living in family groups without a culture of kinship,
their "naturalness" must also have included incest. McLennan therefore
rightly accused Darwin of failing to recognize the necessary *unnaturalness* of
human sexuality. Complaining of Darwin's preference for a primitive culture
resembling the social organization of other primates, he quipped, "The inquiry is, remember, a *human* one."[12]

But Darwin's early culture did have the advantage of allowing the positive
checks to operate, as they do in other species, to effect adaptation through
natural or sexual selection. Darwin went so far as to classify the elements of
McLennan's primitive marriage, which consisted, as we've seen, of Malthus's
preventive checks, as interferences with the normal course of evolution. He
thus implied that if one were to believe McLennan, the onset of culture would
spell the end of natural selection. Even when he turned his attention to sex,
therefore, he was not primarily concerned with the Malthusian sexual question—how can people have sex without making too many more people? Darwin's sexual investigations tended toward a different inquiry: how does sexual
selection keep a thinking species so interested in sex that it will act impru-
dently and press against the limits of its food supply? Darwin, therefore, was
not less Malthusian than McLennan, only differently Malthusian; both carefully traced their views back to the population principle, making the food/sex
conundrum the primeval cultural crux, but (to repeat this point yet again)
they imagined cultures that cohered around opposite sides of the duality.

Such differences in the deployment of Malthus can be found across a range
of early anthropological thought. Edward B. Tylor, for example, followed Darwin by stressing the driving force of the need to increase the food supply, and
he therefore thought cultural evolution was led by technological, linguistic,
and scientific progress. The onset of culture, he implied, was a gradual process
of increasing independence from and control over nature, rather than a sharp
break from it that could be associated with any particular practice. In his
major work, *Primitive Culture: Researches into the Development of Mythology,
Philosophy, Religion, Language, Art and Custom*, Tylor had virtually nothing to
say about human population control; indeed, as the subtitle indicates, he had
remarkably little to say about sexuality or kinship. One of his primary interests
was certainly the origin of the cultic in culture, the early inklings of what

---

[12] Quoted in Stocking, *Victorian Anthropology*, 176. Cites *Studies in Ancient History: The Second
Series* (London, 1896), 51.

would become religion, but far from relating it to exogamy or the incest taboo, he discusses it as an indirect consequence of the development of mankind's general reasoning powers, especially curiosity and self-reflection.

On the other side of the divide, William Robertson Smith followed McLennan's lead and remained focused on reproductive control. The origin and nature of primitive religion increasingly occupied both sides of the anthropological debate in the 1870s and 1880s, but that similarity only brought the differences between the two lines of thought into sharper focus. Whereas Tylor barely mentioned sexual arrangements in his descriptions of religion, Robertson Smith emphasized the immediate connection between exogamy and early cult worship. Those anthropologists who sexed primitive culture, therefore, continued to imagine a more seamless primitive social world than those who concentrated on food production. They left no gaps between the daily life (where the emphasis falls on "life" as in organic being) and ritual observance. To be sure, the culture they depicted was full of violence—infanticide, war, and rape—but that, according to Robertson Smith, only stimulated cults that inspired a fierce devotion and sense of absolute obligation to the group. Exotic, bizarre, and even repulsive as McLennan's and Robertson Smith's representations sometimes were, their consistency and their strong sense of cultural difference from nature proved compelling enough to survive several decades of Darwinian skepticism. And—most importantly for our purposes—they continued to inspire the kind of comparative anthropology whose picture of primitive culture was eventually to merge with that other Victorian culture concept, which took the "works and practices of . . . artistic activity"[13] as its object.

That later merger depended especially on the increasingly daring sexualization of religion. By emphasizing the connection between primitive reproduction and religious impulses, sexuality was brought more insistently into the heart of the culture concept, where it was surrounded with the aura—the scandal as well as the allure—of late nineteenth-century *scientia sexualis*. Robertson Smith, a Presbyterian theologian by training, elaborated McLennan's ideas and applied them to the primitive Hebrews in 1880, arguing that their ritual practices proceeded not from some divinely inspired ideational realm of beliefs but organically from the everyday world of kinship and genealogy. Finding evidence among Semitic tribes of vestiges of all the features of McLennan's primitive culture, he argued that the very people who eventually invented monotheism, began by celebrating rites that sustained a matriarchal, probably either communal or polyandrous, culture, based on female infanticide and rules of exogamy mandating marriage by capture between different totemic groups.

---

[13] Raymond Williams, *Keywords: A Vocabulary of Culture and Society,* 2nd ed. (New York: Oxford University Press, 1983), 90.

The Presbyterian Church Assembly reprimanded Robertson Smith in no uncertain terms for casting such obscene aspersions on Christianity's own theological forefathers: "First, concerning marriage and the marriage laws in Israel, the views expressed are so gross and so fitted to pollute the moral sentiments of the community that they cannot be considered except within the closed doors of any court of this Church."[14] The matriarchal sexuality and murderous means of population control described were bad enough, but the rites themselves, consisting in sacrifices of totemic animals who were considered both gods and blood relations, were even more distressing: "Secondly, concerning animal worship in Israel, the views expressed by the Professor are not only contrary to the facts recorded and the statements made in Holy Scripture, but they are gross and sensual—fitted to pollute and debase public sentiment."

One suspects, however, that it was the similarities, rather than the differences, between these rites and the idea of Christ's sacrifice that exercised the church leaders. The primitive, totemic Hebrew practice was simply too recognizable in modern Christian theology, and in 1889, eight years after his indictment by the church and removal from his post as professor at Aberdeen, Robertson Smith clarified that very likeness: "That the God-man dies for His people and that his Death is their life, is an idea which was in some degree foreshadowed by the oldest mystical sacrifices . . . [T]he voluntary death of the divine victim, which we have seen to be a conception not foreign to ancient ritual, contained the germ of the deepest thought in the Christian doctrine."[15] Robertson Smith dropped the apple of Christianity uncomfortably close to the tree of primal but unnatural sexuality.

The scandalousness of Robertson Smith's ideas no doubt helped disseminate them and formed part of their appeal for a generation intent on studying human sexuality in all of its varieties. But many comparative anthropologists, including, crucially, Tylor, continued to oppose the first premise of the McLennanite line of thought: that early humans wanted to limit the rate of their own increase. Nevertheless, they also seem to have felt mounting pressure to explain exogamy; that is, even the orthodox Darwinians were forced to turn their attention to the sexual organization of culture. Tylor, especially, became interested in the evidence collected by the proponents of totemism and began to write about the culture of reproduction seriously in the late 1880s. In 1889, he credited the existence of a matriarchal stage of development and speculated on the origins of exogamy, but he refused to accept the female infanticide hypothesis. He proposed instead that the arrival of exogamy demonstrated the potential evolutionary importance of *over*population, since it gave the territorial advantage to groups who formed alliances and could

[14] Quoted in Kuper, *Invention*, 85.
[15] From Frazer's 1894 obituary of Robertson Smith and quoted in ibid., 88.

thus overwhelm smaller endogamous groups by sheer force of numbers. Tylor stressed that cultural evolution could only work in a crowded environment: "Again and again in the world's history, savage tribes must have had plainly before their minds the simple practical alternative between marrying-out and being killed out."[16] When he addressed himself to the sexual side of the Malthusian dilemma, he thus emphasized the need to outbreed one's neighbors, exhausting one's own food supply and creating the pressure to assimilate or annihilate the other. A tribe intent on population increase would be more likely to survive, and so a high cultural premium would have to be placed on fertility all around: the growth of the food supply and the enlargement of the human group. Thus Tylor almost rescued the incest taboo from its link to primitive perversity, while placing culture back on a smooth continuum with nature and maintaining Darwin's use of Malthus as the theorist of expansion.

Judging by the next development in the sexualization of culture, the reiteration of this orthodox Darwinian use of Malthus seems to have won the day; far from diverting attention from sexual matters, though, the idea of a culture devoted to increase in general actually resulted in what we might call the sexualization of the food supply. That accomplishment belonged to James G. Frazer, who combined the two terms of the Malthusian dichotomy in a remarkably durable compound that became synonymous with British comparative anthropology for three decades. The synthesis was based on the assertion that in primeval times people did not have a strong sense of separation between themselves and the surrounding natural world, especially between themselves and their food supply. The primitive magic that constituted their culture aimed to make all of nature, including themselves, fecund through the observance of rites that applied human sexual intercourse to the vegetable world and reciprocally conceived human reproduction on the model of vegetation cycles. The rites in which a god was killed and reborn in a new body were the main subject of Frazer's *The Golden Bough*, where it is argued that primitive people thereby ritually imitated and controlled the vitality of the primeval forest while also ensuring that the main representative of their own human group—the god-man—remained young and vigorous. Frazer speculated that these rites often included not only the slaying of the divinity before he or she grew old and feeble and thereby the transfer of his or her potency to a younger body, but also the literal or simulated coupling of representatives of the gods and the orgiastic sexual behavior of the group in the interval between the god's death and rebirth. All of the gods he discussed—Baal, Adonis, Osiris, Dionysus, Artemis, Ceres, and Persephone—turn out to be fertility gods, whose rites combined sexuality and sacrifice. Thus Frazer accommodated the expansionist version of primitive culture, organized by Darwin and Tylor around the food side of Malthusianism, while retaining much that

[16] Ibid., 100.

had earlier belonged to the reproductive limitationist version, concocted by
McLennan and Robertson Smith: initiation rites, human sacrifice, episodes
of group promiscuity, and even the odor of blasphemy emanating from savage
god-men who are killed and resurrected. In short, the premises had changed,
but the thrill hadn't gone.

THE AESTHETICS OF MALTHUSIAN PLOTS

The Golden Bough, we all know, became a foundational text for modernism,
inspiring works by T. S. Eliot, Virginia Woolf, and Sigmund Freud, to mention only a few of the many authors who developed its implications for that
other culture concept: the inward process that creates and understands a
realm of symbolic representations persisting from age to age. Although the
comparative anthropologists apparently used a concept of culture stressing
synchronic relations, seeking, as Tylor put it, the "complex whole" forming
a specific people at a given place and time, a large part of their appeal to
modernists lay in their explanation of how, and where, representations and
their corollary states of mind abide through time, outliving the cultures of
their origin. Modernists scornful of Matthew Arnold's naive formulation of
culture as "the best that has been thought and said" could rescue the idea of
cultural universals by turning to the likes of Frazer. Universalism was built
into the method that he learned from McLennan, who articulated a theory
of cultural symbolism in the introduction to *Primitive Marriage*, which was
then expanded by Tylor as the doctrine of "survivals"; it was the theory that
made the comparisons of the comparative anthropologists possible. McLennan's version stressed that the primitive ways of a people not only survive
their utility but are manifest in later times as apparently meaningless symbols;
he insisted on their incomprehensibility and claimed that the explanations
given by the people who now use the symbols are always wrong. Anything,
according to McLennan, can turn into a symbol. For example, the Khonds
still occasionally practiced female infanticide in the nineteenth century, integrating it into a religious ritual. To McLennan, the infrequency of the
practice and its elevation out of everyday life into the sacred indicated that
it had lost its utility as part of a system of polyandrous kinship. Preserved in
the nineteenth century merely out of "reverence for the past,"[17] the earlier
expedient was transformed into a sacrifice, but the meaning of the surviving
and now merely symbolic action—not so much an action as the representation of an action—could be understood only by discounting its stated religious significance and discerning its original Malthusian use: "It is of no

---

[17] McLennan, *Primitive Marriage*, 7.

consequence [McLennan claims] by what theories the races who practice infanticide now defend the practice. There can be no doubt that its origin is everywhere referable to that early time of struggle [for survival] and necessity which we have been contemplating."[18] McLennan invented the method of interrogating symbols, or "forms" or "fictions," as he sometimes calls them, by dismissing their overt significance and canvasing reports from the least civilized tribes to assemble shards and remnants of the "system" of which they were once a functional part. Eventually, the religious infanticide of the Khonds should give way to a higher level of symbolism—perhaps merely exposing infants to some innocuous danger—and a new specious meaning might be attached.

The comparative method, therefore, began by puzzling over a symbolic form; *Primitive Marriage* starts with symbols of bride capture that can be found in European countries (think, for example, of throwing shoes and rice after the bride and groom as they leave the church), and then moves into the ethnographic literature.

> [W]henever we discover symbolical forms, we are justified in inferring that in the past life of the people employing them, there were corresponding realities; and if, among the primitive races which we examine, we find such realities as might naturally pass into such forms on an advance taking place in civility, then we may safely conclude . . . that what these now are, those employing the symbols once were. (7)

Much has been written about the spatialization of time that this comparative method achieved, about the hierarchy of cultures and races it created, and the expectation of a uniform line of development it encouraged, but I want to call our attention to its impact on how British people began to imagine their own culture. The modernists were intrigued by the idea that the most highly developed peoples misunderstand the forms and symbols by which we live and that they are motivated to adhere to them by ancient promptings beyond their ken. Estranged from the symbols it encounters, modern consciousness was supposed to have lost the clue to their meaning while still feeling their mysterious force. Frazer's stress on "fertility" in deciphering them held a strong appeal because it seemed to imply that some spring of generativity lay hidden in the realm of the "symbolic," existing apart from contemporary society's functional systems. One might then, without having to activate Arnold's cultural piety, understand why art—the largest depository of cultural symbols—inhabited a separate sphere, safe from the more perishable practical arrangement of modern life. And one could even assert, on the basis of the symbol's necessary impenetrability, art's consignment to specialists for inter-

---

[18] Ibid., 68.

pretation and elaboration. Its meanings could be thought of as at once superficially unavailable and universal. The storehouse of primal energies, ancient
human impulses, and remnants of fertility rituals, art was also reconceived, in
the early twentieth century, as sublimated sexuality. What modernism assimi-
lated from comparative anthropology, therefore, was the Malthusian obsession
with fertility metamorphosed into a theory of the symbolic.

I start with the modernists because the impact of anthropological Malthusianism is easiest to see in their writing: we can trace the genealogy from
Malthus to McLennan to Frazer to the Cambridge theorists of literature and
T. S. Eliot, Virginia Woolf, and so on. Or, in a slightly different genealogy,
we can move from Malthus to Darwin to Frazer to Freud. Either way, we
arrive not only at a surprisingly Malthusian modernist literature but also at a
Malthusian literary criticism. Modernism reminds us of the stake that we have
as a discipline in the ideas I have been outlining. Through psychoanalysis,
through the various myth and ritual schools of criticism of the first half of the
twentieth century,[19] even through American naturalism and, later, the influence of Northrup Frye (a complete Frazerian) on North American theories of
literature, the comparative anthropologists' theories flourished in the literary
imagination long after they had been discredited and completely abandoned
by anthropologists in the wake of the First World War. As late as 1961, literary
historians pointed to that source as "the deepest influence upon modern poetry."[20] Indeed, while writing these chapters I have repeatedly been overtaken
by the queasy sensation of watching, in the Malthusian gyrations of the Victorian comparative anthropologists, the primal scene of the conception of the
discipline I am practicing.

If the line of descent from Malthus to the modernist idea of culture via
Frazer, and from there to twentieth-century criticism, is perceptible, there is
yet another route that I want to trace, which is perhaps more typical of the
actual incorporation of the Malthusian dilemma into the literary imagination.
That route emerges in the realist novels of the last half of the century, especially those of George Eliot, George Meredith, Samuel Butler, and Thomas
Hardy. I'll concentrate on the beginning of that list, analyzing George Eliot's
first published fiction, *Scenes of Clerical Life*. Appearing before Darwin's *Origin of Species*, it gives us a chance to look at "cultural" Malthusianism on the
eve of its evolutionary redemption and to suggest that the novel might have
helped shape the anthropological stories. It may seem odd to go back, in the

---

[19] In 1912, for example, Gilbert Murray recounted the birth of tragedy in Frazer's familiar terms:
"[T]ragedy is in origin a Ritual Dance" that is "centrally that of Dionysus," whose agon "represents
the cyclical death and rebirth of the world, including the rebirth of the tribe." "Tragedy," moreover,
is only "one instance of the splendid art that arose from the . . . ritual." See Murray's "Excursus" in
Jane Ellen Harrison, *Themis: A Study of the Social Origins of Greek Religion* (Cambridge: Cambridge
University Press, 1912), 341–63.
[20] Introduction to *Aristotle's Poetics* (New York: Hill and Wang, 1961), 39.

last chapter of this book, to George Eliot's early stories—especially since the previous chapter concentrated on her last novel—but I hope the chronological reversion will allow us to see how novels with "anthropological" ambitions joined the strands of bioeconomics and somaeconomics.

George Eliot's novels have always been recognized as "ethnographic"; no one ever doubted that she went to considerable lengths to depict cultures as whole ways of life. In *Scenes of Clerical Life*, moreover, she also seems to expect her readers to be familiar with the idea of cultures as graduated stages in human development: one early nineteenth-century English town, we are told, is "in a state of Attic culture," while another has reached only a Boeotian level, where "men's minds and wagons alike moved in the deepest ruts."[21] Eliot's narrator can gently satirize her own ethnographic pretensions, but she is nevertheless careful to identify the delicate filaments connecting material to mental formations, showing, for example, how the richness of a dairy farmer's cream assuages all spiritual aspirations and turns Christianity into a complacent paganism. Eliot began by trying to meet the standards for fiction that she had established in her own 1856 review of Riehl's *Natural History of German Life*, standards that included a consequentialist materialism in delineating consciousness, which tended to exclude the appearance of high levels of moral sensibility among people at low levels of social progress. George Eliot's attention was not riveted on the scene of the earliest emergence of culture, as, for example, McLennan's was, but she concentrated nevertheless on the systematic connections between the way a people make their livings, form their families, and create their gods.

To be sure, earlier novelists had also proclaimed that they were rewriting the historical record to include the ways of life, the manners and morals, of common people. But Eliot's intellectual formation had implanted an unusual determination to depict the intimate life of the people, including their struggles for survival and their means of adjusting reproduction to resources. She was educated in the early nineteenth-century Evangelical tradition of social thought that we associate with Thomas Chalmers.[22] As Boyd Hilton demonstrates in *The Age of Atonement*, it was a school of social analysis and Protestant activism saturated with "moral restraint" Malthusianism, in which the suffering attendant on overpopulation was presented as part of God's divine plan to bring about moral progress. Hence, it was a religion that used political economy to emphasize the relation between sexuality, suffering, and spiritual development. By the time George Eliot began her career as a fiction writer,

---

[21] *Scenes of Clerical Life* (New York: Penguin, 1977), 83. Page numbers for other quotations are given in the text.

[22] On Chalmers, see, in addition to Hilton, Robert M. Young, *Darwin's Metaphor: Nature's Place in Victorian Culture* (Cambridge: Cambridge University Press, 1985), 31–39; and Mary Poovey, *Making a Social Body: British Cultural Formation, 1830–1864* (Chicago: University of Chicago Press, 1995), 99–106.

she had already abandoned her Evangelical religion for an equally ardent humanism, which only strengthened her need to believe in the advancement of the species. If Evangelical social theory had stressed the need for the sublimation of fleshly passions, though, the later secular developmentalism emphasized instead the need for spiritual longings to find flesh-and-blood objects of veneration. Her novels consequently tend to feature the humanization of spiritual ambition. Indeed, following a suggestion of Gillian Beer's, Boyd Hilton sees Eliot's novels as expressions of the milder popular Christian political economy of the end of the century; sometimes indistinguishable from secular humanism, it abandoned the ethos of "Atonement" for that of the "Incarnation."[23] But she did not, I shall argue, drop the Malthusian considerations that were part of the fabric of her earlier beliefs.

Eliot underwent no Malthusian epiphany comparable to Darwin's; she did not mention Malthus in her notebooks, and there is only one very late and utterly enigmatic reference to Malthus in her journal; an 1880 entry reads, "A quiet afternoon. Finished Prose Edda, etc./Akkadians/Malthus."[24] But Malthusianism was inescapable in her milieu by midcentury; various strands of it pervaded thinking on social and historical topics, in addition to energizing religious polemics. Moreover, there is plenty of evidence in *Scenes of Clerical Life* that Eliot considered moral-restraint Malthusianism an important component of the Evangelical consciousnesses she set out to depict in those fictions. In "Janet's Repentance" (set, like all three stories, in the years before the New Poor Law), for example, the heroine hears the wisdom of Thomas Chalmers from an Evangelical neighbor, who considers it part of his religious duty to dispense charity according to rules even stricter than those Malthus himself promulgated to "keep industrious men an' women off the parish" (402). The homespun, religiously inspired political economist declares, "I'd rether given ten shillin' an' help a man to stand on his own legs, nor pay half-a-crown to buy him a parish crutch; it's the ruination on him if he once goes to the parish" (402). Chalmers developed and preached his radical antagonism to parish relief on the basis of Malthus's arguments. In *Janet's Repentance* this hard-line abolitionist stance toward the Poor Laws places the character in a particular historical milieu, functioning as a detail of historicist realism. Its presentation as a perfectly reasonable, indeed admirable, position to hold, however, also implicates the narrator in that historical moment and represents an instance of what Harry Shaw has called the narrator's submission to the

[23] Hilton, *The Age of Atonement*, 316–17. See also Gillian Beer, *Darwin's Plots: Evolutionary Narrative in Darwin, George Eliot and Nineteenth-Century Fiction* (New York: Routledge and Kegan Paul, 1983), 154. On Eliot's relation to her earlier Evangelicalism, see U. C. Knoepflmacher, *Religious Humanism and the Victorian Novel: George Eliot, Walter Pater, and Samuel Butler* (Princeton: Princeton University Press, 1965), 24–71.

[24] *The Journals of George Eliot*, eds. Margaret Harris and Judith Johnston (Cambridge: Cambridge University Press, 1998), 201.

history depicted.[25] The point is not that Eliot (or her narrator) was in favor of abolishing the Poor Laws, but that moral-restraint Malthusianism can only be understood by placing it in a sympathetic light as a sincere, if outdated, mode of caring about the poor.

Moreover, *Scenes of Clerical Life* contains other Malthusian reflections on poverty and charity. In "Mr. Gilfil's Love-Story," a widow and her children are evicted from their farm, despite her tears and pathetic pleas, and we are made to understand that the landlord would be doing no one any good by giving in to the widow and allowing the farm to become unprofitable. She and her children would merely decline into the pauper state by such misguided generosity. Moreover, it is clearly her fecundity that makes her unfit to run the farm; the same landlord happily rented to her childless, spinster aunt. He will, it seems, eventually rent the widow a cottage, but instructs her first to find a small place where she and her many children may live economically. Once again the vignette functions as a "historicist" detail, that allows us to witness the enlightened philosophy of an unusually thoughtful late eighteenth-century landowner, one who spends his time on serious improvements rather than wine and hunting dogs. The whole tenor of this historicist realism is antisentimental and favors a clear-eyed rational progressivism.

In her later novels, Eliot's Malthusian utterances seem to belong even more overtly to the narrator. Less the indications of specific historical mentalities, they become a more seamlessly integrated part of the narrative commentary, as in this typically consequentialist passage from *Felix Holt*: "[T]here is no private life which has not been determined by a wider public life, from the time when the primeval milkmaid had to wander with the wanderings of her clan, because the cow she milked was one of a herd which had made the pastures bare."[26] The expansion of the idea of "life" in this passage as it moves from the "private life," denoting individual human lots, to the "wider public life" encompassing a herd of cows and their pastures, meets the Malthusian demand that private lives be recognized, not only as parts of human cultures, according to the common historicist insight, but also as pieces of "Life," an organic, material totality that necessitates constant struggle. Moreover, in the quietly unorthodox way in which the passage briefly plays with the myth of the expulsion from Eden, Eliot's narrator substitutes a purely Malthusian reason for primeval wandering: "pastures bare." The primeval milkmaid, symbol of fecundity, has exhausted the food supply. Overpasturing, or the transition to pastoralism itself from the savage stage of hunting and gathering, is this demythologized Eve's original sin. As soon as the tribe had cows, they were doomed to wander.

[25] Harry E. Shaw, *Narrating Reality: Austen, Scott, Eliot* (Ithaca, N.Y.: Cornell University Press, 1999), 238–46.

[26] *Felix Holt, The Radical* (New York: J. M. Dent and Sons, 1967), 45.

Eliot's narrator here can be succinct, can pithily refer to the aggregate process, because the passage echoes a commonplace of the late eighteenth-century philosophical histories that had been modified by Malthus himself for use by developmentalists. Discussing "the early migrations and settlements of mankind," Malthus emphasized that in pastoral societies, "[t]he women live in greater ease than among nations of hunters, and are consequently more prolific. . . . The . . . causes soon produce their natural and invariable effect, an extended population. A more frequent and rapid change of place then becomes necessary. A wider and more extensive territory is successively occupied. A broader desolation extends all around them. . . . Young scions are then pushed out from the parent stock, and instructed to explore fresh regions." And then he concludes by quoting Milton: "The world is [*sic*] all before them where to choose."[27] Malthus, in other words, had already made the point that pastoralism was the material reality out of which the myth of the expulsion from the garden grew. Eliot's narrator only needs to gesture in that direction.

In Eliot's later novels, Malthusian dynamics are taken for granted; they are part of a generally accepted problematic rather than being relegated to historically limited consciousnesses. The more localized Malthusianism of *Scenes of Clerical Life* points, in contrast, to the continuing controversy surrounding the implications of Malthus's ideas in the 1850s, which went far beyond changes in the Poor Laws to the heart of developmentalism. Before Darwin showed how Malthus could help explain the mechanism of evolution, Malthus's doctrines, as we've already noticed, were generally thought to be *anti*-evolutionary. Malthusians tended to stress balance rather than dynamism in the economy; they seemed allied with agricultural interests rather than industry; and they were often heard pointing out the limits of progress. Only by integrating them, as Chalmers had, into a religious, as opposed to naturalist, dynamic could they be folded into a narrative of improvement. Consequently, overcoming Malthusianism seemed a necessity of naturalist evolutionary thought. Even before the developmentalism of the 1850s gathered a wide following, its characteristic themes could be heard in attacks on Malthusians. Here is one early assault, for example, on what seemed the intrinsic limitationism of Malthusian orthodoxy: "[W]e do not see that nature has contented herself with establishing little groups of organized beings in snug corners to thrive there in security and content, through a nice adjustment of their numbers to the food within their reach. . . . No! Abundance, extension, multiplication, competition for room, is the order of creation."[28]

The debate over what was seen as the Malthusian impediment to the evolutionary hypothesis gathered force through the 1840s and was very much in the intellectual air Eliot breathed when she arrived in London and took up

[27] Malthus, *Principle of Population*, 62.
[28] Review of Chalmers in *Quarterly Review* 48 (October/December 1832), 64.

her editorial duties at the *Westminster Review* in 1851. Indeed, each of the first two issues she edited contained one essay dealing with Malthus; the first defended him against a recent detractor and the second attempted to substitute its own population principle in place of Malthus's. The second essay was by Eliot's intimate friend Herbert Spencer, who began his argument with an anti-Malthusian blast worthy of Dr. Pangloss: "That the human constitution should include some condition which must ever continue to entail either physical or moral pain, is at variance with all that a wide experience teaches [us]. . . . Faith in the essential beneficence of things is the highest kind of faith."[29] He then went on to argue that individuation, which he links to the self-preservation instinct, and reproduction, connected to the sexual instinct, vary inversely. Organisms strongly motivated by one, he asserts, will be only weakly motivated by the other. Since the progress of civilization encourages and thrives on individuation, on self-seeking, reproduction and its attendant passions will be correspondingly curtailed.

We can recognize in Spencer's solution the revival of the Godwinian thesis that provoked Malthus's *Essay on Population* in the first place: that sexual passion diminishes as civilization advances. Unlike Godwin, though, Spencer based his version of the argument on physiological grounds, maintaining that a highly developed nervous system detracts from the reproductive capacity: The more organic matter that goes into your nervous system, the less will be available in your semen. And the more advanced your nervous system, the less you will care about the state of your semen. Never one to discount the importance of goads to competition, however, Spencer both maintained that the drive to reproduce would soon abate and admitted that population pressure is responsible for the species' past and even current progress:

> [A]fter having caused, as it ultimately must, the due peopling of the globe, and the bringing of all its habitable parts into the highest state of culture . . . after having . . . developed the intellect into complete competency for its work, and the feelings into complete fitness for social life . . . we see that the pressure of population, as it gradually finishes its work, must gradually bring itself to an end. (501)

In this pre-Darwinian account of how population pressure causes social improvement as its unintended consequence, Spencer appeared to be half a Malthusian. Just as Darwin and Tylor would two decades later, Spencer articulated an account of the past development of intellectual and social forms that relied on the pressure of population to motivate increasing mastery over resources. Unlike Darwin and Tylor, he imagined that the mastery would become complete and that Malthus was wrong to say that greater population growth would be the result. Although the process might have been miserable, Spencer

---

[29] *Westminster Review*, n.s. 1 (1852), 469–70.

thought that belief in "the essential beneficence of things" required one to imagine a happy ending, with a contented ever-after in which the very desire for reproduction would cease.

There is no record of George Eliot's immediate response to this essay,[30] although it may be relevant that her contemporary correspondence is strewn with sarcastic remarks about such optimistic accounts of the course of nature. The gender politics of Spencer's essay would probably also have distanced Eliot from his conclusions. Maintaining that the investment in reproduction arrests the development of mental faculties, he speculated that females are particularly handicapped by the antagonism between intellectual and reproductive activity, since nature early deducts a reserve of nerve cells from women's brains in order to supply the needs of possible future progeny. It's not likely that Eliot would have found such opinions congenial, or that they would have inclined her to prefer Spencer's new population theory to Malthus's old one.

Indeed, judging from the evidence of her later statements as well as from her early fiction, she seems to have quarreled with Spencer's fundamental postulate that we should reject any theory "requiring that the human constitution should include some condition which must ever continue to entail either physical or moral pain." Eliot maintained that reproduction, especially the suffering of sexual passion and maternity, far from being inversely related to cultural achievement, goes hand in hand with mental grandeur,[31] and hers is certainly the more Malthusian view. The misery entailed in the population principle, Malthus had infamously maintained in the first edition of his essay, is necessary to make mind out of matter. Eliot repeated almost exactly that sentiment in an 1867 letter to John Morley:

> [A]s a fact of mere zoological evolution, woman seems to have the worse share in existence. But for that very reason, I would the more contend that in the moral evolution we have "*an art that does mend nature.*" It is the function of love in the largest sense to mitigate the harshness of all fatalities, and in the thorough recognition of that worse share, I think there is a basis for a sublimer recognition in women and a more regenerating tenderness in man.[32]

Although this might superficially sound like a Darwinian gloss on domestic ideology—women are morally superior because they suffer disproportionately—Eliot's fiction takes the idea in a different direction. If evolution has

[30] For a full discussion of Eliot's relation to Herbert Spencer, see Nancy L. Paxton, *George Eliot and Herbert Spencer: Feminism, Evolutionism, and the Reconstruction of Gender* (Princeton: Princeton University Press, 1991).

[31] On differences between Darwin, Spencer, and Eliot on the question of gender, see Beer, *Darwin's Plots*, 196–218.

[32] *The George Eliot Letters*, ed. Gordon S. Haight (New Haven: Yale University Press, 1978), 4:364. The allusion is to Act IV of *The Winter's Tale*, in which Hermione appears to "come back to life." Hence, the theme of a "dying" and reviving woman is included in the word "art" in this passage.

given the heavier reproductive burden to women, it has also given them a correspondingly "sublimer recognition," which brings to Eliot's mind that important word, "art." Eliot's allusion here is to Shakespeare's *The Winter's Tale*, where "art" refers to the skill of reviving and preserving Hermione, presumed dead in childbirth. In Eliot's earliest fiction, the lethalness of childbirth is similarly associated with the artistic impulse, as in the first two stories of *Scenes of Clerical Life*. For Eliot, as for Malthus, the most admirable traits of human nature arise from the identity of the source of both happiness and misery. For Malthus, as for Eliot, love and suffering spring from the same impulse not because (as earlier thinkers claimed) we cannot control our passion or assuage an unreasonable appetite for pleasure, but because the reproductive drive is itself admirable and its emotions are among the noblest of our nature. Hence, especially when they take some fatal turn, those emotions generate the "sublimer recognition" that becomes a central cultural feature, often taking the form of religion. Eliot's implied Malthusian argument against Spencer is that we should not necessarily simply seek personal happiness; if we were happy, if life were not a perpetual encounter with dead mothers and babies, we would have no need for the art that mends nature.

On these grounds, it would seem, Eliot offered, especially in *Scenes of Clerical Life*, not only an overtly fictionalized form of anthropological conjecture, but also yet another way of thinking about sexuality and culture, especially culture as an achievement of consciousness. Before the evolutionary anthropologists began the train of speculations that would inspire the modernists, Eliot had already begun to link art to sacrifice and sacrifice to sexual passion. Before Darwin made one sort of secular theodicy out of Malthus's dilemma, justifying the evils attendant on population pressure as the condition of mankind's evolution and acculturation, Eliot had already made another, in which specifically procreative suffering forged the social bond and prompted the creative impulse. Eliot was acquainted with McLennan in the years just before she eloped with George Henry Lewes, and of all the comparative anthropologists, his vision was closest to hers, for both thought of culture as an immediate outgrowth of generativity. To be sure, Eliot did not speculate about how the earliest human societies were formed, nor did she imagine a people so savvy about the population principle that they twist their way of life into an impediment to their own increase; but she shared with McLennan a view of culture as an attempt to make sense of suffering, especially female suffering, and both thought that the idea of sacrifice had its origin there. They both, moreover, sought in their own culture the arcane customs and habitual, encrusted forms that could be deciphered as the remnants of lost organic unities, and consequently they looked with special interest at the connection between religion and eros.

All three stories in *Scenes of Clerical Life* probe modern Christianity for its core of procreative or sexual unhappiness. The pattern is perhaps easiest to see in "The Sad Fortunes of Amos Barton," with its impoverished clerical hero, whose wife struggles to feed and clothe their six children decently on a curate's salary and ultimately dies trying to give birth to a seventh. The repellent Barton is a failure as a clergyman; he insists on reforms, but cannot explain their purposes or benefits to his parishioners. He is tactless, vain, and inarticulate, so when a rumor takes hold that he has an improper attachment to a gentlewoman who sponges off of him, his parishioners ostracize him and deny him any help as the family's financial crisis deepens. But far from blaming the parishioners for their pettiness or the Bartons for their improvident over-breeding and ineptitude, the narrator tries to turn our attention away from the specific chain of causation leading to Milly Barton's death and to focus us instead on its result, the change that takes place in the husband and his congregation once "the sweet mother with her baby in her arms" (109) is in her grave. Milly Barton becomes a female Christ, who cheerfully accepted her sacrifice, and her husband's mourning becomes an object of pity to the parishioners, who are able to enter into a community of suffering with him, which makes him the center of their religion for the first time. "Milly's memory," we are told, "hallowed her husband, as of old the place was hallowed on which an angel from God had alighted" (101). As the oddness of that formulation indicates, Barton still isn't quite their priest because none of his personal qualities are transformed by the casualty. He is, rather, a "place," a gathering spot for the remembrance of suffering. The cult that forms around him has moved from its ossified Christianity to a spontaneous form of devotion to the dead woman, a modern counterpart to a mother goddess, whose resurrection is effected by the narrator.

The story bears traces of a number of influences on George Eliot's early fiction. It is most obviously indebted to Ludwig Feuerbach's *Essence of Christianity* (which Marianne Evans translated in 1854), especially to the section on "The Mystery of the Suffering God." Explaining that Christianity, like all religion, is only a way of worshiping humanity by projecting human traits onto an imaginary god, Feuerbach finds the innovation in Christianity to be the emphasis on suffering: "The Passion of Christ . . . represents not only moral, voluntary suffering, the suffering of love, the power of sacrificing self for the good of others [reads Eliot's translation]; it represents also suffering as such, suffering in so far as it is an expression of passibility [human openness to external impressions] in general. The Christian religion is so little superhuman that it even sanctions human weakness."[33] In other words, the cult that forms around suffering gets closer than any other to acknowledging that religion is the worship of the human; consequently, as the formalistic Christianity in "Amos Barton" gives way to the cult that is devoted to Milly's

[33] *The Essence of Christianity*, trans. George Eliot (Amherst, N.Y.: Prometheus Books, 1989), 62. See also Sally Shuttleworth, *George Eliot and Nineteenth-Century Science* (Cambridge: Cambridge University Press, 1984).

fatal passibility, the germ of all religions manifests itself. Eliot's art is designed not only to reveal this essence of Christianity and express emotional solidarity with it, but also to begin, unobtrusively, shifting its energies toward a secular humanism.

I want to dwell for a moment on that word, "passibility." It refers to the capacity of something to be changed from without, to take an impression. The incarnation, according to certain Christian heresies, might be seen as the moment when God ceases to be unchangeable and takes on the trait of passibility, which is then further expanded in Christ's passion and crucifixion. In *Scenes of Clerical Life*, Eliot uses the figure of the pregnant woman as the ur-instance of passibility—the giving over of the self to a change wrought by others. And when that change becomes fatal, it only seems to work out its inherent logic. Impassibility implies immortality; passibility, on the other hand, quickly runs toward the "passing" of mortality. As Feuerbach points out, Christians, despite their orthodox disclaimers to the contrary, seem to be worshiping such a feature in the suffering Christ and might therefore be said to worship human mortality itself.

Important as Feuerbach's influence was, though, he did not provide a precise understanding of what makes human suffering both unavoidable and sublime, the motive force of "zoological" and "moral evolution" alike. Any suffering would have made the Feuerbachian point, but what is striking about George Eliot's early fiction is its systematic linking of suffering with motherhood, sexual passion, or both, and for that connection she seems to have relied, either consciously or unconsciously, on Malthus. With unfailing consistency, suffering in these stories derives from the procreative urge. In "Mr. Gilfil's Love-Story," the young heroine, Caterina, rejected by the thoughtless young man who earlier made love to her, converts her anguish into the "full, deep notes" of her singing and finds temporary relief. A figure for the sorrowing artist whose misery enhances her music, giving added pleasure to her listeners, the love-sick Caterina is also, like Milly Barton, destined to die in childbirth: "[T]he delicate plant had been too deeply bruised, and in the struggle to put forth a blossom it died" (243). Her former room is the holy shrine that the Reverend Mr. Gilfil keeps in pristine condition. Although he alone worships there, the truly religious part of his character, like that of the Reverend Amos Barton, is devoted to the woman dead in childbirth. Knowing this essence of humanistic reverence from the outset, Gilfil makes an amiable but listless parson.

The third story gives us yet another variation on the same tune. Lest we begin to think that women might avoid suffering by avoiding motherhood, "Janet's Repentance" gives us the story of the childless woman, abused by her husband, who first becomes an alcoholic and then struggles to regain her moral integrity. Suffering cannot be avoided by the nonreproductive woman, either, for she will be morally vulnerable in a way that her reproductive sister is not: "Mighty is the force of motherhood! Says the great tragic poet to us across the ages, finding, as usual, the simplest words for the sublimest fact. . . . It transforms all things by its vital heat" (334). Janet's heat has to come from another source: her identification with the consumptive agony of a clergyman, the Reverend Mr. Tryan, who sacrifices his life to his parishioners in atonement for the sin of seducing, ruining, and causing the death of a young girl. Like Mrs. Barton in the first story, Mr. Tryan, in his anguish, gives his followers the idea of the divinity of suffering. He becomes a focus of sacrificial fervor, and after his death, Janet, we are told in the last paragraph, is his "memorial." This time the woman suffers from the frustration of her maternal longing, but, denied sacrificial status, she becomes, like the clergymen in the other stories, the memorial ground impressed by the retributive sacrifice of Tryan and the young woman he sacrificed to sexual passion.

There is a striking resemblance between these figures and McLennan's, Robertson Smith's, and Frazer's agonized gods who represent human generation; like those comparative anthropologists but in a much more demure way, Eliot also explored the buried common source of *cultus* and eros. *Scenes of Clerical Life*, though, not only uncovers generative suffering at the fountainhead of religious worship but also goes on to insinuate that the art of the stories themselves should gently replace the religion that must misrecognize its object. Art alone, it implies, can put humanity back at the center of its own worship, and novels, as conjectural microhistories of intimate life, have a special mission to reveal and preserve the sacrificial impulse.

Later novelists, indeed, went so far as to imply that the novel was the modern equivalent of primal sacrifice. In Walter Pater's *Marius the Epicurean*, for example, the narrator explains that the human sacrifices of earlier times had become the popular amusements of the Roman amphitheaters; these amusements, in turn, were:

> The novel-reading of that age—a current help provided for sluggish imaginations, in regard, for instance, to grisly accidents, such as might happen to one's self; but with every facility for comfortable inspection. . . . If the part of Marsyas was called for, there was a criminal condemned to lose his skin. It might be almost edifying to study minutely the expression of his face, while the assistants corded and pegged him to the bench, cunningly; the servant of the law waiting by, who, after one short cut with his knife, would slip the man's leg from his skin, as neatly as if it were a stocking. [34]

Although the form's decadence is strongly implied in this passage, the novel's likeness to earlier forms of sacrifice is also clearly delineated. Like novels, the Roman long shows and earlier human sacrifices featured symbolic suffering.

---

[34] Walter Pater, *Marius the Epicurean: His Sensations and Ideas*, ed. Ian Small, 2nd ed., 1885 (New York: Oxford University Press, 1986), 137.

In the shows, as in the rituals, the victims were not only themselves but also figures for gods and other mythical persons, so even though they literally died, their deaths were symbolic. Moreover, in novels, executions, and sacrificial rituals the victims also represent the audience, who can experience the suffering and still remain unhurt. Thomas Hardy made the same link, both in *Tess of the d'Urbervilles*, where he gives us our final vision of the heroine on a sacrificial altar at Stonehenge, and in an essay on reading fiction, which explains that passion in the novel allows "the nerves and muscles of figures . . . [to] be seen as in an *écorché*."[35] The vicarious sensations of the novel reader, Hardy suggests, are linked via sacrifice to the "supreme fact in nature"—what one reviewer of Frazer's *The Golden Bough* referred to as "the eternal succession of birth and death, of verdure and decay, of reaping and sowing, of destruction for the purpose of reproduction."[36] We crave the sensations of our ancestors (the primitive somaeconomics of sacrifice) because our instincts lead us to reproduce their bioeconomic rituals with their underlying logic of forfeiting a life to fertilize the world.

Turn-of-the-century writers like Hardy judged those impulses far more harshly than George Eliot had in *Scenes of Clerical Life*, and by the early twentieth century, literary Malthusianism became truly bleak. In Hardy's poem "The Germ," for example, reproductive matter—sperm and egg—is the real cause of all we imagine to be human thoughts, feelings, and actions. The germ merely uses our subjectivities to make a series of new creatures to inhabit and consume. Even the later, less sanguine George Eliot never reached conclusions as dismal as these. Nevertheless, we can trace a continuity between "Amos Barton," sentimental as it certainly is, and Hardy's *Jude the Obscure*, in which Father Time hangs himself and his siblings with a sign around their necks explaining, "Done because we are too menny." If the consciousness that comes from such suffering is no longer "sublime," its novelistic representation carved out the space of the modernist avant-garde, with its sexual radicalism and disdain for bourgeois pieties.

So by the time T. S. Eliot met comparative anthropology in the twentieth century, the central themes were already well established in English literature; the sacrificial suffering connecting fertility with death had been explored in the novel for decades. Long before modernism, fiction writers were busy tracing genealogies for "culture" that were similar to those being uncovered by the evolutionary anthropologists, and they were similar because Malthus inspired both sets of authors. By using Malthusian plots to explain religion, in particular, as an epiphenomenon of reproduction, the framers of both culture concepts outflanked their religious competitors, proclaiming science and art,

---

[35] "The Profitable Reading of Fiction," *Thomas Hardy's Personal Writings: Prefaces, Literary Opinions, Reminiscences*, ed. Harold Oral (New York: Macmillan, 1966), 110–25.

[36] "Review of *The Golden Bough*," *Edinburgh Review* 172 (1890): 552.

respectively, the authorities on human motives, behavior, and spiritual ambition. Each sought to replace religion, not by attacking it as error, but by interpreting it as a recently superseded mode of confronting an intractable human dilemma. The writers on culture, moreover, promised not to resolve the dilemma but only to reinscribe it in their own terms. And so by the opening of the twentieth century, the dismal science had spawned an equally dismal culture in which the elements of the Malthusian condition—the melancholy of procreative desire, its quasi-sacred status, the suffering it exacts, and the self-consciousness and guilt it compels—were the miseries and the splendors of the human condition.

Afterword

Looking back over these chapters, we can see that political economists and the British literati were fellow travelers in a long migration that transferred speculations about life, death, and the passions from the realms of theology and moral philosophy to those of biology, comparative anthropology, and psychology. And yet we don't think of economics today as sharing much with these "life sciences," so what became of bioeconomics and somaeconomics as economics disciplined itself?

Unlike their literary contemporaries, the political economists had no ambivalence about developing a "discipline," and hence they tended to keep track of their changing intellectual environment so that they could distinguish themselves from it. Moreover, the group of political economists most deeply concerned with bioeconomics and somaeconomics—Malthus, Senior, McCulloch, Chadwick, Jennings, Spencer, and Jevons—tended, in their very modes of shifting into new intellectual vicinities, to firm up their disciplinary borders. If we trace, for example, the connections linking a set of incidents we have already encountered, we can observe how, when they broke their ties with the eudemonic position inside moral philosophy, they both made an opening toward psychophysiology and established the condition on which they could forget all about "sensation."

Nassau Senior's 1836 *Outline of the Science of Political Economy*, began, it will be recalled, by trying to delimit his subject, explaining that political economy cannot be a science until it knows and respects its place in relation to "the Sciences and Arts to which it is subservient"[1] (4), for it was only one small subset of "the theory of morals and government" (2). When he insisted that "the subject of the Political Economist is not Happiness, but Wealth" (2), and that the question of the good of wealth itself must fall outside the confines of his inquiry, he was trying to move the focus of political economists from their surroundings (ethics) to the insides of their own discipline. Let those concerned with other branches of "moral philosophy" answer the question of "[t]o what extent and under what circumstances the possession of Wealth is, on the whole, beneficial or injurious to its possessor, or to the society of which he is a member" (2).

The apparent modesty of Senior's formulation, its reference to the "subservience" of the discipline, was thus calculated to exempt political economy

---

[1] Senior, *Outline of the Science of Political Economy* (New York: A. M. Kelly, 1836). Subsequent page numbers are given in the body of the afterword.

from the demands of being an ethical inquiry and to ward off the criticisms directed at its shortcomings in that regard: "it has often been made a matter of grave complaint against Political Economists, that they confine their attention to Wealth, and disregard all consideration of Happiness or Virtue. It is to be wished [he acerbically remarks] that this complaint were better founded" (3). Most political economists err in the opposite direction, "not in confining [their] attention to Wealth, but in confounding Wealth with Happiness" (4). Once free of these eudemonic chains—the burden of answering queries about the true nature of human happiness—political economy could finally settle its own first premises, ignore its critics, and let others decide for themselves what its practical applications might be. The disciplinary ambition at the heart of this modest proposal is then made explicit: "the more strictly a writer confines his attention to his own Science, the more likely he is to extend its bounds" (4).

Freedom from moral philosophy, however, did not result in liberation from an interdisciplinary context or in exemption from speculations about economic emotions. J. R. McCulloch, seemingly following Senior's lead, marched directly into a new area of discourse about emotion, which was no longer to be situated, as talk of the passions had been, inside ethics but rather in the incipient field of psychology.[2] The announced objective was to explore our real mental nature rather than to recommend some hierarchy of emotions, the subject matter shifting from what should motivate us (What will make us happy?) to what does motivate us (What are the economic emotions?). The first was clearly a value-laden question; the second tried to confine itself to the facts:

> But whether the attainment of wealth . . . be favourable or unfavourable to happiness, there can be no doubt of its pursuit being eminently congenial to human nature. . . . "The natural flights of the human mind are not from pleasure to pleasure, but from hope to hope"; and at every step of this progress man discovers new motives of action, new excitements of fear and allurements of desire.[3]

Political economy's retreat from the territory of moral philosophy, in short, opened an extensive and fertile border with psychology.

That border was frequently traversed over the next four decades, and it was increasingly filled in by ideas about the physiology of the mind, which found their most influential spokesman in William Stanley Jevons, whose explicit purpose, like that of Senior and McCulloch, was to rid political economy of extraneous metaphysical baggage. But if McCulloch's psychology seemed to

---

[2] Thomas Dixon, *From Passions to Emotions: The Creation of a Secular Psychological Category* (Cambridge: Cambridge University Press, 2003).

[3] McCulloch, *The Principles of Political Economy* (London: A. Murray and Son, 1970), 532–33.

posit an active and driving imagination, Jevons's psychology connected such imaginings to the physiology of the nervous system and therefore further extended political economy's interdisciplinary reach. Once again, the border crossing was achieved through declaring the necessary independence of economics from moral science; and once again the rhetorical tactic was propitiatory modesty. There is, Jevons insisted, a hierarchy of feelings, and the pleasures and pains with which the economist deals are of "the lowest rank," concerned only with "supplying the ordinary wants of man at the least cost of labour."[4] "A higher calculus of moral right and wrong would be needed to show how he may best employ that wealth for the good of others as well as himself" (93). In order to fall within the purview of economics, Jevons claimed, a felicific calculus must be a matter of "moral indifference." Like Senior and McCulloch, he thus tried to make peace with the moralists by establishing separate sovereignties: "we may certainly say, with Francis Bacon, 'while philosophers are disputing whether virtue or pleasure be the proper aim of life, do you provide yourself with the instruments of either' " (93).

What is the significance, though, of the fact that Jevons was not as careful as Senior and McCulloch to avoid the term "happiness"? Indeed, in a passage that seems to reflect on McCulloch's notion that gratification lies in anticipation, rather than achievement, of pleasure, Jevons simply *equates* hope with happiness: "We may safely call that man happy who, however lowly his position and limited his possessions, can always hope for more than he has, and can feel that every moment of exertion tends to realize his aspirations" (99). "Everyone must have felt," Jevons continues, "that the enjoyment actually experienced at any moment is but limited in amount, and usually fails to answer to the anticipations which have been formed," for "'Man never is but always to be blest' " (98). Although the use of the aphorism here makes the psychological insight seem merely the common knowledge of reflective people, Jevons's remarks about anticipatory happiness and the decrease in enjoyment upon possession of a commodity were central to the marginal revolution and were given a thoroughly scientific basis in the psychophysiology of Alexander Bain, which had earlier been linked to political economy by Richard Jennings.

It was this self-confident reliance on "science" that allowed Jevons to be somewhat freer with the words "happy" and "happiness" than Senior and McCulloch had been. Despite the fact that he shared their ambition to shield their discipline from ethical deliberations, he indicated that the problem with the turn-of-the-century Utilitarian rhetoric of happiness had been merely its refusal to admit a hierarchy of happinesses: "Motives and feelings," he wrote,

---

[4] Jevons, *The Theory of Political Economy*, ed. and intro. R. D. Collison (Baltimore: Penguin, 1970), 93. Subsequent page numbers are given in the body of the afterword.

"are certainly of the same kind to the extent that we are able to weight them against each other; but they are, nevertheless, almost incomparable in power and authority"; thus, "a single higher pleasure will sometimes neutralize a vast extent and continuance of lower pains." But by the same logic, of course, the opposite might also be the case. It is, indeed, precisely because psychophysiology provided a theory in which pains and pleasures do become fungible at the margins that an idea of general happiness can creep back in. For example, a weak moral, intellectual, or aesthetic pleasure might be "neutralized" by a strong physical need. Consequently, the statement that higher and lower pleasures are "almost incomparable" is not really strong enough to keep the question of overall human happiness at bay. Ironically, in other words, the attachment of economics to physiology might have given an opening for the return of the issue of happiness, but that return had become unproblematic because happiness itself had ceased to be a moral issue and had become a psychological datum.

Unlike moral philosophy, psychophysiology did not require the "subservience" of political economy or pester it with unanswerable questions, so the change of disciplinary context consolidated the autonomy of economics (which could then drop the "political" term). After having served as the raison d'être for the mathematical operations of marginal utility theory, psychophysiology was gradually and quietly forgotten. As John Maynard Keynes remarked in an essay on Jevons's immediate successor, F. Y. Edgeworth,

> Jevons, the Marshall of the seventies, and the Edgeworth of the late seventies and the early eighties *believed* the Utilitarian Psychology and laid the foundations of the subject in this belief. The later Marshall and the later Edgeworth and many of the younger generation have not fully believed; but we still trust the superstructure without exploring too thoroughly the soundness of the original foundations.[5]

The convenient thing about this new interdisciplinarity was that, after a decade, you could simply ignore it. Keynes, inhabiting an intellectual world in which quite different psychological models prevailed, seems only mildly embarrassed by the discrepancy. Indeed, he might have seen the recession of the psychological as the very thing that protected economics from the antipsychologism of certain vigorous strains of early twentieth-century British intellectual life.

Marginal utility theory also absorbed important elements of Malthus's bioeconomical thought without leaving any lasting interdisciplinary residue. Malthus's critique of the orthodox theory of value (which I've analyzed as a paradoxical clash between somaeconomic assumptions regarding the value-

---

[5] John Maynard Keynes, *Essays in Biography*, ed. Geoffrey Keynes (London: R. Hart-Davis, 1951), 230.

producing pains of production and bioeconomic considerations regarding the maximization of life) was read by Jevons as an argument for the priority of demand, and as such it partly inspired his reformation of the discipline:

> There were Economists, such as Malthus and Senior, who had a far better comprehension of the true doctrines . . . but they were driven out of the field by the unity and influence of the Ricardo-Mill school. It will be a work of labour to pick up the fragments of a shattered science and to start anew, but it is a work from which they must not shrink who wish to see any advance of Economic Science.[6]

Keynes also identified what he saw as Malthus's chief concerns—defense of unproductive consumption, respect for empirical data, and advocacy of the stimulating effects of government spending—as fundamentals of his own revolution. Echoing Jevons, he exclaims,

> If only Malthus, instead of Ricardo, had been the parent stem from which nineteenth-century economics proceeded, what a much wiser and richer place the world would be to-day! We have laboriously to rediscover and force through the obscuring envelopes of our misguided education what should never have ceased to be obvious![7]

But what became of Malthus's more explicit emphasis on "Life"? Unlike "happiness," "Life" never became a conscious bone of contention among political economists. In hindsight we can see that its ascendence as a god term, a self-evident value beyond the reach of questions, was something of a novelty, but it was not controversial at the time. As we have seen, Malthus's argument was immediately challenged on religious grounds—How could a just God at once command the multiplication of human life and attach so much unavoidable suffering to it?—and he reworked it into a theodicy of soul-making through suffering, which became a staple of the moral-restraint Malthusianism spread by Thomas Chalmers. One strain of Malthus's thought, therefore, stayed within religious discourse and allowed for the dissemination of certain political-economic ideas far beyond the discipline. The ideas that Ricardo developed from the bioeconomic repertoire—the theory of rent, the tendency of the rate of profit to fall, the wages fund theory—became fundamental to the "orthodox" classical position; they also tended to inspire certain somewhat eccentric polymaths, such as Edwin Chadwick and Herbert Spencer, who claimed that political economy's future lay further into the domain of physiology. In Spencer's career, Darwin's appropriation of Malthus's bioeconomics marked the beginning of that notorious biologization of economic thought known as "social Darwinism." But there were other, to my mind more respect-

---

[6] *Theory of Political Economy,* 2nd ed., lvii; quoted in Keynes, 291.
[7] Keynes, 120–21.

able, offshoots of Malthus's stress on the economics of life and death, including Chadwick's protoecological experiments, comparative anthropology, and, later, the evolutionary science of "ecology" itself, the very name of which was modeled on the word "economy" by its coiner, the German Ernst Haeckel. If somaeconomics edged toward materialist psychology through a series of disciplinary discriminations and was consequently able to disregard its "interdisciplinary" context, bioeconomics exported Malthus into fields whose interest in political economy was only fleeting.

In short, somaeconomics served as a portal through which political economy took in psychophysiology and then forgot about it, whereas bioeconomics was an opening through which certain economic ideas were exported into biology and anthropology. In both cases, the location of the traffic was on the borders of the life sciences rather than inside the broad spectrum of "moral philosophy," where political economy began. The traffic with the life sciences, though, seems to have left economists with the impression of freedom from both their old and their new interdisciplinary commitments.

As a discipline that has achieved a high level of autonomy by taking its axioms for granted and ignoring competing accounts of human behavior, postwar economics has irritated literary critics. Even among scholars who have learned to appreciate nineteenth-century political economists or those interested in the economics of literature, twentieth-century economists are reputed to be "scientistic" technicians. One widespread narrative, for example, charts a decline in economic thought from Adam Smith to the late nineteenth century, lamenting the break with moral philosophy and blaming mathematical analysis for making academic economics inaccessible to the rest of us.[8] Economists' attachment to rational-choice thinking in recent decades also made them appear to be the epitome of that limited Anglo-American imagination identified by Lionel Trilling in 1950: "As it carries out its active and positive ends it unconsciously limits its view of the world to what it can deal with, and it unconsciously tends to develop theories and principles, particularly in relation to the nature of the human mind . . . that justify its limitation."[9]

Thus, in the academy of the twentieth century, despite the rich history of nineteenth-century interactions between political economy and literary culture, English studies revived the Romantics' disdain for the "mechanistic" operations of economists and proposed its own subject matter as the antidote to their disciplinary narrowness. For Trilling and for many other literary critics of his day, continental philosophy and Freudian psychology held important

---

[8] See Regenia Gagnier, *The Instability of Human Wants: Economics and Aesthetics in Market Society* (Chicago: University of Chicago Press, 2000), and for the earlier construction of numerical representation as peculiarly authoritative, see Mary Poovey, *A History of the Modern Fact : Problems of Knowledge in the Sciences of Wealth and Society* (Chicago: University of Chicago Press, 1998).

[9] Lionel Trilling, *The Liberal Imagination: Essays on Literature and Society* (Garden City, N.Y.: Doubleday, 1957), xi.

analytic keys to the "irrational" side of human beings, but it was literature itself that usually provided the material to be analyzed, for literature was said to possess the fullness and intricacy of human life. Indeed, it was said to be the place where humanity reveals its complexity and its resistance to conceptual categories. Because they valued their objects of study for their unfathomable depth, literary critics, moreover, tended to stress the insufficiency of even their own increasingly technical critical prowess to a full description of the object. If economists simplified their object to fit their analytical categories, academic literary critics professionalized in the opposite direction, insisting on the difference between literature and all analytic modes of thought. The New Critics, for example, recommended the analysis of literature's "inversions, solecisms, lapses from the prose norm of language, and from close prose logic."[10] Moreover, to make the contrast with economics even more explicit, they counterposed literature to all forms of abstraction and exchangeability, especially those practiced in the marketplace. New Critics purported to describe not what made exchange possible but what disabled it, and they held that learning to talk about a work of literature without reducing it to its "prose core" constituted an important form of resistance to the modern tendency—always clearest in economic transactions—toward abstracting fungible values from particular objects, which then became merely disposable.

Looking especially at postwar American universities, we can see how this contrast with "reductive" social sciences served literature departments. They not only gained a veritable monopoly on human "depth," "particularity," "ambiguity," "the unconscious," "the irrational," and so forth, but also became the busiest ports of entry for postwar European intellectual movements precisely because other disciplines had drawn borders that kept, for example, Sartre out of the philosophy curriculum, Freud out of the psychology department, Lukács and Gramsci out of political science, and made Mauss and Lévi-Strauss peripheral in anthropology departments. The ecology of the academy seemed to require such an inclusive discipline, one dedicated to preserving or admitting what had been discarded in the disciplining of other departments.

Of course, it was not long before the salons de refusés that literature departments had become in the 1950s, 1960s, and 1970s took in some guests like Derrida, who challenged the binary structures of thought that gave literature its putative uniqueness; Foucault, who asked us to be more critically self-reflective about our own disciplinary procedures; and Bourdieu, who drew attention to the ways in which the literature/economics opposition enables us to distribute cultural capital. Somewhat chastened out of our sense of occupational moral superiority but nonetheless proud to be the discipline that can practice a rigorous critique of its discipline (What better evidence of depth

---

[10] John Crowe Ransom, "Criticism, Inc.," reprinted in David Lodge, ed., *Twentieth Century Literary Criticism: A Reader* (London: Longman, 1972), 232.

and inclusiveness could you have?), literary critics are now more curious and tolerant about economic logic than they were at any time in the twentieth century.

Just in time to observe a turn toward interdisciplinarity among economists who have lately begun to study the physiology of sensation and emotion again. The press has greeted this development as a striking innovation in the history of economics, and it does seem a departure from rational choice assumptions. Economist George Loewenstein explained in the *New York Times* that "Under the influence of powerful emotions or drives, people often end up doing the opposite of what they think is best for themselves, even at the moment of acting."[11] The reports of this new somaeconomics have an uncannily familiar ring to any reader of McCulloch or Jevons. Here is Loewenstein a few months later on the issue of pleasure and happiness, for example: "We don't realize how quickly we will adapt to a pleasurable event and make it the backdrop of our lives. When any event occurs to us, we make it ordinary. And through becoming ordinary, we lose our pleasure."[12] Although this was Jevons's main point, the new breed of interdisciplinary economists, who often work with cognitive scientists and behavioral psychologists, oddly blame the neoclassicists for banishing feelings from economic consideration: "[The neoclassical economists] couldn't include 'the passions,' or emotions in their models, because they were too unruly, too complex," Loewenstein is reported to have said in yet another *New York Times* article from June of 2003.[13] And yet, the basic insights seem very close to "Utilitarian" psychology, with its emphasis on happiness and pleasure, that Keynes opted not to disturb at the foundations of neoclassicism.

So is this just a repetition from which we will learn nothing new? Perhaps not; the current partnership with psychology and brain chemistry has led to some conclusions that depart from the nineteenth-century theorists. For example, whereas McCulloch and Jevons thought that constantly being propelled from one *expectation* of pleasure to another was a positive emotional state driving the economy, and was therefore unproblematic, the economist Daniel Kahneman uses the same insight to question whether or not the economy should be entirely reliant on consumers' desires, since they are such notoriously bad "affective forecasters": "If people do not know what is going to make them better off or give them pleasure . . . then the idea that you can trust people to do what will give them pleasure becomes questionable."[14] Economist Richard Thaler proposes that "public and private institutions should gently

[11] Sandra Blakeslee, "Brain Experts Follow the Money in Studying Decision Making," *New York Times* (6/17/03): D4.

[12] Jon Gertner, "The Futile Pursuit of Happiness," *New York Times Magazine* (9/7/03): 47.

[13] Stephen J. Dubner, "Calculating the Irrational in Economics," *New York Times* (6/28/03): B9.

[14] Quoted in Gertner, "Futile," 86.

steer individuals toward more enlightened choices. That is, [consumers] must be saved from themselves."[15] And who can be entirely indifferent to the research that models economic interactions by studying brain activity during game playing, discovering, for example, that "in a game of mutual trust, women's brains show a big dopamine or reward response when they are trusted by others; there is no such response in men's brains."[16] Surely there is a novelist somewhere building a plot around that breakthrough. Hence, resisting the impulse to throw up my hands with a dismissive *"Plus ça change,"* I'll hope that there really are things to be learned from the new interdisciplinary mixture. After all, haven't we learned that anticipating something new will always make us happier than attaining it?

[15] Dubner, "Calculating," B9.
[16] Blakeslee, "Brain Experts," D4.